Alfred Hitchcock and the Making of **PSYCHO**

Alfred Hitchcock
and the Making of
PSYCHO

STEPHEN REBELLO

SOFT SKULL PRESS | BERKELEY

Alfred Hitchcock and the Making of *Psycho*
Copyright © 1990, 2012 by Stephen Rebello

Library of Congress Cataloging-in-Publication is available.
ISBN 978-1-59376-511-8

Interior design by Elyse Strongin, Neuwirth Associates, Inc.

Soft Skull Press
An imprint of COUNTERPOINT
1919 Fifth Street
Berkeley, CA 94710
www.softskull.com

Printed in the United States of America
Distributed by Publishers Group West

10 9 8 7 6 5 4 3 2 1

TO MY FAMILY,

who keep me honest.

CONTENTS

"Film should be stronger than reason."

—ALFRED HITCHCOCK

PREFACE

Los Angeles, California. April the Fifth. 10:30 a.m.

I'm sitting in a 20th Century Fox Studios executive boardroom at one end of an imposingly long, mighty, gleaming conference table. Atop the table are place cards printed with the names of invitees, the project title *Hitchcock*, and an illustration depicting the eponymous film director and his wife-collaborator, Alma, as the stern-looking couple in an edgy, witty, contemporary sendup of Grant Wood's painting *American Gothic.* Also on the table sit copies of *Hitchcock,* the screenplay for a feature film based upon the book you are now reading. Forty or so people are gathered for a table read of that script. Eight days remain before principal photography begins on Friday the thirteenth—a date of which the late director himself might have approved.

The faces of many gathered at the table are instantly recognizable. To my left sit Sir Anthony Hopkins and Dame Helen Mirren, who play Mr. and Mrs. Hitchcock. Flanking them to the right are costars Jessica Biel (playing actress Vera Miles), James D'Arcy (in the role of actor Anthony Perkins), and Wallace Langham (as graphic designer Saul Bass). To their left sit Danny Huston (screenwriter-adapter of two Hitchcock films, Whitfield Cook), Richard Portnow (Paramount boss Barney

Balaban), and Michael Wincott (Ed Gein, the real-life multiple murderer and *Psycho* inspiration). Missing due to prior commitments or logistical challenges are the actors set to play our *Psycho* leading lady Janet Leigh, longtime Hitchcock production associate Peggy Robertson, Hitchcock's fearsome agent-turned-studio-mogul Lew Wasserman, and *Psycho* screenwriter Joseph Stefano—Scarlett Johansson, Toni Collette, Michael Stuhlbarg, and Ralph Macchio, respectively.

The conference room is also packed with less instantly-identifiable talents but even a partial list of the credits, nominations, awards, and accolades amassed by the director, producers, studio and production executives and associates, technicians, specialists, and craftspeople is impressive. There have been warm, even high-spirited introductions and hugs but make no mistake: The room buzzes with anticipation and a healthy dose of nerves. We're all aware that this is a big moment, a labor of love, and a gathering of very heady company.

So heady, in fact, that I secretly pinch my arm under the table just to prove that I'm not dreaming. It's been quite a long time since I've done that—not since January of 1980, in fact, when, through an equally unlikely and miraculous series of events, I sat down as a budding, fresh-faced journalist to talk with Alfred Hitchcock himself in his suite at his Universal Studios office bungalow. The master filmmaker, even at age eighty and diminished by fading health, displayed remarkable wisdom, brilliance, powers of imagination, playfulness, valor, and tolerance for all sorts of persistent, possibly annoying questions. He remained such an inveterate ham and showman that he had even arranged a prank. Minutes before I was ushered into his office, a secretary, on cue, opened Hitchcock's inner office door just long enough to make sure that I would glimpse the suspense maestro sitting in a tall chair with his head thrown back and his fleshy neck exposed to his barber's shiny straight razor. Shades of *Spellbound* meets *Sweeney Todd*.

That interview went on to become the very last one Hitchcock ever gave. Our talk inspired me to capture, on audiotape and on paper, Hitchcock and everyone responsible for making *Psycho*— before it would be too late. My "relationship" with Hitchcock went a few years back. As a young child, with the indulgence of my loving, incredible parents, I would call the director's offices at Universal after school (yes, *really*, but more about that another time, in another venue). And it had been *Psycho* that led me to explore other Hitchcock films as well as those of the great (and not so great) directors of the 20th century.

In 1986, my *Cinefantastique* cover story on *Psycho* further opened the doors to many of Hitchcock's associates. And that access, as well as access to the director's personal papers and production files, in turn, led to the 1990 publication of *Alfred Hitchcock and the Making of Psycho*. I enjoyed first-hand the kindness, charm, and wry, playfully macabre wit of *Psycho* novelist Robert Bloch and the intelligence, warmth, humor, and complexity of screenwriter Joseph Stefano. Janet Leigh personified grace, generosity, and supreme professionalism, especially when I had the privilege of traveling coast to coast with her for television and promotional appearances. I resonated with the acerbic, uptown intellect, edge, outsider vibe and turbulence of Anthony Perkins, and I deeply respected the focused, visionary, endlessly creative talent of graphic designer Saul Bass. The recollections of delightful, no nonsense veteran actress Lurene Tuttle, lovely, erudite costume designer Rita Riggs, and modest but keenly insightful script supervisor Marshall Schlom, were particularly precise and expansive. Also invaluable in so many ways were Paul Jasmin, Joseph Hurley, Margo Epper, Robert Clatworthy, Jack Barron, Harold Adler, Helen Colvig, and Tony Palladino.

Those alliances led to treasured times spent with Hitchcock's associates on other films, like Ernest Lehman, the impossibly bright, irascible, complicated, and irreplaceable screenwriter-producer-director who brought me into his life, mentored me as a screenwriter, dazzled and shocked me with war stories of the joys and perils of working with the *real* Hitchcock, introduced me to the joys of the best *zabaglione* to be found outside of Italy, and introduced me to the terrors and hilarity of receiving one of his own infamous middle-of-the-night faxes. At his invitation and insistence, I also nearly collaborated with him *twice,* once on a book and once on a new version of a never-completed original screenplay for Hitchcock. Both projects derailed when Ernie became skittish about competing with his own impeccable body of work. And, of course, from Hitchcock, too, came the privilege of my friendship with the intensely private *Vertigo* star and film icon Kim Novak.

Those vivid past and current voices, the indelible memories shared by these Hitchcock collaborators, and more, inform every paragraph of *Alfred Hitchcock and the Making of Psycho.* Back when I immersed myself in research for the book at such places as the Margaret Herrick Library of the Academy of Motion Picture Arts and Sciences, there were times when I almost felt as though I had slipped back to 1959 when *Psycho* was in pre-production and actual production. As I read Hitchcock's handwritten script notes, intra-studio memos, daily "call sheets" listing the addresses and phone numbers of the cast and crew, the censorship notes, and memos on musical scoring and dubbing, it seemed as though I was transported to a time when *Psycho* had not yet stunned international movie audiences and changed the way we look at film thrillers. Those studies, I hope, enliven and enrich everything I contributed to *Hitchcock.*

Sitting in the Fox conference room, as the script reading is about to begin, I also allow myself a brief moment to muse about how in the world I landed here. Let's call that saga *The Making of*

Alfred Hitchcock and the Making of "Psycho" or, since we've now simplified that mouthful of a title to *Hitchcock, The Making of the Making of Hitchcock*. Let me collapse that long, bloody saga into bullet points. In 2004, independent producers Alan Barnette and Tom Thayer were among several suitors pursuing the idea of turning my 1990 nonfiction book into a film. Don't ask why it had taken fifteen years for this possibility to manifest itself, but I credit my extraordinary and persistent literary agent, Mary Evans, for keeping the book in the public eye with the publication of a 1995 edition. Alan Barnette especially struck me as a rare, experienced moviemaker who prefers getting films made rather than *talking about* getting them made.

I was originally hired to consult and to give notes on screenplay drafts written by the screenwriter the producers had hired. Producer Alan Barnette figured out pretty quickly that I had more to offer and my role expanded. And expanded. The project circulated around Hollywood and attracted the attention of household-name, heavyweight talents and some lesser-known but outstanding young guns. A number of those household-name directors and actors eventually balked at the prospect of going up against the ghost of Hitchcock, especially after the debacle of the ill-advised 1998 remake. Others fought to step up. Eventually, one of the more offbeat, unexpected, and fearless of those producer-directors became attached. What did I want most? To see the "making of" aspect serve as backdrop to a tale revolving around the complex personal and professional relationship of Alfred and Alma Hitchcock. I wanted to help build a film that would pull back the curtain on the relationship of two of the most private and gifted collaborators who ever worked in Hollywood. I also wanted it to be fun, stylish, witty—a love story with a knife hovering over it, if you will.

In the succeeding years, our project found homes at several

studios, was given two separate green-light start dates, got derailed by a contentious 2007 Writers Guild of America strike, and, in the end, lost its original director. From then on, once again, *Hitchcock* got courted by—and rejected by—directors of both the household-name and up-and-coming varieties. Through the *sturm and drang*, I was always grateful and never doubted that the movie would get made.

But now here we finally all sit in this 20th Century Fox conference room, listening to a scene in which Helen Mirren's loving, strong, charming, bracingly intelligent Alma fires off some home truths to Anthony Hopkins's loving, obsessive, pressured Alfred. The actors clash with such craft, art, and intensity that I sense many in the room wanting to applaud. The moment is even sweeter for me because it has always been one of my half-dozen or so favorite (and most personal) moments in the screenplay. Now these spectacular actors take it and run with it, making it their own. I get that adrenaline rush again and again not only when Sir Anthony and Dame Helen work their magic, but when Richard Portnow as the powerful, ramrodding, righteous head of Paramount Pictures goes head to head over *Psycho* with Anthony Hopkins's equally fearsome, intransigent Hitchcock. Bells also go off when both Jessica Biel and James D'Arcy prove to be so touching in their scenes with Sir Anthony. The barbed dialogue and the jokes get laughs. *Intended* laughs. The emotional moments sting and move us. There's excitement, release and, okay, more than a little cautious euphoria.

The table read ends in sustained applause, congratulations, sniffles, guarded optimism, and excited anticipation about the challenges ahead. Sheer adrenaline alone could have propelled me all the way home, but I took the conventional method and drove my car off the Fox lot, thinking how far *Alfred Hitchcock and the Making of Psycho* has traveled since it's publication twenty-two years ago after dozens of publishing houses had turned it down. Thanks to my then agent, the late Julian Bach (elegant, boundlessly energetic, justifiably legendary) and the late S. Arthur "Red" Dembner, a straight-shooting former *Newsweek* executive turned independent book publisher, the book got published, although modestly and without fanfare. But our audience found us, especially after May 9, 1990, when the *New York Times* published Christopher Lehmann-Haupt's favorable review on the front page of its "Books of the Times" section. To commemorate the thirtieth anniversary of the theatrical release of *Psycho,* I was soon invited as a guest on several national and international TV shows, and the book became a college course curriculum staple. To this day, not a week goes by without at very least one person contacting me with a question or a comment about the book. And if my current literary agent, the wise, ferociously supportive, and indefatigable Mary Evans, hadn't spurred the book's reissue, die-hard producers Alan Barnette and Tom Thayer might never have found it.

All these years later, I still want to tinker with the text of this book, clarify the chronology, fix glitches, and describe how my reactions to *Psycho* have shifted over time. In fact, if allowed, I'd rewrite it from page one. As a kid, I considered the film a brilliant, one-of-a-kind hair-raiser but now see it as far more. However, it is always gratifying to learn that so many readers—and *some* critics, anyway—appreciate that I deliberately chose not to analyze, dissect, deconstruct, or, especially, wring the life out of *Psycho.* Twenty-two years after the book's first publication, it was an immensely powerful, moving, and sometimes surreal experience to watch the director, cast, and crew of *Hitchcock* recreate on locations and on the soundstage certain documentary aspects of the book, as well as images, dialogue, scenes, and sequences created specifically for the script. *Wait*, I sometimes wanted to say, that isn't how this character looked or sounded. This isn't what they said or how they sounded saying it. At other moments, everything felt eerily, precisely right.

I'll share some favorite on-set moments—spoiler-free, I hope. Some of the best of these unfolded on the lot and on soundstages at Hollywood's historic Red Studios, opened in 1915 as Metro Pictures Backlot #3, later owned by Desi Arnaz and Lucille Ball and renamed Desilu Studios, and still later, called Ren-Mar Studios. It was a filming site for such TV shows and films as *I Love Lucy, The Dick Van Dyke Show, The Andy Griffith Show, The Jack Benny Program, I Spy, The Golden Girls, Seinfeld, Weeds,* and *Who Framed Roger Rabbit?*

I eye-witnessed the shooting of some satisfying moments, like a scene where Sir Anthony as Hitchcock and the brilliant Toni Collette playing longtime Hitchcock production assistant Peggy Robertson watch as the fiercely independent beauty Vera Miles (played by Jessica Biel) gets ushered onto the set and into her dressing room to begin her first day of shooting. Biel's movements, even the tilt of her head, subtly inform us about Miles's bloodied but unbowed attitude toward having fallen out of favor with her would-be Svengali, Hitchcock. Sir Anthony regales Collette with choice, snide observations—some scripted, some improvised—about Miles, making Hitchcock irascible, nasty, but absolutely human, using malicious humor to hide his hurt at being rejected by Miles, whom he had hoped to rebrand in the chic, cool, Grace Kelly glamour-girl mold. As Robertson, Collette defends her gender, defends Miles, and deflects Hitchcock's petty barbs; her chemistry with Sir Anthony is electric. The work of these actors is simple and unfussy, yet it's a master class.

I cherish the memory of watching Helen Mirren's eloquent expression and body language when, as Hitchcock's indispensible and largely silent collaborator, she watches the tall door of a sound-stage slide closed, shutting in her husband and his fellow movie-makers while shutting her out. There was the lovely moment of Dame Helen's Alma confiding to Huston the pain and pleasure of being married to an obsessive, flawed, and fallible man who also happens to be a famous director. And to watch Anthony Hopkins pace and fret in a movie theater lobby while secretly listening to an early movie audience react to *Psycho*, allowing himself only a moment of satisfaction when he hears the crowd erupt in a bloodcurdling scream—does it get much better?

There were smaller moments, too, that felt equally rich, such as producer Alan Barnette walking me through a dark, genuinely creepy set depicting the horror-chamber Wisconsin home of Ed Gein, the 1950s killer. Wandering into the reproduction of Hitchcock's production suite, I noticed on the receptionist's desk a dozen or so vintage-style envelopes hand-addressed to Alfred Hitchcock. Audiences will never see them but a smart, detail-oriented prop or set person cared enough to make certain they were there. Richard Chassler told me that, before playing his scene as actor Martin Balsam, he touched for good luck the original *Psycho* stairway newel post, rented for our film from the Universal prop department. Walking into the makeup and hair headquarters presided over by Howard Berger and Julie Hewett, a life-sized dummy of Mrs. Bates sat in a chair. Spotting a male extra dressed in one of Julie Weiss's meticulous period costumes, I saw that his stance and attitude captured the vibe of the era—solid acting, even when the cameras weren't turning. The cast and crew took such care to recreate the glamour and excitement, as well as the career pressures on Hitchcock, during the 1959 movie premiere of *North by Northwest,* let alone that of an early New York showing of *Psycho*. For the latter, the exterior of a downtown Los Angeles movie house was decorated with posters, standees, and door panels recreating Hitchcock's influential advertising campaign—only with the images of the cast of *Hitchcock* substituted for the cast of *Psycho*.

I spent many solitary hours writing *Alfred Hitchcock and the Making of Psycho*. There were many more spent working on various aspects of *Hitchcock*. Some might say that I was obsessed, perhaps even a little mad, but, to quote one of *Psycho* screenwriter Joseph Stefano's many now-famous lines of dialogue, "We all go a little mad sometimes." Watching the director, the cast, crew, producers and studio team members invest passion, love and professionalism into making *Hitchcock*, how gratifying to know that this time, I didn't go mad alone.

STEPHEN REBELLO
September, 2012

1. The Awful Truth

The Atrocities of Ed Gein

> There was a young man named Ed
> Who would not take a woman to bed
> When he wanted to diddle,
> He cut out the middle
> And hung the rest in a shed.
>
> ANONYMOUS, 1957

In late November 1957, no one would have marked Plainfield as unlike any other hardscrabble, rawboned Wisconsin farm hamlet. That winter was especially raw. Ask any of the friendly townies of third-and fourth-generation German and French stock. In flat, laconic tones, they recite litanies of burst water mains and permafrost; of nights spent hunkering down against slashing winds and rains that blew east along Canada's border. But that November also saw Plainfield mentioned in newspapers across the country. Remind these dairyland types about *that* little bit of business and their open faces wall up. They begin to study their shoes or make excuses before they beg off. That month, in 1957, Plainfield police smoked out an oafish fifty-one-year-old, odd-job-and-errands man named Ed Gein (rhymes with mean) as one of the grisliest mass murderers America ever spawned.

Long before the headlines were to brand Gein as a bogeyman, his rural, God-fearing community of seven hundred had chalked him off as a crank. A perpetually grinning, unmarried recluse, Gein rambled over 160 ruined acres once farmed by his parents and brother. Even locals who never gave a second thought to hiring Gein for errands or baby-sitting had wearied of his hare-brained theories. He liked to rag on the whys and wherefores of criminals who fouled up, or yammer endlessly, and pitifully, about women. Plainfielders recall his clinical obsession with anatomy and with the sex-change operation of Christine Jorgensen. But there was more to Gein than loony talk. That came home with a vengeance with the discovery of bloodstains on the floor of Bernice Worden's general store on November 16.

Customers *had* marked it as odd that Worden's store had been closed since before noon that Saturday, her busiest day. No one had seen the steady, well-liked storekeeper since the previous day. Her pickup truck was missing from its usual spot. Concerned, Worden's deputy sheriff son, Frank, let himself into the store. A late entry in Worden's sales book ("½ gall. antifreeze") triggered Frank's recollection of Ed Gein's loafing about the store the previous week. Gein had asked whether Frank would be out deer hunting on Saturday. When Frank answered that he would, Gein casually mentioned he might be back for a can of antifreeze.

On Frank Worden's tip, Sheriff Art Schley and Captain Lloyd Schoephoerster made tracks for Gein's lonesome, decaying hermitage. The hand of death had first passed over the stark farmland when Gein's father succumbed to a stroke in 1940. Four years later, a fire claimed the life of Ed's older brother, Henry, and, the following year, Gein's hellfire-and-brimstone-spouting mother met her maker, too. Now, Gein lived alone—or so it had seemed.

Gein was elsewhere when the law came to call. Schley and his officers lighted the way with kerosene lamps and flashlights; the old house was only partly jerry-wired for electricity. The lawmen picked their way through a rat's nest of browning newspapers, pulp magazines, anatomy books, embalming supplies, food cartons, tin cans, and random debris. Upstairs, five empty, unused rooms slept under blankets of dust; by contrast, the bedroom of Gein's late mother and a living room, both nailed shut, were kept pristine.

Raking the rubble of Gein's kitchen and bedroom, the officers uncovered sights for which no highway wreck or Saturday night special shoot-'em-up had prepared them. Grinning, loose-toothed Ed Gein did not live alone, after all. Sharing his abode were two shin bones. Two pairs of human lips on a string. A cupful of human noses that sat on the kitchen table. A human skin purse and bracelets. Four flesh-upholstered chairs. A tidy row of ten grimacing human skulls. A tom-tom rigged from a quart can with skin stretched across the top and bottom. A soup bowl fashioned from an inverted human half-skull. The eviscerated skins of four women's faces, rouged, made-up, and thumb-tacked to the wall at eye level. Five "replacement" faces secured in plastic bags. Ten female heads, hacked off at the eyebrow. A rolled-up pair of leggings and skin "vest," including the mammaries, severed from another unfortunate.

In the adjacent smokehouse shed, police found what they would later identify as having once been Bernice Worden. Nude, headless, dangling by the heels, she had been disemboweled like a steer. Sitting atop a pot-bellied stove in the adjacent kitchen was a pan of water in which floated a human heart. The freezer compartment of the refrigerator was stocked with carefully wrapped human organs.

"I didn't have anything to do with it. I just heard about it while I was eating supper," mumbled Gein when Frank Worden located and confronted him about the discovery of Bernice's corpse. Worden arrested Gein on the spot. In no time flat, Plainfield's Caspar Milquetoast underwent a lie detector test, a murder charge, and psychiatric examinations at Central State Hospital for the Criminally Insane. Until then, no one had credited the mutterings of a shiftless crank about his "collection of shrunken heads." No one paid any mind to his inside knowledge of the area's many unsolved disappearances of women. The Gein farmhouse offered testimony not only to man's fathomless capacity for the barbaric, but also to the ability of an entire community to deny its very existence. "It can't happen *here*," insists the satiric lyric of a Frank Zappa song, "Help I'm a Rock." The "here" in question is the human heart and mind.

Gein met the probing of his examiners with barely audible, monotone ramblings. His memory was murky. He admitted to only two murders, claiming he was "in a daze" during both. No law officer, psychiatrist, or court examiner could penetrate Gein's motivations. Yes, he admitted to dismantling Bernice Worden's cash register and removing $41. Yes, he had also exhumed his first cadaver with a farmer crony, Gus. Yet his rationale for both was identical: He liked "taking things apart" to see "how things work."

Deep in the night, while his hard-working neighbors made love, snored, studied the Good Book, and fretted over bills, bland, simple Ed Gein delved into the mystery of "how things worked" by traipsing around the farm with the skin, hair, and face mask of newly exhumed corpses strapped to his naked body. Authorities discovered that Gein's first graveyard visit led to forty-odd other digs—always graves of females—often just a stone's throw from the final resting place of his mother. He told his examiners that he and Gus (who had died several years earlier of natural causes) buried the bones and incinerated less-interesting body parts in the Gein stove. When newspapers reported that Gein claimed "I never shot a deer," how many locals shuddered at the memory of plastic bags packed with tasty "venison" given them by Gein?

Gein made his first kill in 1955 when, late one bitter winter night, his .32 rifle drew a bead on a bosomy, fifty-one-year-old, divorced tavern owner. Using a sled, Gein dragged the body of Mary Hogan to his "summer kitchen" shed. Police suspected Gein of torturing and murdering at least ten other victims between Mary Hogan and Bernice Worden. He never owned up to them before being judged criminally insane and sentenced to life at Central State Hospital.

Local newspapers, some of which dubbed Gein "the mad butcher," reported only his murders and alleged cannibalism. Transvestism, grave robbing, and, as some speculated, an incestuous relationship with Mom apparently went beyond the limits of even big-city reportage of the 1950s. For "America's dairyland," such topics were literally unspeakable. But what the newspapers suppressed, back-fence rumors and sick jokes spelled out. The press and the ambulance chasers attached themselves to Plainfield like piranha on a drowning sumo wrestler. Cars packed with the curious drove miles to aim Brownie cameras and to stone Gein's "murder house." Outraged locals circled the wagons and closed their minds. Yet many natives were known to drive miles out of their way to bypass the Gein farm. Inevitably, there were cracks in the wall of denial. Physicians throughout the state found their offices packed with patients complaining of gastrointestinal symptoms. Local psychiatrists treated many ids scrambled by Gein's penchant for "spare parts."

Sick jokes, "Gein-ers" the locals called them, ran rampant. Setup: "How were Ed Gein's folks?" Payoff: "Delicious." Or "What's Ed Gein's phone number?," which drew the response: "O-I-C-U-8-1-2." And this to defuse another unspoken terror: "Why could no one ever keep Gein in jail?" Punchline: "Because he'd just draw a picture of a woman on the wall and eat his way out." Bar hounds roused boozy yuks by ordering Gein Beer ("Lots of body, but no head"), and corn-fed tykes with faces like Campbell's Soup can kids jumped rope, chanting:

'Twas the night before Christmas
And all through the school,
Not a creature was stirring
Not even a mule.
The teachers were hung
From the ceiling with care
In hope that Ed Gein
Soon would be there.

To the day of Gein's quiet, uneventful death on July 26, 1984 in the asylum, hospital workers described him as "tractable," "harmless." His awareness of the outside world was minimal. Of his crimes he was virtually an amnesiac. Perhaps hoping to purge Plainfield of the Gein legacy, unknown persons torched the farm over two decades ago. To this day, the morbid, the crime buffs, the thrill seekers, and the marginals make pilgrimages to the ruins. And locals admit a Yuletide never passes without some child's warbling, "Deck the halls with limbs of Mollie."

No one can measure the shock waves unleashed by Ed Gein's monstrous acts or the anguish he inflicted upon his victims or their survivors. In 1957, most Americans preferred to perceive themselves as God-fearing, clean-living men in gray flannel suits, or perfectly perfect Doris Day wives, or wholesome kids next door like Shirley Jones and Pat Boone in *April Love*. We elected a president named Eisenhower, twirled Hula Hoops, and watched *Ozzie and Harriet*. But in a town less than forty miles from Plainfield, at least one man stared hard into the bathroom mirror while shaving. He brooded over Gein, thought of himself, and shuddered.

2. THE NOVEL

Yours Truly, Robert Bloch

Weyauwega, Wisconsin, lies thirty-nine miles from Plainfield. Robert Bloch—an unassuming, literate, forty-year-old writer— was unsettled by what he glimpsed of his soul as he stared into the bathroom mirror one morning. Bloch had just finished writing a new novel. He perceived that he had perhaps disinterred nasty, unvoiced things—about himself, about the human spirit. True, this new book was not the first time he had trafficked with the dark side. An acolyte/protégé of the High Priest of fantasy-horror fiction, H. P. Lovecraft, Bloch had been exploring the underbelly since 1934 with "Lilies," a story he sold to *Marvel Tales* at age seventeen. When he had read the first newspaper reports of the Ed Gein case, Bloch was best known for *The Scarf*, a novel he had written eight years earlier. That book opens with the lines: "Fetish? You name it. All I know is that I've always had to have it with me."

Although Bloch and his wife were not subscribers to the local mouthpiece, the *Weyauwega Chronicle*, the writer had hungrily searched out a few meager paragraphs about Gein that lay buried among in-depth accounts of church bazaars and daily homilies-to-live-by. When Bloch scoured the bigger, Milwaukee papers, he puzzled over how even *they* played down the case. A wry, elfin man with a sonorous voice, Bloch recalls, "Facts were sparse, since the news didn't care to play up unsavory local happenings. All I could learn was that a man had been arrested after murdering the proprietress of a local hardware store found hanging in his farm dressed out like a deer. Then, the police found other, 'unspecified' evidence which led one to believe he had not only committed previous crimes but perhaps dug up some graves."

The raw facts so gripped Bloch, he began to take notes furiously. The writer observed: "I wondered how this man, never suspected of any kind of wrongdoing, in a town where if someone sneezed on the north side of town, someone on the south said 'Gesundheit,' was only *suddenly* discovered to be a mass murderer. I was also puzzled by how unanxious his neighbors were to speak about these crimes. I said to myself: 'There's a *story* here.'"

Starting off with the few scraps he had gleaned about Gein, Bloch plunged himself into imaginings about a central character for a proposed novel. At the time, Bloch never dreamed that this character was to tap into the heart of a peculiarly American darkness. He recalled: "In my mind, the character would have been the equivalent of a Rod Steiger–type at that time, who lived alone—a recluse more or less, who didn't have a lot of friends. How would he select his victims? I came up with his being a motel keeper because of easy access to strangers. At the time, I was not positively aware that the actual murderer had also been a grave robber. Besides, it wasn't considered exactly polite to discuss those sorts of things in newspapers, not to mention fifties mystery fiction."

Following his bent for abnormal psychology, Bloch began to spin feasible—if sensational—means and motivations for his bizarre main character. The writer explained: "In itself, his living alone and victimizing transient customers wouldn't be enough to prevent discovery of the crimes. I thought, what if he committed these crimes in an amnesiac fugue with another personality taking over? But *whose* personality? Now, in the late fifties, Freudian theories were very popular and, although I much prefer Jung if I have to stick with anybody, I decided to develop the story along Freudian lines. The big Freudian concept was the Oedipus fixation, so I thought, 'Let's say he had a thing about his mother,' based strictly on the kind of inverted personality he was. Let's suppose mother was dead—naturally for story convenience, you didn't want her hanging around—but suppose he *imagined* she was still alive? The reason he had amnesiac fugues was that he *became his mother* while committing the crimes. He might have talked to her when alone. Then I thought, 'But wouldn't it be nice if she were actually present in some form?' And that is when I came up with the notion that he had actually *preserved* her body."

Taxidermy as a major plot device assured that Bloch had crossed the dividing line between the polite "parlor mystery" of the day and the flat-out "shocker." Bloch next toyed with the device of telling the story employing the first-person "voice" of his mama's-boy central figure. If the gambit worked, Bloch's surprise ending might put a whole new Freudian spin on the whodunit genre. If it failed, Bloch would land on the bones of other writers unable to bring off what Edgar Allan Poe or Jim Thompson in *The Killer Inside Me* had done to diabolical perfection.

Although Bloch backed down from his original intent, he deployed nearly as risky a tactic. He explained: "I realized I *had* to have multiple viewpoints—a hero *and* a heroine—so I devised a heroine from another town who'd come to stay at this particular motel on a mission. It occurred to me to do something not generally done in fiction: establish a heroine, give her a problem, make her more or less likable so that the reader would have some kind of empathy for her, then kill her off about one-third of the way through the story. Readers would say, 'My God, *now what?* We've lost her.'"

Bloch was to pull off a fiendish masterstroke in stage-managing not only the *timing* but also the *manner* of the demise of his heroine. "I had the notion that a person is never more defenseless than when taking a shower," he recalled, pride tugging at the corners of his mouth. "Naked, in a confined space, we feel we're alone and then—well, a sudden intrusion is a *very* shocking thing. I hit upon a device, which worked in print, of ending the chapter by having a shower curtain flung aside. The knife cut off her scream. And her head.* Now that's a shockeroo. I had not thought of a film at that time; in fact, they weren't making films with that graphic violence in those days."

Once Bloch had invented the characters of a snoopy sister and the lover who search for the missing heroine, his story beats fell perfectly into place. "The story basically wrote itself," observed Bloch of the first draft, on which he worked six weeks. "I added various embellishments as I went along to strengthen the story. The moment I finished it, I sent it off to my literary agent, Harry Altshuler, who handled me in science fiction, fantasy, and suspense."

---

*As written, the passage actually reads: "Mary started to scream, and then the curtains parted further and a hand appeared, holding a butcher knife. It was the knife that, a moment later, cut off her scream. And her head."

Altshuler, based in New York, promptly sent the Bloch manuscript, titled *Psycho*, to Harper & Row. Almost as promptly, the
publishing house rejected it. On the rebound, Altshuler tried
Clayton Rawson, an editor at Simon & Schuster and a noted
mystery writer himself. Rawson snapped up *Psycho* for Simon &
Schuster's popular, one-per-month Inner Sanctum Mystery book
series.** "I received the staggering advance of $750," recalled
Bloch. To acknowledge the speedy sale his agent had made,
Bloch inscribed *Psycho* with the dedication: "10% of this book is
dedicated to Harry Altshuler who did 90% of the work."

At Simon & Schuster, the corridor talk pegged *Psycho* as a sensational read and a highly exploitable commodity. Art director
Jeffery Metzner hired graphic artist Tony Palladino to design a
title concept that would convey the shock aspect of the storyline.
Palladino's distinctive title logo evoked letters slashed by a knife
or shattered by a scream, or even madness itself. In fact, Palladino's graphic was to become synonymous with the title *Psycho*
and remained so for three decades. The illustrator recalled: "The
book and title were on the tongues of a lot of people at Simon &
Schuster at the time. That title was so descriptive, I let the title
become the graphic. It was much stronger than any illustration
one could do. The guy [in the novel] was quite cracked up, so,
in the graphic, I cracked up the lettering to reinforce the title."

Simon & Schuster published *Psycho* in the summer of 1959,
just months before the second anniversary of the discoveries
at the Ed Gein farmhouse. In the novel, Bloch transformed

**Simon & Schuster's Inner Sanctum imprint took its title from a popular for-
ties radio mystery series. From the 1940s through the 1970s, the line published
top writers Anthony Boucher, Ira Levin, Philip MacDonald, Ellery Queen,
Craig Rice, and lesser lights. In the early forties, Universal Pictures produced
a series of Inner Sanctum shockers as second features (*Weird Woman*, *Pillow
of Death*, *The Frozen Ghost*). TV had a go at an Inner Sanctum series in 1953.

Midwestern Plainfield into "Fairvale," a graceless, humdrum town in the American Southwest. The writer fictionalized real-life Gein into the pudgy, mother-dominated motelkeep, Norman Bates, whose flights of madness are fired up by liquor, pornography, Saint-Saëns, and Beethoven. Bates encounters a pretty, vulnerable guest, Mary Crane (Gein's first victim was named Mary), en route—with forty thousand stolen dollars— to her lover who owns a hardware store (Gein's second victim owned a hardware store). During a supper and conversation, Mary arouses the compassion—and the lust—of the pathetic Bates. After Mary begs off, she is slashed to death in a shower stall, apparently by Bates's possessive, maniacal mother. When an insurance sleuth is also knifed to death while tracking Mary, the boyfriend and sister of the dead girl pursue the mystery. They eventually unmask Norman Bates as a matricidal, trans- vestite, multiple murderer.

The first printing of ten thousand copies of *Psycho* enjoyed brisk sales and, Bloch observed, "some very flattering reviews, including one in the *New York Times*." Indeed, on April 19, 1959, writer and anthologist Anthony Boucher, in his "Crimi- nals at Large" column of the *New York Times Book Review*, raved: "[Bloch] is more chillingly effective than any writer might rea- sonably be expected to be . . . [and] demonstrates that a believ- able history of mental illness can be more icily terrifying than all the arcane horrors summoned up by a collaboration of Poe and Lovecraft." The *Herald Tribune* critic marked the novel as "adroit and bloodcurdling," and *Best Sellers* thought it "A terribly chilling tale . . . may well be the most unusual story of the year." Fawcett picked up the book for a paperback version that sped through nine printings of its first edition.

Among most of the mainstream literary cognoscenti, *Psycho*, a genre piece, was rebuffed. As Raymond Chandler described the lot of fellow mystery writers in a 1944 letter: "However well and expertly he writes a mystery story, it will be treated in one paragraph while a column and a half of respectful attention will be given to any fourth-rate, ill-constructed mock-serious account of the life of a bunch of cotton pickers in the Deep South." However, such contemporary writers as Stephen King compare Bloch's trio of psychological novels (*The Scarf, The Deadbeat, Psycho*) to James M. Cain's *The Postman Always Rings Twice, Double Indemnity, Mildred Pierce*). "In their own way," wrote King in *Danse Macabre*, "the novels that Robert Bloch wrote in the 1950s had every bit as much influence on the course of American literature as did the Cain 'heel-with-a-heart' novels of the 1930s."

Measured by the yardstick of contemporary horror literature, when readers have been Stephen King-ed and Clive Barker-ed to a bloody pulp, *Psycho* now looks like a model of restraint. Yet in 1959, Mickey Spillane or Agatha Christie were about as far as mainstream thriller literature went. *Psycho* came on like something on which Edgar Allan Poe and William Gains, master of the horrifying E. C. Comics of the fifties, might have collaborated while hopped-up on Krafft-Ebing. Robert Bloch had sexed-up and Freudianized the Gothic, revitalizing such creaky elements as the rattletrap Old Dark House, the stormy night, and the crackpot madwoman locked in the dank basement. Into the brew, Bloch stirred a motel on the skids and a randy, alcoholic, mama's boy whose scrambled psyche and way with taxidermy could keep several shrinks in summer houses in the Hamptons for years.

Despite howls of protest from critics who believed that their genteel sensibilities had been violated, Bloch actually tidied up and made palatable the far more unsavory facts of the Gein case.*** Explains Bloch, "In my novel, following on Freudian precepts, I made Norman Bates a transvestite who dressed up as his mother with a wig and dress whenever he committed these crimes. Much to my surprise, I discovered that the actual killer dressed up also, but he allegedly wore the breasts and skins of his mother. I also discovered he was subject to amnesiac fugues and had no memory of committing these crimes. He was a necrophiliac and a cannibal. Busy, busy, busy! He had a fixation on his mother, who had died twelve years previously. He kept her room inviolate and untouched since that time and the gentleman was also given to perversions in the time-honored tradition of the Nazi death camps."

It was when Bloch realized the weird similarity between the true-crime revelations and his own novel that he began to find himself staring into mirrors and wondering about himself. "In other words," Bloch mused, "in inventing my character I had come very close to the actual persona of Ed Gein. It horrified me how I could think of such things. As a result, I spent the next two years shaving with my eyes shut. I didn't want to look in the mirror."

During mid-February 1959, Bloch's agent, Harry Altshuler, had sent out advance copies of *Psycho* to several movie studios. A typical response to the book was script reader William Pinckard's; on February 25, he offered this opinion to Paramount executives: "Too repulsive for films, and rather shocking even to a hardened reader. It is original, no doubt about that, and the author practices clever deceptions upon the reader, not revealing until the end that the villain's mother is actually a stuffed corpse. Cleverly

---

***Bloch's fascinating account of the Gein case alone makes *The Quality of Murder* (Dutton, 1962) worth reading. Edited by Anthony Boucher, the book compiles some of history's most fascinating crimes and criminals, as seen by members of the Mystery Writers of America.

plotted, quite scary toward the end, and actually fairly believable. But impossible for films."

"Impossible" or not, in April 1959, Music Corporation of American (MCA) agent Ned Brown tendered a $7,500 "blind bid" to Altshuler for the screen rights. Bloch recalled his agent's buoyantly phoning him with the news: "When I asked who was buying the book, he said, 'They won't tell me.' I said, 'We've got to get more than $7,500. Why don't you try $10,000?'" Altshuler complied and, in a wire dated May 6, agent Brown counteroffered a sum of $9,000. Altshuler advised Bloch to accept. "Harry came back and said, 'I can't get them any further.' I said I'd take it and signed the contract believing agents are supposed to know about such things. I'd sold nothing to films before that. So, under the terms of my contract, Simon & Schuster got 15 percent off the top and my agent got 10 percent, which left me with about $6,750 before taxes. In the end, I imagine I wound up with about $5,000."

At roughly the time that Bloch learned that his contract with Simon & Schuster included no bonus or percentage of profits in the event of a sale to Hollywood, the writer reeled from another blow. "It was then," said Bloch with a sigh, "I learned that *Psycho* had been bought by Mr. Alfred Hitchcock."

3. THE DIRECTOR

The Trouble With Alfred

Why Alfred Hitchcock and *Psycho*? Most would understand the glee of a relatively obscure author on learning that one of the world's most celebrated directors had snapped up the film rights to one of his books. Yet even to a flattered novelist, *Psycho* and the Master of Suspense seemed an odd coupling. In the spring of 1959, Alfred Hitchcock had the movie world wrapped around his pudgy finger. Having been a household name for decades, Hitchcock earned $250,000 per picture, plus a healthy chunk of the gross. Since 1953, after several bumpy years at Warner Bros., Hitchcock and his retinue had presided over a knotty-pine-paneled suite in the Producers' Building of Paramount at 5555 Melrose Avenue, Hollywood.

Paramount gave Hitchcock carte blanche over story selection, screenwriter, cast, editing, and publicity for any project costing

$3 million or less. The studio superstructure so coveted the director's services that they also turned over to him the highly lucrative rights to *Rear Window, The Trouble with Harry, The Man Who Knew Too Much,* and *Vertigo* after release. No wonder a Paramount executive had written to a counterpart at MGM, while Hitchcock was making *North by Northwest* in 1958, "Paramount functions practically as a studio setup for him."

In the late spring of 1959, Hitchcock was gearing up for the July release of *North by Northwest,* a $3.3 million Technicolor chase featuring Cary Grant, Eva Marie Saint, James Mason, and Mount Rushmore in a larky Ernest Lehman screenplay involving spies, microfilm, and sex. Having mushroomed into MGM's biggest-budgeted project of 1959, aside from *Ben-Hur,* the picture went on to become one of the great Hitchcock audience pleasers. But there is reason to suspect that the fifty-nine-year-old suspense maestro felt bullied by his brilliant present and past.

Forty-six feature films and three successful seasons on television had put Hitchcock on constant guard against repeating himself. To "recharge the battery," as Hitchcock put it, he had already confined the action to microcosms (*Lifeboat, Rope, Rear Window*) and gleefully splashed it across public spaces and national monuments (*Blackmail, The 39 Steps,* the British and American versions of *The Man Who Knew Too Much, Saboteur, Foreign Correspondent*). He had gussied-up melodrama with ruffles and flourishes (*Jamaica Inn, Under Capricorn*) and tricked-out stageplay adaptations with such technical gizmas as the ten-minute take or 3-D (*Rope, Dial M for Murder*). He had pumped up the adrenaline with chamber pieces about neurotics (*Rebecca, Suspicion, Notorious*) and full-on psychopaths (*Spellbound, Shadow of a Doubt, Strangers on a Train*). He had played comedy light (*Mr. and Mrs. Smith*) and autumnal *The Trouble with Harry*). He had tried on semidocumentary (*The Wrong Man*) and haunting, sexy metaphysics (*Vertigo*). There had even been a couple of lumbering musical numbers (*Waltzes from Vienna, Stage Fright*); Hitchcock's hand was so practiced, he made top-ten Neilsen ratings for *Alfred Hitchcock Presents* on CBS look like something one does in one's sleep.

Alfred Hitchcock was only half joking when he told the press, "If I made *Cinderella*, the audience would be looking for a corpse to turn up in the coach," or ruefully observed of the trap in which he had caught himself, "Style is self-plagiarism." H. N. Swanson, friend to Hitchcock and agent to such suspense novelists as Raymond Chandler and Elmore Leonard, put it this way: "Hitch never casually looked for 'something different.' He was *relentless*." Another longtime Hitchcock associate, agent Michael Ludmer, insisted, "We scoured everything—plays, novels, short stories, newspaper clippings. 'Whodunits' were out of the question and he mistrusted science fiction, the supernatural, or anything to do with professional criminals. Since one couldn't second-guess what little spark might turn him on, it was terribly back-breaking tracking material for him."

Enter *Psycho*. "It certainly seemed like a departure," admitted Bloch in recalling the director's interest in his despairing story of lives played out in dingy offices, run-down motels, and a decrepit house. "He had been doing big color films, with big stars and all the box-office insurances deemed necessary. Although I had no idea what to expect, I knew his film adaptations from novels were very much changed—*The Secret Agent* (which became *Sabotage*), *Suspicion*, or *Spellbound*, for example. However, I felt that there wasn't much point in him buying this particular book unless he meant to use the storyline. There was hardly anyone else in the world I would have preferred to Hitchcock, except [director] Henri-Georges Clouzot, who had done *Les Diaboliques*."

Yet in 1959, virtually no one but Hitchcock could answer

"Why *Psycho*?" Cameraman Leonard South, whose first of fifteen Hitchcock assignments was *Strangers on a Train* (1951), explained: "Hitch had promised Universal a picture and decided that *Psycho*, a small project, would get that commitment out of the way." Another reason for *Psycho* is that, for a director frantically in search of the unexpected, the Bloch novel came to his attention not a minute too soon. Earlier that year Paramount lost small fortunes on two aborted Hitchcock projects. *Flamingo Feather* had been an adventure-chase involving diamonds and tribal unrest in Africa that the director envisioned as a giddy, John Buchan-esque (*The 39 Steps*) fandango. Unfortunately, while busily combing Africa for suitable chase locations, Hitchcock had delegated the screenplay to screenwriter Angus MacPhail (*The Wrong Man*, *Vertigo*), who never managed to deliver a completed manuscript. No such problems awaited the sparklingly malicious murder comedy, *No Bail for the Judge*, based on Henry Cecil's book about a lawyer who must defend her magistrate father against charges of strangling a streetwalker. The script by Samuel Taylor (*Vertigo*) was camera-ready when intended star Audrey Hepburn announced her pregnancy. Then British law cracked down on street prostitution—Hitchcock's MacGuffin, the plot device that greased the wheels of suspense. In private Hitchcock railed. To the public he made light, as when he told the *New York Times* about his frustration in finding suitable material: "Newspaper headlines tell too many outlandish stories from real life that drive the spinner of suspense fiction to further extremes. I always regard the fact that we've got to outwit the audience to keep them with us. They're highly trained detectives looking at us out there right now."

Another fly in Hitchcock's ointment was competitors who strayed onto his turf and competed for material. Directors William Castle (*When Strangers Marry*), Robert Siodmak (*The Spiral*

Staircase), George Cukor (*Gaslight*), Otto Preminger (*Laura*, *Whirlpool*), and dozens of others, had each "pulled a Hitchcock" with varying degrees of finesse. And what about the 1955 French import, *Les Diaboliques*, one of the first breakaway hits from the art-house circuit, that had critics praising director Henri-Georges Clouzot as "the Gallic Hitchcock?"

Hitchcock had also soured at being held hostage to the salary demands of such stars as Cary Grant and James Stewart, or of Grace Kelly, whom he considered his once and future leading lady until she defected to Monaco to marry the dashing prince. "Stars' salaries are becoming unthinkable," the director complained. "The minute you put a star into a role you've already compromised because it may not be perfect casting . . . In television we have a greater chance to cast more freely than in pictures. Star names don't mean all that much in television, at least in dramatic terms."

Alfred Hitchcock trusted the film instincts of few. One of his inner circle was Peggy Robertson, a production assistant to him since *Under Capricorn* (1949). The wife of film editor Douglas Robertson, the razor-sharp, occasionally acerbic aide was one of three women—Alma Hitchcock, the director's wife, and screenwriter-producer Joan Harrison being the other two—whose sensitivity to Hitchcock's distress signals bordered on the telepathic. "I've never dealt with whodunits," he often explained of his choice of material. "They're simply clever puzzles, aren't they? They're intellectual rather than emotional, and emotion is the only thing that keeps my audience interested. I prefer suspense rather than surprise—something the average man can identify with. The audience can't identify with detectives; they're not part of his everyday life."

Hitchcock depended on Robertson to wade through prospective material. In a year in which the Hitchcock office logged

2,400 submissions, Robertson passed on only thirty to the boss. Hitchcock often groused: "I can't read fiction without visualizing every scene. The result is it becomes a series of pictures rather than a book." Robertson had been on the alert for material that might make what her boss had called a "typically un-Hitchcock picture."

With that in mind, Robertson circled in ink Anthony Roucher's strong review in his "Criminals at Large" column. She had read the "coverage" of the novel by Paramount reader William Pinckard (he of the "impossible for films" verdict), but brushed that aside. She also ignored the fact that the novel was reviled by the studio decision-makers. Robertson was an assistant well attuned to how her boss often resonated to obscure material rather than to classics by better-known mystery writers. *Psycho* began to impress Robertson all the more.

Hitchcock holed up with the novel for a weekend in his home on Bellagio Drive in Bel-Air. The working-stiffs milieu, two shocking murders, a twist finale peppered with transvestism, incest, and necrophilia—these were catnip to a man who fancied himself a connoisseur of abnormal psychology. Hitchcock would observe: "I think that the thing that appealed to me and made me decide to do the picture was the suddenness of the murder in the shower, coming, as it were, out of the blue. That was about all." Elaborated Robert Bloch: "[Hitchcock] said that the things that attracted him to *Psycho* were that it had characters with whom the reader could identify and care about. He felt it was very important for shock value that the audience care about the characters who get killed. Then, of course, the cleverness of the device of transvestism." Bloch's novel spoke to Hitchcock's savage sense of irony as had few pieces of material in ages. "I am aware," Hitchcock said, "that I am equipped with what other people have called a fiendish sense of humor."

MCA agent Ned Brown, who struck the deal for the Hitchcock acquisition of the book, once said: "Hitch was fascinated by the idea that the story starts out as one thing—the girl's dilemma—then, after a horrible murder, turns into something else. But frankly, we all thought he would keep the shower murder of the girl and come up with a whole new situation and characters!" Michael Ludmer, who also assisted Hitchcock in finding suitable material, observed: "Often, all Hitchcock was looking for was a springboard or a trigger, even just a relationship. Raw material was all he ever needed." Despite the consternation of some of his colleagues, Hitchcock—to keep the surprises of *Psycho* as surprises—reportedly ordered Peggy Robertson to buy up as many copies of the novel as possible from the publisher and from bookstores.

Hitchcock had finally laid claim to something he had craved since 1955. That year, French director Henri-Georges Clouzot (*Quai des Orfèvres; The Wages of Fear*) had beaten Hitchcock to the punch by buying the rights to a recently translated French suspense novel, *Celle Qui N'Etait Plus* (*The Woman Who Was No More*) by Pierre Boileau and Thomas Narcejac. On the rebound, Hitchcock purchased *D'Entre Les Morts* (roughly, *From Amongst the Dead*), another book by the same authors. Clouzot turned *The Woman Who Was* into *Les Diaboliques*, a gimmicky shocker with a surprise ending that won in 1955 surprising worldwide success with both audiences and critics. In 1958, Hitchcock turned *his* Boileau-Narcejac property into the haunting, elegiac *Vertigo*, which took a drubbing from most critics and the paying public. Alfred Hitchcock had a score to settle with Clouzot.

Although he rarely acknowledged the influence of any sound-era films or directors, Hitchcock clearly scrutinized *Les Diaboliques* (released in America by United Motion Picture Organization as *Diabolique* or *The Fiends*) as well as its publicity campaign as if with a jeweler's loup. Clouzot and cinematographer Armand Thirard photographed *Les Diaboliques* in moody, dirty-dishes-in-the-sink black-and white. Boileau and Narcejac's serpentine plot hinges on the strange bond between birdlike Christina Delasalle (Vera Clouzot) and cool, predatory Nicole Horner (Simone Signoret), respectively the wife and the mistress of a venal schoolmaster, Michael Delasalle (Paul Meurisse). The two women conspire to murder the rotter, but when the wife unravels from a case of the jitters, Nicole drowns her lover in the bathtub. The screws turn as snoopy Inspector Fichet (Charles Vanel) asks too many pointed questions and the dead man's presence seems to cry out from beyond the grave for vengeance.

The set pieces of *Les Diaboliques*—the murder in the bathroom of a grimy hotel room, the hidden corpse that is almost discovered by the schoolboys in a foul swimming pool—build to a finale that made audiences gasp and scream aloud. In France, newspaper ads discouraged moviegoers from seeing the picture except from the beginning. Theater entrance doors were closed at the start of each performance. Titles at the conclusion chided, "Don't be diabolical yourself. Don't spoil the ending for your friends by telling them what you've just seen. On their behalf— Thank you!" When the United Motion Picture Organization imported the film and opened it in New York at The Fine Arts Theater on E 58th Street between Park Avenue and Lexington on November 20, 1955, both the ad campaign and end titles emulated the exploitation gimmicks that had worked so well in Europe.

Films and Filming from England called the thriller "beastly and brilliant" and Bosley Crowther of the *New York Times* thought it "one of the dandiest mystery dramas that has shown here in goodness knows when. To tell anybody the surprises . . . is a crime that should be punishable by consigning of the culprit to a diet of grade-B films." The *Los Angeles Herald-Examiner* critic wrote: "If director Henri-Georges Clouzot isn't the master of the suspense thriller today, then who is? True, Hitchcock is suaver; but this Frenchman is joltier, a master of timing and building an almost unbearable suspense." How could Hitchcock help but feel a bit superannuated when the "joltier" Clouzot and *Les Diaboliques* won the prestigious Delluc Prize in France for highest achievement in originality?

Soon after the release of the movie, Hitchcock would cast the actor who played the shabby detective of *Les Diaboliques*, Charles Vanel, in a small role as Bertani, another enigmatic character, in *To Catch a Thief*. But the director would later appropriate much more from the directorial competitor whom writers were already calling "the French Hitchcock."

Hitchcock had also been carefully tracking the box-office figures of low-budget horror pictures turned out by Universal-International, American-International, Allied Artists, Hammer Film Productions, and others. Such shockfests as *Macabre*, *I Bury the Living*, and *The Curse of Frankenstein* drew crowds while many Hollywood "A"-budget pictures barely drew flies. Hitchcock had begun to quiz his associates—everyone from his limousine driver and barber to agents and studio executives—as to how profitable they thought a first-class, low-budget shocker by a major director might be? Other "name" directors had gone that route before: Howard Hawks (with Christian Nyby) on *The Thing* (1951), Charles Laughton on *The Night of the Hunter* (1955), or Mervyn Leroy on *The Bad Seed* (1956). Hitchcock's colleagues were accustomed to the puckish Buddha's posing rhetorical questions solely for his own amusement. They passed off these new queries as more of the same. But when the egocentric Hitchcock, hardly given to self-criticism or self-analysis, began to dismiss his recent James Stewart or Cary Grant pictures as "glossy Technicolor baubles," associates of the director realized that Hitchcock had something else up his sleeve.

Hitchcock lived a hermetic life: driven to the studio daily for story conferences or shooting, or to Chasen's for dinner with his wife, gossiping with the high-rollers of the business while puffing imported cigars. But even a monied man who viewed the world through the windows of a suite at Claridge's Hotel in London or a home whose walls were lined with Klees and Vlamincks must have sniffed change in the wind. Television news and franker, more adult movies from Europe were shifting the expectations of audiences toward a grittier reality on screen. All the better for *Psycho* that it exposed the grinning skull beneath the rhythms and routine of the ordinary—workaday jobs, make-do relationships, dreams deferred, backwater locales. *Psycho* took place in a world much closer to the one in which most moviegoers lived. Having been born the son of an East End greengrocer in a second-floor apartment above the shop, Hitchcock was as much fascinated as horrified by that world.

Considering a recent track record that included the successful *Rear Window*, *To Catch a Thief*, and *The Man Who Knew Too Much*, Alfred Hitchcock was surely confident when he met with the Paramount bosses on an early June afternoon to announce *Psycho* as his fifth and final commitment under his existing contract. Studio president Barney Balaban and vice-president George Weltner had reason to arrive at that meeting with some confidence themselves. Balaban had come up through the ranks. A run-of-the-mill Chicago band singer, he hit paydirt when he and partner Sam Katz opened a chain of nickelodeons in 1916. Years of trafficking in Mafia payoffs had steeled Balaban to tough negotiations. While television had many rival studios on the ropes, Balaban had steered Paramount to a $12.5 million profit in 1958, the studio's largest takings in nine years. But even in a relative boom, to the Paramount brass, Hitchcock and *Psycho* sounded like a bad mix. Corridor talk at the studio had leaked the rumor that Hitchcock wanted to try "something different." Similar motivations had led to *The Wrong Man* at Warner Bros, and to *The Trouble with Harry* and *Vertigo* at Paramount—three box-office busts. Hitchcock's enthusiasm for an "impossible" property sent Balaban, Weltner, and other Paramount moneymen into executive apoplexy. What was *with* Hitchcock and his cockamamie potboiler about a knife-happy madman who dresses up like dear old Mom? This was worse than *Vertigo*, which at least had class. "They *were* very unhappy about it," admitted novelist Bloch in a classic understatement. "Hitchcock's associate producer, Herbert Coleman, told me Paramount *absolutely* didn't want to make it. They didn't like the title, the story, or anything about it at all. When Hitchcock became insistent, they said, 'Well you're not going to get the budget you're used to having for this sort of thing.' Hence, no Technicolor, no Jimmy Stewart, no Cary Grant. Hitchcock said, 'All right, I'll make do.'"

Hitchcock loathed anyone's making a "scene." He terminated the meeting with icy politeness. It had been decades since anyone, even someone as powerful as producer David O. Selznick, had the temerity to squelch the mighty Hitchcock. In private, the director may have fumed, but not for long. The score Alfred Hitchcock had to settle now went beyond H. G. Clouzot and *Les Diaboliques.*

4. THE DEAL

Hitchcock Outmaneuvers

Developing passion for a movie property can be like falling madly for someone who leaves one's friends cold. Hitchcock had been battling indifference, or outright bewilderment, toward his projects from the start. Producer David O. Selznick, who railed constantly against the director's "damned jigsaw cutting," seemed to have imported Hitchcock from England without comprehending that the sort of talent who can create *The 39 Steps* or *The Lady Vanishes* does not tend to flourish on a leash. Cary Grant complained throughout the shooting of *North by Northwest* that he could make neither heads nor tails of the script. A Paramount executive admitted: "I never saw what Hitchcock did in *Rear Window* until I saw the finished movie." Lack of vision is one thing. Across-the-board contempt for a proposed Hitchcock movie was something new.

Hitchcock refused to kowtow to Paramount. After all, studio executives came and went like this year's starlet. Hitchcock had become a legend for being right more often than wrong. The director and his production staff quietly began exploring how to minimize the investment downside of *Psycho.* Hitchcock hit on the solution: plan his new production as scrupulously as he would any big-budget feature film, but shoot it quickly and inexpensively, almost like an expanded episode of his TV series, *Alfred Hitchcock Presents.*

That popular anthology series, which debuted on CBS on October 2, 1955, had been a master plot of Hitchcock's MCA agent, confidante and father confessor Lew Wasserman, nee Lewis Robert Wasserman. A former burlesque-house usher and sweets peddler, Wasserman had been promoted by Jules Stein to vice-president of MCA after two years. Wasserman had risen to becoming one of the shrewdest, most powerful and respected power brokers in the trade. In 1946, Stein appointed the tall, spindly Wasserman head of MCA, and his style and comportment became the house style. It pleased Hitchcock that Wasserman negotiated charmingly and relentlessly in a dark suit, white shirt, and slim tie. MCA agents became known as "the black-suited Mafia."

In 1951, despite a storm of controversy over a bylaw of the Screen Actors Guild that prohibited agents from producing films without a Guild waiver, MCA created its first television show, *Stars Over Hollywood,* through its newly formed Revue Productions. Granted a waiver by then-president of SAG, Ronald Reagan, MCA premiered *GE Theater* in 1953; Wasserman hired Reagan to host that series. Soon, MCA and Revue enjoyed an ongoing arrangement with NBC, for which they produced such popular TV series as *Wagon Train, Wells Fargo,* and *M Squad.*

Lew Wasserman had been waiting for an opportunity to capitalize on the offbeat charisma given off by Hitchcock's manner of a macabre cherub. The director had recently agreed to lend his name to *Alfred Hitchcock Mystery Magazine*, an enterprise funded by a rich Floridian, in which Hitchcock played no role in story selection or editing. Even the first-person story lead-ins were penned by attorney-novelist Harold Q. Masur. But the Hitchcock name was sufficient to send circulation skyward. Movie audiences, too, awaited the walk-on appearance the director made in each of his films. Wasserman understood Hitchcock's seemingly contradictory dynamic of the exhibitionist and the recluse. "About his appearance," observed an associate of the director, "Hitch was very contradictory. He seemed sometimes to delude himself into thinking that because he *directed* Cary Grant that he looked like him."

Lew Wasserman also avidly hoped to give MCA a greater toehold in the production side of film and television. In the late fifties, top Hollywood talent generally steered clear of the "over exposure" that TV appearances seemed to threaten. But in 1959, when Wasserman orchestrated the sale of Universal-International Studios and absorbed the Revue production facilities for MCA for $11,250,000, Hitchcock took notice. "We ought to put Hitch on the air," Hitchcock biographer John Russell Taylor quoted Wasserman as saying. The conglomerate mogul contended that a top box-office draw like Hitchcock would lend class to the weekly half-hour suspense-mystery series he envisioned for Revue. Bristol-Meyers readily agreed to bankroll the show, provided Hitchcock act as host as well as director of "several" episodes per season. Certain that Hitchcock would balk at any activity that he perceived as a diversion from feature-film making, Wasserman pitched the proposition masterfully. All rights to each of the episodes, budgeted at $129,000 each, would revert to the director after the first broadcast. Hitchcock consented.

The director installed himself as president and chief executive officer of Shamley Productions, named after a summer place he and Alma, his wife, had bought in a village south of London in 1928. Housed in a modest bungalow, Shamley Productions was entirely separate from the Hitchcock Production Company, the corporation under which Hitchcock did his film work. To make certain he kept his schedule clear for movies, Hitchcock brought on Joan Harrison, who had risen from his secretary in 1935 to script collaborator (*Rebecca, Foreign Correspondent, Suspicion*) to independent producer (*Phantom Lady, They Won't Believe Me*). Sharp, worldly, handsome, experienced, and genre-wise—Harrison was the wife of mystery writer Eric Ambler—she was a matchless choice.

Hitchcock limited his role in the series to reading droll, macabre segueway monologues scripted by playwright James Allardice and to directing the scripts selected and developed for him by Harrison. A crack cadre of technicians made certain the boss needed to lavish no more than three days—one for rehearsals, two for shooting—on such episodes as "Revenge," "Breakdown," and "Back for Christmas."

In forming a creative team for his TV endeavors, Hitchcock duplicated the situation that he enjoyed on his feature-film work. Movie cameraman Leonard South explained: "[Hitchcock] was ill at ease around people. That's basically why he had the same camera crew for fifteen pictures. After we finished *Vertigo* at Paramount, Hitch told us he was going to be inactive for a while because he had to have gallbladder surgery. So George Tomasini [editor], Bob Boyle and Henry Bumstead [art directors], Bob Burks [chief cinematographer], and I were signed to a two-picture deal with the producers William Perlberg and George Seaton. In the middle of our making for them *But Not for Me*, with Gable and Carroll Baker, Hitch decided to make something out of nothing: *Psycho*. "

Among members of his TV team were cinematographer John L. Russell, assistant director Hilton A. Green, set designer George Milo, and script supervisor Marshall Schlom. Schlom, son of one of the prolific RKO B-movie producers, Herman Schlom, observed: "Mr. Hitchcock was the biggest thing around, especially on TV. To the studio, he was a hands-off client who got anything he wanted. The crews for the other Revue TV shows, *The Jane Wyman Show*, *The Millionaire*, kept changing, but he said, 'I want my own little family.' While we were doing the hour and half-hour shows, we kept hearing rumblings that he was toying with the idea of doing something different. One day, word came that he was about to make a feature and those of us that were close to him were going to do it with him."

With a trusted, competent talent pool at the ready, Hitchcock devised the idea of shooting *Psycho*—his "smallest" project since *The Wrong Man*—utilizing his television collaborators. The director reconvened the heads of production at Paramount to present this new cost-conscious option. He suggested that he thoroughly prepare the project at Paramount, then import his TV crew to shoot the picture on the studio lot, where he would also complete the editing and postproduction. The executives made it clear: Paramount would not finance *Psycho*. Further, they told Hitchcock that every studio soundstage was either occupied or booked, even though everyone on the lot knew that production was in a slump.

Hitchcock was ready for them. He agreed to finance *Psycho* personally and shoot at Universal-International if Paramount agreed to distribute the picture. As the sole producer, Hitchcock would defer his director's fee of $250,000 in exchange for 60 percent ownership of the negative. Such an offer Paramount could not—and did not—refuse.

In his book *Dark Victory: Ronald Reagan, MCA, and the Mob*, Dan E. Moldea weaves a politically nefarious, byzantine plot regarding the financing of *Psycho*. In interviews conducted by the FBI for an investigation of ties between MCA and Paramount, a source told Antitrust Division attorney Leonard Posner, "[*Psycho*] was produced on the Universal lot by MCA . . . Financing for the picture came from the company that is going to distribute the picture—Paramount . . . In other words, MCA represented Hitchcock and told Paramount that if it wanted to finance and release the Hitchcock picture, it would have to be produced on the Universal lot so that MCA could get its cut from the below-the-line facilities. This arrangement was made in spite of the fact that Paramount had a lot that was half empty at the time. Obviously, Paramount would have preferred to have had the picture made on its own lot, so that it could have gotten some of its money back toward overhead."

If Hitchcock savored his coup, few in his inner circle shared his glee. Producer Herbert Coleman, perhaps the director's closest on-line associate, had served as second-unit director on all Hitchcock productions since *Rear Window*. Coleman had been with Paramount for over thirty years, having risen from the script department to assistant director to William Wyler on such films as *Roman Holiday*. Throughout the summer of 1959, the seasoned, exacting Coleman helped Hitchcock steer *Psycho* through the straits of preproduction. Having worked several times on abandoned Hitchcock projects in the past several years, Coleman apparently hoped this might be another of them. As *Psycho* looked more and more like a "go" project toward the fall, Coleman withdrew. He intended to establish an identity within the movie community outside of Hitchcock. He also had objections to the direction the dark project was taking. Similarly, Shamley production head Joan Harrison reportedly refused profit points in *Psycho* in lieu of a raise. "This time, you're going too far," Harrison reputedly advised Hitchcock about his new project. Not even his closest colleagues envisioned just how far Hitchcock planned to go.

5. THE SCREENPLAYS

Writing Is Rewriting

The deeper Hitcock waded into preproduction on his forty-seventh picture, the more obvious it became that to make it would cut him adrift from his moorings: long-time associates, plush production values, picture-postcard locations, major stars, and expensive screenwriters of the reputation of Samuel Taylor (*Vertigo*) or Ernest Lehman (*North by Northwest*). By necessity, *Psycho* would mark Hitchcock's break with his moviemaking past and put the industry on notice that a sixty-year-old directorial workhorse could shock and innovate with the best of the youngbloods. For an insulated and entrenched creature such as Hitchcock, one might liken that prospect to the dizzying attraction-repulsion that acrophobic Scottie Ferguson (James Stewart) experienced when he looked down from the heights in *Vertigo*.

Hitchcock kept secret the specifics of his new project from all but his closest remaining associates, and began to search for a suitable screenwriter. "This is going to need someone with a sense of humor," the director insisted. According to Hitchcock, "When you mention murder, most writers begin to think in low-key terms. But the events leading up to the act itself might be very light and amusing. Many murderers are very attractive persons; they have to be in order to attract their victims." Among writers whom Hitchcock considered to adapt *Psycho* was novelist Robert Bloch, who was eking out a living in the Midwest. According to Bloch, a client of another agency, MCA agents advised Hitchcock that the writer was "unavailable." The "black-suited Mafia" played upon Hitchcock's loyalty (and frugality) by suggesting that he hire from their wide client list.

In the end, Joan Harrison and MCA prevailed upon the director to hire thirty-eight-year-old client James P. Cavanagh, which Hitchcock did on June 8, 1959. Cavanagh had impressed Harrison with his flair for macabre comedy in teleplay credits for Shamley, including "The Hidden Thing" (broadcast May 20, 1956), "The Creeper" (broadcast June 17, 1956), and "Fog Closes In," all *Alfred Hitchcock Presents* episodes, and the last an Emmy-winner. *Psycho* would mark Cavanagh's motion picture screenplay debut.

To bolster the case for Cavanagh, Harrison reminded her boss that he had directed the writer's teleplay, "One More Mile to Go," based on a story by F. J. Smith, in January 1957. Broadcast on April 7, 1957, the show virtually suggests a dry run for *Psycho*. In it, David Wayne plays a henpecked husband who—when his wife dies accidentally—stuffs her corpse into a sack in his car trunk, then heads for a lake to dispose of the body. En route, a menacing motorcycle cop hounds him and a burned-out taillight leads to disclosure of his cargo.

A *Hollywood Reporter* squib on June 10 announced that Hitchcock had signed Cavanagh, who was en route from Paris to begin work on his next film. The same article leaked the title of the project as *Psyche*, which led some observers to wonder whether Hitchcock might be turning to Greek tragedy in search of unusual suspense material. The director teased: "It's the story of a young man whose mother is a homicidal maniac." While on a publicity tour to promote *North by Northwest* and awaiting a first draft of the Cavanagh script in late July, Hitchcock dropped the first hints about his new project to the general public in a June 22 *New York Times* piece by A. H. Weiler. Although he suppressed the title of the Bloch novel ("It would undo any effects I will try to put into the picture"), Hitchcock showed uncharacteristic candor when he promised a film "in the *Diabolique* genre."

"It takes place near Sacramento, California, at a dark and gloomy motel," elaborated the director. "Some very ordinary people meet other ordinary people and horror and death ensue in a manner that can't be unraveled unless you have the book as a guide." Making virtue of necessity, he underscored how modest a budget he planned for the project. Observed Hitchcock: "Nothing about it to distract from the telling of the tale, just like in the old days." In other words, just like in the years in England before Hitchcock came to expect the posh production values that only a Selznick or a Paramount could provide him.

An undated, first-draft screenplay by James Cavanagh, stamped "Revue Studios," not only provides a glimpse of a *Psycho* that might have been but also illustrates the early stages of the development of Hitchcock's visual scheme. As in the novel, the action begins with Mary Crane's absconding with cash from her banker boss, Mr. Lowery, to free her to marry her lover, Sam. By the twelfth page of the script—or, approximately, twelve minutes into the film—the fugitive Mary has traded in her car and, in a rainstorm, taken shelter at the brooding Bates Motel. As she unpacks, Mary overhears Norman Bates and his invalid mother bickering viciously, then joins Bates for an awkward late supper. Much of Cavanagh's script has a sketched-in, tentative feel with little of the density of detail common to Hitchcock scripts. Yet the supper bill-of-fare is oddly specific: "sausage, cheese, pickles, and rye."

During the supper conversation, the empathy that develops between Mary and Norman deepens when Bates reveals that the bank is about to foreclose on the motel. Both Mary and Norman are trapped by lack of money. Their sympathy toward each other builds and peaks when Norman makes an embarrassing pass, that Mary only *just* rebuffs. "You don't like me, do you?" he asks. "As a matter of fact, I do," she replies. "But I wouldn't like you to think your mother was right about me." As Mary begs off and returns to her cabin, it is apparent that she intends to return the stolen cash. As she begins to undress, Cavanagh employs tedious description to misdirect the audience as to Norman's action and whereabouts. With frequent cuts to a ticking clock, Cavanagh details Norman checking in on mother ("a sleeping figure lying in bed") and, later, drinking himself into oblivion after reading the foreclosure letter.

At this stage of the screenwriting process, Hitchcock and Cavanagh took so indecisive a tone as to suggest that one or both of them were questioning whether the ideal venue for *Psycho* would be theaters or TV. One almost hears them hedging their bets: "How much should we moralize on the actions of Mary?," "How much or little can we 'show' of Mother Bates without tipping off the audience?," "How graphically can we depict the murders?" As described by Cavanagh, the shower scene is quite cinematic, complete with the slashings of an "old-fashioned straight razor" that slits Mary's throat. And this: "For a brief moment, we see the mad figure of old Mrs. Bates and hear her high, shrill, hysterical laughter."

After the killing, Norman wakes from "a drunken stupor," discovers Mary's cabin door ajar, then finds a bloody dress and razor in Mother's room. In the finale of the first act, Bates sinks Mary's car in the nearby swamp. Unlike the earlier sections of the script, the latter scene reads like a virtual blueprint for filming—down to the moment when "The car stops sinking. Norman's terror mounts."

Unfortunately, Cavanagh himself sinks in the second and third acts of the script. Scene after scene fritters away the action to detail an unconvincing romance between the dead girl's lover, Sam, and her sister, Lila. Rather than propel us headlong toward the Bates horror house, Sam and Lila discuss whether Mary was "good" or "bad" as if they were team captains in a high school debate. The pot boils anew when "Mrs. Bates comes walking down the stairs" toward private detective Arbogast: "Now that she is this close, even in the dim light, the grotesque makeup, the disordered hair and mad eyes makes [sic] him take a step back almost in fear."

In the matter of Mother, the Cavanagh script cheats. In a scene in which two policemen confer outside the room in which the corpse of Arbogast lies (unlike in the film, the motel and house are connected), Bates and Mother "converse" in frantic whispers, "his head buried against her breast." In other matters, the script fumbles. When Arbogast fails to return, Sam and Lila carry on the investigation. As they approach the office of the motel— despite their fear/certainty that Norman is lurking just out of sight and that he is behind the disappearances of Mary and the detective—they kiss passionately. Finally, in Mary's cabin, Sam and Lila turn up a clue in a bloodstained earring; in the film, a scrap of paper with "figuring" on it serves the same function. Then, Sam confronts Norman, who bashes Sam with a liquor bottle and drags the body into a closet. From there, the thrills unfold much as they do in the novel and in the finished film, except that the local sheriff, not a psychiatrist, explains Bates's psychological kinks for the audience.

Hitchcock spent a weekend at home pondering a script that straddled the then-distinct line between episodic television and feature films. But long before he reached the climactic revelation of Mrs. Bates as "a dummy with staring glass eyes and the blank face of a huge doll," Hitchcock undoubtedly knew the script did not play. In fact, the script falls so short of the mark, one might question the motivations of Joan Harrison. After all, she was neither a fan of the project nor did she lack for experience in matching a writer with a project. Yet Harrison had taken special pains to recommend to one of *the* most exacting directors in the business *this* inexperienced, inexpensive writer. Did she hope that the collaboration might persuade Hitchcock to get *Psycho* out of his system by doing it for TV? Or to drop it altogether?

Despite the letdown Hitchcock surely experienced, many typical details that had presumably evolved during story conferences with Cavanagh were to find their way into the completed film: the elaborate details of the heroine's harrowing car trip; the poignant, impactful supper conversation between Bates and Mary; the obsessive cleanup by Bates after the shower murder; and the swamp's gobbling Mary's car. Even the shower murder sequence anticipates the intricate camera movement that ends in a close-up of blood mingling with shower water gurgling down the drain.

Presumably, Cavanagh enjoyed access to eight pages of handwritten notes by Hitchcock in which the director laid out precise camera movements and sound cues for certain key sequences. In the scene in the used-car lot, writes Hitchcock, "The CAMERA pans along a series of California plates." He emphasizes "The relief of the traffic cop's whistle" that breaks the tension when

Mary's boss peers at her through the windshield of her stopped car, stolen money in her purse. And to describe Mary's car journey after stealing the money, Hitchcock writes:

> The long traffic-laden route along Route 99—the roadside sights—the coming of darkness. Mary's thoughts about Monday morning and the discovery of her flight with the money. The rain starts.

So assured and cinematic are his concepts that Hitchcock even inserted an intriguing bit of self-parody or foreshadowing here and there. In a scene in which Norman Bates prays for the swamp to gulp down Mary's car, a small plane buzzes overhead like a deranged fly. The moment simultaneously recalls the pursuing crop duster in Hitchcock's previous film (*North by Northwest*); refers to Mother Bates, who "wouldn't even harm a fly," in the last line of his present film; and anticipates the winged furies of his next (*The Birds*). In the precise notes to the sound editor that the director dictated months before he cut *Psycho*, Hitchcock would continue to insist on the insertion of the buzzing of the plane.

Hitchcock might well have puzzled over the deficiencies in Cavanagh's draft. Where were the self-confidence, insouciance, and black wit of the writer's TV work? There seemed no percentage in commissioning a rewrite. Without so much as a personal word of explanation to Cavanagh, Hitchcock cashiered him, to the tune of $7,166, on July 27. Michael Ludmer, to whom the director often delegated the responsibility of dropping writers, observed: "It was very difficult for Mr. Hitchcock to express his feelings. There was a *great* deal of input that Mr. Hitchcock gave a writer. He didn't know how to say, 'I'd like to tell you how I feel about these pages,' if there was a problem. He knew that a writer would be upset or disturbed if he were to find out that somebody else was coming on the script. So he would delegate the delivery of that message." Cavanagh was to write the scripts for several of the more well-received Hitchcock TV shows, including "Arthur," "Mother, May I Go Out to Swim?," and "Coming, Mama." He died at age forty-nine, in 1971.

On the rebound, MCA agents suggested to Hitchcock another young client, Joseph Stefano, a thirty-year-old former actor (stage name: Jerry Stevens) and pop music composer. Exuberantly cocky, volatile, and streetwise, Stefano, who had only owned a television for two years, had harbored no writing aspirations outside of music. Then, he had watched a live telecast of *Playhouse 90*, at the time a leading showcase for promising playwrights, directors, and actors, and thought; "I can do that." Stefano recalled: "I wrote a one-hour teleplay and within two weeks, the boss of a secretary friend of mine had made a deal for me with [producer] Carlo Ponti. I'd never even *read* a screenplay. Somebody had to tell me about 'Long shots,' 'Exterior,' and 'Interior.'"

Stefano won respectable notices for his first produced screenplay for Ponti, *The Black Orchid*, a moonlight and Mafia soap opera, released by Paramount, starring Anthony Quinn and Sophia Loren. He also won awards for his own *Playhouse 90* script, "Made in Japan," also a relationship story. Still bemused today by how quickly things happened, Stefano said, "I was offered a seven-year contract at 20th Century-Fox without knowing who the hell I was as a writer or even knowing that much about films." Stefano's wife, then pregnant, had always wanted to live in California; with the security of the movie contract, the writer abandoned his music career and moved west.

Stefano grew so "miserable" with his first studio assignment, a Sam Engle production called *A Machine for Chuparosa*, he asked his agent to secure a release from the contract with Fox. Fox agreed. The neophyte writer fretted that such an action might blackball him within the industry, yet the same studio immediately hired him to adapt a J. R. Salamanca novel, *The Lost Country*, as a vehicle for rising young actor Anthony Perkins. Perkins never made the movie. Elvis Presley did, as *Wild in the Country*, from a script by Clifford Odets.

Stefano hopped to MCA, where he was represented by Ned Brown, the very agent who had finessed the acquisition of *Psycho* for Hitchcock. Stefano presented Brown with a list of ten directors "who could teach me something." Meetings for Stefano with William Wyler and Otto Preminger had short-circuited when Lew Wasserman alerted Brown to Hitchcock's immediate need for a writer. Hitchcock rejected Stefano sight unseen, telling agent Brown, "My fear about Mr. Stefano is that, from the work of his I've seen, maybe he doesn't have a sense of humor." The director had lumped Stefano with what he termed "the Reginald Rose–*Playhouse 90* crowd—humorless, self-important types with Something to Say.

To Stefano's rescue came formidable agent Kay Brown. Brown, among her many accomplishments, had steered David O. Selznick toward the acquisition of the Margaret Mitchell novel, *Gone With the Wind*, and toward Daphne du Maurier's *Rebecca*. Brown had also negotiated Hitchcock's first American contract with Selznick, and had influenced the director to hire playwright Samuel Taylor as screenwriter for *Vertigo*. "I hadn't done *anything* to support my writing *Psycho*," Stefano said, "but my agents felt I was exactly what Hitchcock needed—someone who could do characterizations. They thought it was a very inferior book, a very sleazy kind of property. Hitchcock was strange about a lot of things. He only liked to work with people he knew and wasn't about to meet any new writer. Finally, there was enough pressure put on him by Lew Wasserman and everybody else, who kept saying, 'Just meet him, that's all.'"

Yet when Stefano read the Robert Bloch novel as a preinterview preparation for Hitchcock, the writer puzzled over the big lobbying effort on his behalf. "I was very disappointed," Stefano recalled. "Having loved all Hitchcock's work, I had in mind *The 39 Steps*, *Rebecca*, and *North by Northwest*, not some strange little pulp fiction. [*Psycho*] didn't even ring of a Hitchcock picture. I let [Hitchcock] know how disappointed I was as soon as we met." "[Hitchcock] told me that he had a script by Robert Bloch that hadn't worked out," Stefano asserted. Bloch, who was living in Wisconsin at the time, today denies he wrote any such script. An intra-Revue Studios correspondence by Peggy Robertson dated December 19, 1959, confirms, "It is my understanding that Mr. Stefano has not been exposed to the James Cavanagh first draft screenplay. It is further my understanding that no synopsis, treatment, or material of the like has been written for this film other than the above two items."

But when they met, Hitchcock offered Stefano no suggestion that he saw in *Psycho* anything more than a chance to show the low-budget horror *schlockmeisters* a thing or two. Stefano said: "I told him part of the problem was that I really didn't like this man, Norman Bates. I really couldn't get involved with a man in his forties who's a drunk and peeps through holes. The other problem was that there was this perfectly horrendous murder of a stranger I didn't care about either. I just kept talking to him in the vein 'I wish I knew this girl,' I wish Norman were somebody else.'"

As to the writer's qualms about the central male character, Hitchcock pacified Stefano with a question: "How would you feel if Norman were played by Anthony Perkins?" The writer recalled: "I said, 'Now you're talking.' I suddenly saw a tender, vulnerable young man you could feel incredibly sorry for. I could really rope in an audience with someone like him. Then I suggested starting the movie with the girl instead of Norman."

A great screenwriting collaborator of Hitchcock's, Charles Bennett, (*The 39 Steps, Young and Innocent*) once described the director as "literate" only to the extent that "he liked to read the dirtiest parts of *Ulysses*." Instinctively, Stefano played to the sexual imp that lay inside the director. Stefano recalled: "I told him, 'I'd like to see Marion shacking up with Sam on her lunch hour.'* The moment I said 'shack up'or anything like that, Hitchcock, being a very salacious man, adored it. I said, 'We'll find out what the girl is all about, see her steal the money and head for Sam— on the way, this horrendous thing happens to her.' He thought it was spectacular. I think that idea got me the job."

Neither writer nor director committed to another meeting beyond the first. Hitchcock seemed particularly wary about repeating his experiences with James Cavanagh. But Stefano felt that he had penetrated the Hitchcock armor. "He found that I was very funny and we had a lot of laughs together," said the writer. Soon after, the Hitchcock office arranged a second meeting, which the director began by excitedly proposing: "What if we got a big-name actress to play this girl? Nobody will expect her to die!" Stefano observed: "He wanted somebody much bigger than Janet Leigh—someone I didn't think was terribly good. But once he mentioned Janet Leigh, the whole thing really began to get me: She was someone with no association with this kind of movie—a suspense-horror movie—and neither were Perkins, Hitchcock, nor I."

By mid-September 1959, Hitchcock had been sufficiently convinced: He hired Stefano, but only on a week-to-week basis. The arrangement was hardly secure for Stefano, but it gave Hitchcock a ready escape hatch if their collaboration failed to ignite. Yet, ignite it did, and the writer was eventually to receive $17,500

---

*In the final script, the name Mary Crane was changed to Marion Crane.

for his labors. But Stefano continued to harbor hopes that he and the director would expand, deepen, and glamorize the source material into what Stefano called "a real Hitchcock movie, where a lot of money is spent just because it's *there*." But, no. "When I asked him why he had bought the book, he said he noticed that American-International was making movie after movie for under a million dollars, yet they all made ten or thirteen million. Then I saw it: He had bought this tight little novel and had no intention of blowing it up."

Hitchcock completely scuttled the James Cavanagh first draft, and, according to Revue intraoffice correspondence, that draft was never shown to Stefano. "He told me there was no point in reading it," Stefano explained. "Even in [Robert Bloch's] book, I don't think Bloch was aware of some of the things he came up with, like the shower scene. But the dynamics of it *were* there. What excited me was the thought of taking this warm, sympathetic woman away from the audience and replacing her with Tony Perkins, not the Norman Bates of Bloch's book."

For his part, Hitchcock was more charitable toward Bloch and his novel. The director told writer Charles Higham in *The Celluloid Muse*, "*Psycho* all came from Robert Bloch. Joseph Stefano . . . contributed dialogue mostly, no ideas." Robert Bloch attributes Stefano's peckishness to simple turf rivalry. "It's a good thing Mr. Stefano didn't adapt the *Bible*." But it had long been Hitchcock's tendency to appropriate any good idea as his own.

Hitchcock and Stefano held five weeks of daily story conferences at Paramount, beginning at 10:30 A.M., the hour to which the director agreed to accommodate Stefano's ongoing sessions with a psychoanalyst. According to the writer, "When it got down to 'Let's get some work done,' he was never very eager. He was very hard to pin down. I wanted him to tell me what he expected this movie to be like, but he preferred gabbing, gossiping, and he *loved* to laugh. I think he really got a kick out of me. He told me his last writer, Ernie Lehman [*North by Northwest*], was a worrier and a bitcher. But I was laughing all the time, thinking to myself, 'You didn't expect to be in movies in the first place and here you are working with Hitchcock.'"

For Stefano, keeping Hitchcock's quicksilver mind attuned to *Psycho* was an uphill battle all the way. According to the writer, when Hitchcock talked about the job at hand at all, it was usually to throw out "wild ideas" that he expected one to weave into the scenario. It almost seemed as if the director felt it necessary to "school" a writer in the world according to Hitchcock: his brand of wit, wisdom, flippancy, and power. Stefano said, "One of the easiest times for anyone to get in to see Hitchcock was whenever he was in conference with a writer. Lew Wasserman used to come in and they'd talk stocks and money, money, money!" Yet despite the director's quirky timetable, certain "givens" fell into line. "Purely for budgetary reasons, I knew he had decided to do the movie in black and white," Stefano explained. "And without too much conversation, we decided this was going to be a picture of Gothic horror, something he had not really done before."

Stefano perceived that the way to engage Hitchcock's imagination was to conceptualize and verbalize the story in terms of visuals. According to Stefano, "He was not interested in characters or motivation at all. That was the writer's job. If I said, 'I'd like to give the girl an air of desperation,' he'd say, 'Fine, fine.' But when I said, 'In the opening of the film, I'd like a helicopter shot over the city, then go right up to the seedy hotel where Marion is spending her lunch hour with Sam,' he said, 'We'll go right into the window!' That sort of thing excited him."

Left to grapple on his own with complexities of structure and character, Stefano found the freedom disarming and exhilarating. "I worked on a level of characterization that was probably unheard of for what turned out to be a horror movie. In fact, I felt like I was writing a movie about Marion, not about Norman. I saw Marion as a girl getting on in years working at a dull job around undelightful, unimpressive people. She is in love with a man who won't marry her because he has financial problems. The greatest thing about Marion is that she never stops to think 'Can I get away with this?,' which is exactly the way that someone performs an act of madness when they themselves are *not* mad. Once we got to the motel, the whole game changed for me. From then on, we were into manipulation of the highest order. Torturing the audience was the intention. Because there was no precedent for *Psycho* in Hitchcock's body of work, I went at it with an incredible and surprising amount of freedom."

In other details of script construction, however, Hitchcock was the complete detail man. "We worked out the story piece by piece," Stefano observed. "He was very big on technicalities, like the elaborate business of the girl's trading in her car. He would say, 'I think we ought to see her get important papers when she goes to her house to pack up. A pink slip, and such.' He never wanted audiences asking questions. His theory was 'Think what the audience is going to ask and answer it as fast as possible.'"

To make certain Stefano got the details right, Hitchcock hired a Hollywood-based detective as a technical adviser. The Hitchcock office also had the screenwriter observe the style and manner of a used-car dealer, Ralph Outright, at 1932 Wilshire Boulevard in Santa Monica. Stefano was also provided with data on every foreseeable plot point, from the topography of Route 99 (including names, locations, and room rates of every motel) to details of the administration and physical appearance of real estate offices; from traffic citations and mother fixations to amateur taxidermy.

Stefano quickly found that no plot twist tickled Hitchcock more than predesigning the murder sequence. The writer recalled

Hitchcock's relish for the scene that would eliminate a sympathetic character—played by a star actress—*one-third of the way into the story.* "We had the longest discussion about laying out the shower murder," Stefano recalled. "Both of us wanted to know exactly what was going to be on film. I remember sitting on a couch at his Paramount office where we were working this particular day, discussing the murder in great detail. He rose from his desk, came round toward me, and said, 'You be the camera. Now, we won't have her really lying on the bathroom floor. We'll show him lift up the shower curtain . . .' And Hitchcock acted out every move, every gesture, every nuance of wrapping the corpse in the curtain. Suddenly, his office door flew open behind him. In walked his wife, Alma, who rarely came to the studio. Hitchcock and I yelled, *'Aaaaaaaaaggggghhhhh!!!'* The shock of the intrusion at that moment was so great, we must have laughed for five minutes!"

After the second week of story conferences, Hitchcock departed without explanation for a two-week commitment. "I had the feeling this was going to be my screen-test," Stefano recalled, chuckling. "He said, 'Why don't you start writing the scene with the girl and her lover in the Phoenix hotel?' So I wrote it, right to the point where she walks out of the hotel room. When Hitchcock came back, I handed him the pages and we went on talking. The next day he said, 'Alma loved it.' He never said *he* loved it, but he kind of made me feel if he didn't, I wouldn't have been at the meeting."

The director's *sangfroid* came as no surprise to the writer, who thought the Hitchcock staff "a strange organization." According to Stefano, "They weren't into compliments. It was like royalty. The compliment was that you were *invited.* Hitchcock was talking about John Michael Hayes one day—someone who had written several of his huge hits [*To Catch a Thief, Rear Window,* etc.]. Hitchcock said, 'Oh, he had *one* good line in *The Trouble with Harry* where Shirley MacLaine says, 'I've got a short fuse.' Right there, I said to myself, 'If you think you're going to get any applause, Stefano, forget it.'" Longtime Hitchcock collaborator, screenwriter Charles Bennett (*The 39 Steps*) summed up that quality in Hitchcock as "a character flaw." Bennett told journalist Pat McGilligan in *Backstory*, "And a very ungenerous character flaw, actually, because as I said, he is totally incapable of creating a story or developing a story. He has got good ideas—but he will never give credit to anyone but himself."

While attending to last-minute details on the foreign release of *North by Northwest*, Hitchcock dispatched a small crew to Phoenix, Arizona, to shoot additional "atmosphere" and research photographs. Stefano completed a first draft screenplay in three weeks and turned it in on December 19, 1959. Despite the screenwriter's cavils about the original novel, he clearly helped himself to the best of Bloch—structure, characters, atmosphere, tone—while enlivening the dialogue with gallows wit and deepening the characterization. Whatever Stefano had believed about Hitchcock in terms of being a "time-waster," certainly something of the director's influence informed the screenplay.

"He only asked me to change one scene and one word," Stefano recalled of Hitchcock's response to the script. "He didn't think a scene where the highway cop wakes the girl after she's been sleeping in the car was suspenseful enough. I had the cop as a handsome young guy coming on to her, preventing her from moving on. Hitch liked the idea during our discussions, but after reading the script, he wanted the cop to be more menacing. The offending word was in the first scene where the heroine is telling Sam she won't see him anymore and he makes a crack about writing each other 'lurid' love letters. Hitch said, 'I don't like "lurid."' I said, 'Do you think it's wrong for the character?" No, no,' he said, 'I just don't like the word.' So I said, 'If that's your only justification, I won't cut it.'" Stefano didn't. Surprisingly, neither did Hitchcock.

Although Stefano read Hitchcock's response as satisfactory, the director streamlined or dropped while shooting (or editing) the writer's many attempts to challenge the censors and to enrich the complexity of the characters, context, and texture. In the opening scene—the tryst between Sam and the heroine (called Mary in the script) in the Phoenix hotel room—Stefano foreshadows the closing line of the movie ("Why, she wouldn't even harm a fly") by interrupting a long kiss with ". . . the buzzing and closeness of an inconsiderate fly." (The idea was cut.) The stodgy, unappealing Sam waxes eloquent about his and Mary's being "a regular working-class tragedy" and tells her: "You know what I'd like? A clear, empty sky . . . and a plane, and us in it . . . and somewhere a private island for sale, where we can run around without our—shoes on. And the wherewithal to buy what I'd like." (The lines were cut.)

In the scenes set in the real estate office as written by Stefano, the vulgar oil man, Mr. Cassidy, makes a blatantly sexual remark to Mary that was cut from the film. In the scene as written, Cassidy leers at Mary, saying, "What you need is a weekend in Las Vegas," to which she replies, "I'm going to spend this weekend in bed." The oil man retorts, "Only playground that beats Las Vegas." Stefano also tried to sustain the suspense of Mary's flight with the stolen money by having her stop at a gas station to fill up, only to flee when a pay phone jangles; but this was cut. And lengthier than in the completed film was the scene in which the highway patrolman ("his face dispassionate," although he is not described as wearing sunglasses) delays her.

In Stefano's description of Mary's harrowing car trip, which Hitchcock would later film like a heavily stylized descent into the underworld, Stefano several times describes quick cuts to the wheels of the car spinning in the driving rain. Hitchcock instead shot the sequence with intense subjectivity, never varying the point of view beyond alternating shots of the heroine with shots of what she sees. Stefano pokes a good deal of phallic fun at Norman. In the scene in which Mary arrives at "Mrs. Bates Motel" in a rainstorm, Stefano describes Norman's umbrella as dangling "limply and uselessly at his side." Later, Norman's elaborate, post-shower-murder cleanup is continued with shots of him hosing away the tire tracks leading to the swamp. And following "An Extreme High Angle" that depicts Norman as he carts Mother's bloodstained shoes and skirt to the basement furnace, Stefano proposes a silent, long shot of the Bates house and chimney, from which an eerie plume of smoke rises. All were cut from the final film. But Hitchcock was also to insert (then later cut) the last image into the screenplays for *The Birds*, *Torn Curtain*, and at least two never-realized projects of the sixties and seventies.

Hitchcock also dropped from the script an elaborate visual pun in a montage sequence in which the rented car of Detective Arbogast continually bypasses Bates Motel as he questions other hotel owners. In a screenplay rife with allusions to the connection between food and sex, Hitchcock cut a line that Norman utters to Arbogast during the interrogation about Mary: "She had an awful hunger." Lost, too, were such touches as Norman tenderly caressing and hiding away a stuffed bird knocked off a lampshade during his conversation with Arbogast; a conversation in the hardware store between Sam and Lila played against a background display of carving knives; a grisly sight gag to occur when Sam leaves Lila in the store in search of Arbogast, "among some bathroom fittings a nozzle from a shower falls to the floor"; and an elegant camera move that begins in a medium shot on

Sam and Lila talking in their motel room, glides past them to the flower pattern on the wallpaper, and ends in a big close-up of Norman's eye peering in at them. The latter shot was to have "echoed" the earlier, similarly voyeuristic moment when Norman watches Mary disrobe.

Throughout the screenplay, Stefano went to some pains to flesh out the characters of Sam and Lila, whom Hitchcock called mere "figures." If James Cavanagh had tried to trump up a flat-out romance, Stefano's more subtle attempts center on a slow thawing of the initial chill between Sam and Lila as they hunt for the missing girl. Coos Lila while she and Sam wait vainly for Arbogast to return from the motel, "Whenever I start contemplating the panic button, your back straightens up and your eyes get that God-looks-out-for-everybody look and . . . I feel better." Sam: "I feel better when you feel better." Before Sam hurries off to question Bates at the motel, Sam advises Lila, who wants to accompany him, to stay behind and "contemplate your . . . panic button."

In a scene late in the action, when the couple drive to the motel to investigate the disappearance of Arbogast, Sam mutters, "I wonder if we'll ever see Mary again—alive." As Lila reminisces about how her sister sacrificed her own college career for Lila's, she says, "Some people are so willing to suffer for you that they suffer more if you don't let them." Sam mumbles, "I wouldn't let her lick the stamps," a reference to one of Mary's absurdly poignant lines in the opening scene in the hotel room. In the penultimate scene, when the psychiatrist explains Norman's illness, Lila "begins to weep softly, for Mary, for Arbogast, for the destroyed human beings of the world."

Hitchcock excised it all, convinced that the audience would tolerate Sam and Lila only so long as they propelled the resolution of the mystery. Stefano regretted the loss of the sentimentality, but Hitchcock clearly preferred Stefano's more subversive side. In that arena, Stefano prevailed. The script is shot through with obvious delight in skewering America's sacred cows—virginity, marriage, the reliance on pills, the sanctity of the family . . . and the bathroom. Stefano said, "I told Hitch 'I would like Marion [Mary] to tear up a piece of paper and flush it down the toilet and *see* that toilet. Can we do that?' A toilet had never been seen on-screen before, let alone flushing it. Hitch said, 'I'm going to have to fight them on it.' I thought if I could begin to unhinge audiences by showing a toilet flushing—we all suffer from peccadillos from toilet procedures—they'd be so out of it by the time of the shower murder, it would be an absolute killer. I thought [about the audience], 'This is where you're going to begin to know what the human race is all about. We're going to start by showing you the toilet and it's only going to get worse.' We were getting into Freudian stuff and Hitchcock dug that kind of thing, so I knew we would get to see that toilet on-screen."

Despite the gusto with which he and Hitchcock took a meat-ax to American taboos, Stefano rejects the claims by Hitchcock critics and biographers that *Psycho* marked a darkening in the worldview of the director. He said, "Hitchcock didn't think we were doing anything that was any different from his *last* movie or would be from his *next*. He didn't seem to think that this was coming from a 'new Hitchcock.' No matter what has been read into Hitchcock's state of mind, I don't think at any time he was making it he was knowingly or unconsciously reflecting any particular darkness from within. He simply had a script and he was shooting it."

Hitchcock accelerated his production plans and schedule while Stefano polished the script to the director's specifications. The writer delivered a slightly-revised second draft dated November 2, 1959. Further modest alterations and refinements were turned in on November 10, November 13, and December 1. Following this, Stefano and Hitchcock convened for a day at the director's home to break down the shooting script. This stage of the development process had always been among the most rewarding, for Hitchcock. "My films are made on paper," the director often told the press. Stefano detailed the process by which Hitchcock created imagery from words. "From my master scenes, he'd say, 'Shall we have a close-up here of, say, a purse?' For the shower scene, we made the decision that you would never see the knife touch the body. I told him I thought there was a point beyond which we would lose the audience, since we *like* Mary, feel sorry for her, and know that she is going to return the money. He told me that Saul Bass, who had done the titles for him on other films, was also going to storyboard the shower scene." By early November, with that sequence in mind, Hitchcock had already sent the first script draft to Bass, the innovative graphic designer who had created title sequences for *Vertigo* and *North by Northwest*, among others.

Stefano recalled how Hitchcock enthused over the chance to manipulate sound to heighten audience involvement and to implicate them, with Norman Bates, as voyeurs. In the scene where peeping Norman watches Mary through the hole in the motel office wall, Stefano wrote, under the direction of Hitchcock: "The SOUNDS come louder, as if we too had our ears pressed against the wall." Stefano claimed that Hitchcock was also very open to suggestions for camera placement—so long as they fit within his overall vision. For instance, the writer said he proposed to Hitchcock that he modify the point of view for the second killing in the movie, the stabbing of Arbogast. "When we got to Arbogast going into the house and up the stairs, I said, 'If you only start pulling the camera up when the woman comes out of the room, I'm going to get suspicious why you're not showing her.' That phrase—I'm going to get suspicious' —was my key to get him to change something. I said, 'When he starts to go upstairs, what if we go way up high like we're removing ourselves from what's about to happen? The audience *knows* what's about to happen to the detective anyway, so the upward movement would already be established when the mother runs out from her bedroom.' He said, 'That's going to cost a lot of money. I'll have to build a thing way up there.' The next day he said, 'It's worth it.' As much as he was concerned about keeping costs down, he wasn't about to do anything that would hurt or detract from the movie."

Writers from Charles Bennett (*The 39 Steps, The Man Who Knew Too Much*) to Raymond Chandler (*Strangers on a Train*) and from John Michael Hayes (*Rear Window, To Catch a Thief*) to Ernest Lehman (*North by Northwest, Family Plot*) have attested to Hitchcock's having been an exasperating collaborator. Stefano recalls only a single flare-up. "He wanted to cheat on something," the writer noted. "It was the scene where Arbogast comes to the motel and he and Norman talk, then Norman goes off to the house to put on Mother's clothes and kills Arbogast. Hitchcock wanted Norman to just go out the door [of the motel office], but I said, 'If we don't see him walking to put the sheets away, I'm going to be suspicious when we go up to the house.' Hitchcock muttered, 'Well it might be one of those things you might want to cut.' I said, *'Shoot it and don't cut it!'* I told him this wasn't going to be the kind of movie where he could get away with stuff like he had in the past."

Within hours, Hitchcock and Stefano had fully broken down the screenplay. Uniquely Hitchcockian was his insistence on turning the script into a virtual blueprint for production. Each scene was composed with the camera—frequently acting as the audience surrogate—in mind. In the third act of *Psycho*, Lila Crane (Vera Miles) is about to do what the entire audience was to hope/fear she will do: search the Bates house—alone. Explained Stefano: "He always thought about making the audience share the point of view of the character." From the screenplay:

EXT. REAR OF MOTEL —S. C. U. [CLOSE-UP] — DAY
Behind the motel Lila hesitates. She looks ahead.

LONG SHOT —DAY
The old house standing against the sky.

CLOSE-UP
Lila moves forward.

LONG SHOT
The CAMERA approaching the house.

CLOSE-UP
Lila glances toward the back of Norman's parlor. She moves on.

LONG SHOT
The house coming nearer.

CLOSE-UP
Lila looks up at the house. She moves forward purposefully.

SUBJECTIVE SHOT
The house and the porch.

CLOSE-UP
Lila stops at the house and looks up. She glances back. She turns to the house again.

SUBJECTIVE SHOT
The CAMERA MOUNTS the steps to the porch.

CLOSE-UP
Lila puts out her hand.

SUBJECTIVE CLOSE-UP

Lila's hand pushes the door open. We see the hallway. Lila
ENTERS PAST CAMERA.

Once Hitchcock and Stefano had completed the breakdown, it was all over but the shooting. "We had lunch and toasted the project with champagne," said Stefano. "He looked very sad, and said, 'The picture's over. Now I have to go and put it on film.'" Despite their long hours of story conferences and kibbitzing, Stefano singled out that particular moment as one of the few during which Hitchcock let down his guard. But in another, after the director had arranged a private showing of *Vertigo* at the writer's request, Stefano believed he had at last glimpsed the man who hid behind the mask. "Here was this incredibly beautiful movie he had made that nobody went to see or said nice things about it," Stefano said. "I told him I thought it was his best film. It brought him to near-tears."

6. PREPRODUCTION

The Studio

Armed with a shootable script that had been annotated with camera movements and elegance of technique honed over three decades of filmmaking, Hitchcock turned his attention to bringing on-line the technical crew. The process had been set in motion by associate producer Herbert Coleman before his departure the previous summer. Although Paramount had agreed to distribute Hitchcock's finished product, the studio heads persisted in denying the director's request to shoot *Psycho* on the lot. Coleman confirmed to novelist Robert Bloch that the action by Paramount was another means of the studio brass's opinion that *Psycho*, with Hitchcock or not, was a dubious project at best.

On the other hand, Universal-International, the studio in North Hollywood that MCA had recently bought for $11,250,000, was only too happy to accommodate a new Hitchcock production. Universal was a far cry from the posh Paramount studios that had boasted such directors as Ernst Lubitsch, Josef von Stern-berg, Preston Sturges, Billy Wilder, and Cecil B. DeMille, or con-tract stars such as Gloria Swanson, Rudolph Valentino, Marlene Dietrich, Mae West, and Gary Cooper. Universal, the home of *Frances the Mule* and *Ma and Pa Kettle*, was a factory-mentality studio that had been built in 1914 by Carl Laemmle on the site of the former Taylor Ranch in North Hollywood Lankershim Township. Laemmle bought the land for $165,000 and chris-tened the acreage Universal City. He charged tourists twenty-five cents to cram bleachers and soundstages to watch the shooting of such silent films as *Damon and Pythias* and such budding stars as Rudolph Valentino.

The head of Universal, Irving Thalberg—at twenty-one the youngest Hollywood mogul—brought class to the studio with Erich von Stroheim's *Foolish Wives* and two great Lon Chaney silents, *The Hunchback of Notre Dame* (1923) and *The Phantom of the Opera* (1925). Despite such occasional classics as *Show Boat* or *My Man Godfrey* (both 1936), Hollywood wags dubbed Uni-versal "The House of Horrors" because of four years of astonish-ingly profitable shockers, beginning in 1931 with *Dracula* and *Frankenstein* and continuing through *The Old Dark House*, *The Mummy*, *Murders in the Rue Morgue* (all 1932); *The Invisible Man* (1933); *The Black Cat* (1935); and *The Bride of Frankenstein* and *Werewolf of London* (both 1935).

The clarion soprano of Deanna Durbin saved Universal from going under during the forties, yet the studio ground out 350 features between 1940 and 1945. Few besides *Destry Rides Again* (1939), *My Little Chickadee* (1940), *Never Give a Sucker an Even Break* (1941), Hitchcock's *Saboteur* (1942) and *Shadow of a Doubt* (1943), and *Phantom Lady* (1944) linger in the memory.

On November 12, 1946, Universal merged with the inde-pendent International Studios. Hoping to spruce up its image for a changing market, the new studio brooms swept away the B-movie unit and most of its contract players. Despite the shift to Technicolor, it was the Ma and Pa Kettle and Abbott and Costello pictures that buttered Universal's bread until 1952, when Decca Records won controlling interest in Universal. New studio heads Milton Rackmil and Edward Muhl knew what the public wanted to see and ushered in the era of profitable science fiction movies (*It Came From Outer Space*, *The Creature From the Black Lagoon*, *The Incredible Shrinking Man*), tearjerkers (*All That Heaven Allows*, *Imitation of Life*, *Magnificent Obsession*), and frothy sex comedies (*Pillow Talk*, *That Touch of Mink*).

However, between 1957 and 1958, when the average movie ticket cost fifty cents, ticket sales plummeted by 12 percent. The Universal soundstages lay vacant, and the studio was $2 million in debt. The bosses of MCA—which was known as "The Octopus" for having its tentacles wrapped around a bit of everything— wanted larger facilities for their television subsidiary, Revue Productions. They tempted Rackmil with a $11.25 million buyout offer and he accepted. The studio, renamed Universal-Revue, was to earn respect from the industry as a moneymaker, if nothing else. Still, the Revue lot boasted Hitchcock's Shamley Production bungalow. Today, the Shamley site has been replaced by a monolithic bank building. In those days, Hitchcock and his staff could watch rabbits and ducks romp on the lawn outside their windows. The director's associates Herbert Coleman and Peggy Robertson had budgeted *Psycho* at $800,000, or roughly three times what the average episode of the TV show *Wagon Train* cost Revue. Given the precision with which Hitchcock had predesigned the film, a thirty-six-day shooting schedule seemed realistic. Every day, the momentum for making *Psycho* built.

In October, the Motion Picture Association of America alerted the Shamley office that the maverick director Sam Fuller (*Pickup on South Street*) had, in late September, registered the title *Psycho* for an original screenplay. The news brought a dignified but unequivocal protest from the Hitchcock staff. The MPAA decided in favor of Hitchcock because the Bloch novel of the same title had been published the previous spring. This was not to be Hitchcock's only contretemps over the title. Following the release of *Psycho*, the Hitchcock office and Paramount lodged a complaint with the Motion Picture Association of America about the registration of the title *Schizo* by none other than Hitchcock's old boss, producer David O. Selznick. The withdrawal of the title by the once-mighty producer of *Gone With the Wind* and *Rebecca*, with whom Hitchcock's relationship had grown increasingly strained during their nine-year association, perhaps gave Hitchcock grim satisfaction.

The Technical Crew

Late October 1959 found Hitchcock absorbed in dictating to the department heads of Revue the precise production requirements of *Psycho*. Vincent Dee would handle costumes, Florence Dee hairstyles, and Jack Barron makeup. Each would receive his or her standard TV-show fee; a check from the Hitchcock office for the princely sum of $300 would be sent to makeup and hairdressing department head Larry Germain, for example, to cover his total costs for the film. Not surprisingly, Hitchcock worked out these details from his swank Paramount suites in Hollywood rather than trudge over the hill to the North Hollywood valley home of rough-and-ready Universal-Revue.

For budgetary reasons, Hitchcock dropped in preproduction several lovingly detailed camera flourishes described in the shooting script. First to go was a helicopter shot of the sort with which he had amused himself on *To Catch a Thief* (1955). Thus, *Psycho* would have to do without a shot in the "absurdist geometry" style that Hitchcock would later display in the aerial views of the heroine's car trip in *The Birds* (1963), or the hero pursuing the hostile widow through the cemetery maze in *Family Plot* (1976). In *Psycho*, the audience was to have viewed the progress of two taxis—one carrying Lila Crane, sister of the heroine, and the other with Detective Arbogast—as they made their way through city streets and converged on the hardware store owned by Sam Loomis.

Hitchcock also scrubbed a 360-degree camera pan that would have begun on Norman Bates darning socks (!) on the front porch of the motel. From there, the camera was to have followed the character's point of view as he watches Arbogast's car thread its way toward the motel. The shot would have ended full circle on the reaction of Bates as the car pulled up before the porch. The director also cut exterior shots of the house and neighborhood of the heroine and her sister, as well as a cat-and-mouse sequence at a filling station where the jittery Mary would refuel en route to Sam. Gone, too, would be scenes at Lila's hotel lodgings in "Fairvale"—a locale that Hitchcock's production notes suggest he planned to shoot in a style that would recall the hotel at which Sam and Mary enjoyed their final tryst.

Although rumblings about what Hitchcock was calling his "thirty-day picture" had emanated from the Shamley office for months, Hitchcock played his intentions even closer to the vest than usual. "Those of us associated with him through television all knew he had his own feature-film crew," explained Hilton Green, whom the director had promoted from a second assistant director with Revue Productions to his first assistant director on his TV show. "He *definitely* didn't like new crew faces around all the time. While he was doing *North by Northwest* at MGM,

I was quietly called in and told, 'He's thinking about doing a low-budget, quality film,' and that I was going to be the assistant director. *North by Northwest* having been a rather expensive film for its day, he wanted to prove to his peers he could make a quality movie without spending a lot of money to do it. So he thought of his television crew because we were more accustomed to shorter schedules."

That October, Hitchcock charged Hilton Green with overseeing a small crew headed by second-unit director Charles S. Gould. Their assignment was to capture a detailed series of stills of Phoenix residents, city streets, and atmospherics. Again, Hitchcock's precisely detailed requirements for these photographs belie the "low budget" trappings of the project. They included a "shoddy hotel exterior, with the street outside with taxis and passersby"; "the interior and exterior of a real estate office, including a bank"; "exterior of a small house in which two girls live [secretaries], including a two-car garage and street; a bedroom of the same house." Further requirements included the details and furnishings of the home of a local sheriff. On the return trip, the same crew obtained information on psychiatric detainment facilities in California. They also scouted possible locations for the Bates swamp, finding one at Grizzly Island off Freeway 40 or along Highway 12 near Travis Air Force Base. Green observed: "Hitchcock wanted to know things like *exactly* what a car salesman in a small town in the valley would be wearing when a woman might come in to buy a car. We went up there and photographed some salesmen against a background. He wanted to know what people in Phoenix, Arizona, looked like, how they lived, what kind of people they were. He wanted to know the exact route a woman might take to go from Phoenix to central California. We traced the route and took pictures of every area along the way." On roadmaps hung on his office walls, Hitchcock traced with pushpins the heroine's exact route. Carefully noted were the precise distances between each point from Phoenix to California, via Blythe, Indio, San Bernadino, Palmdale, Lancaster, and Redding. Hitchcock also obtained from the studio research department information as to whether "a mental case could be kept at a jail until a psychiatrist got there."

On Green and Gould's return, Hitchcock installed Green in the same office at Paramount that producer Herbert Coleman, who had defected from the project, had inhabited since the production of *Rear Window.* The symbolic significance of that move was apparent: Green on *Psycho* was as important to Hitchcock as Coleman had been to the director on previous films. The preproduction details and the intensity with which Hitchcock immersed himself into them suggest the degree to which *Psycho* was a project Hitchcock undertook as a challenge. Hilton Green observed: "He was always looking for something new. The one thing that tickled him the most, that he talked about again and again, was that his leading lady was going to get killed in the first twenty minutes. 'This is really going to throw them for a loop,' he said. He enjoyed fooling the audience like that.

"Another of his pet ideas, and he expounded on it a lot, was his philosophy that deep down, audiences enjoy being frightened. So he liked the *idea* of this movie and saw great possibilities for certain sequences—the staircase killing, the revealing of Mother. He probably knew the moves and technical aspects of a camera as well or better than any cameraman. He started preparing . . . these shots that would be very difficult, especially for that day, when we didn't have the kind of equipment we do now."

In filling other key creative positions, Hitchcock strayed outside of the Shamley "family." In late November, Hitchcock asked composer Bernard Herrmann, his musical alter ego since *The Man Who Knew Too Much* (1956), to score the film. The brilliant, contentious Herrmann, who had magnificently scored *Citizen Kane* for Orson Welles and, for other directors, *The Devil and Daniel Webster* and *The Ghost and Mrs. Muir*, was easily Hitchcock's equal in prickly pride. "Benny had this repertoire of themes he could pull out of his hat," observed actor-producer John Houseman, who worked closely with Welles and Herrmann on *Citizen Kane*. "That is not to say he didn't compose original pieces for films, but directors'needs tended to be quite similar and one of Benny's favorites he called 'frozen music,' an eerie, keening kind of theme for strange sequences in pictures like *The Day the Earth Stood Still*."

Hitchcock was attuned to Herrmann's predilections and wanted nothing by-the-numbers for *Psycho*. In turn, Herrmann balked at the director's offer of near-scale salary. For a while, Herrmann let Hitchcock stew. Finally, the director wired the composer: "Awaited call from you all day Thursday following my call. However unnecessary have agreed to your terms $17,500 the job. We are up to schedule and expect film to finish by mid January or thereabouts and picture must be handed over not later than February 22nd. Yours in sunshine, Hitch."

The preparations of another non-Shamley collaborator, graphic designer Saul Bass, enhanced those of assistant director Green and others. At thirty-nine, Bass had already created a stir by designing bold title sequences for *Carmen Jones*, *The Man with the Golden Arm*, and *The Seven-Year Itch*. "The best thing about the movie is the Saul Bass credits" had almost become a critics' cliché. Superb Bass titles for Hitchcock's *Vertigo* and *North by Northwest* seemed to announce an uncommon meshing of sensibilities. On November 10, 1959, Hitchcock sent Bass the first twenty pages of the Stefano script; on the twenty-ninth of the same month, Bass received pages seventy through seventy-nine. As Hilton Green observed: "Hitch had it completely storyboarded [by Bass]." But internal Shamley memos suggest that the hiring of the designer sparked a territorial squabble or two. Early on, Herbert Coleman had been among several Hitchcock aides who advised their boss to offer Bass a less-substantial salary than $10,000 (plus three 16-millimeter prints of his main titles) for his thirteen consecutive weeks of work under the rubric "Pictorial Consultant." According to a terse memo, Hitchcock, a tight man with a dollar, "vetoed the suggestion."

Bass recalled: "Hitch was generally viewed as a fairly opaque person. He had a curious, dry view. But our relationship was an extremely warm one. He was, of course, the grand 'patron,' I the eager, interested, talented student. On *Psycho*, he came to me with a much more ambitious expectation. He wanted me to do the titles, of course, in addition to which he wanted me to do 'something' with the shower sequence, the Arbogast murder, the revelation of the desiccated body of the mother, and with the 'haunted house.' He had identified those key elements as something that needed special care." Following a series of meetings with Hitchcock, Bass began to draft conceptual sketches at his Hollywood office.

Concurrently, Hitchcock again bypassed his Shamley production roster by choosing editor George Tomasini (*To Catch a Thief, The Wrong Man*) over his TV cutters Edward W. Williams and Richard G. Wray. "Hitch hired George for two reasons," noted an associate of the editor. "His overall cutting expertise and for the shower sequence. He knew that would be *the* stickler." On November 16, Hitchcock hired Tomasini at a salary of $425 per week.

Casting

"Once you cast a star in a part," the director had often groused, "you compromise your original intentions to a great extent." On *Psycho*, Hitchcock had determined that he and the story were to be the stars. "Hitchcock's thing about actors was very strange," observed screenwriter Joseph Stefano of the director who had gotten so much press coverage out of calling actors "spoiled children" or "cattle." Even two of the director's blue-ribbon specimens did not escape his scorn. In private, Hitchcock referred to Ingrid Bergman, the lustrous heroine of *Spellbound*, *Notorious*, and *Under Capricorn*, as "so beautiful, so stupid." After James Stewart gave Hitchcock four of his finest performances, the director rewarded the star of *Rear Window* and *The Man Who Knew Too Much* by denying him the lead in *North by Northwest*, accusing the actor of having "looked too old" to have made a financial success of Vertigo.

Stefano remarked: "It was as though he really didn't live in the same world with them, or they in his. Somehow, we were the moviemakers, they were the 'others.' It was like he had one of England's great houses, now he had to let the tourists loose in it." The first performer that Hitchcock had signed for *Psycho* had done so before he had read the script. Joseph Stefano's screenplay describes Norman Bates as "somewhere in his late twenties, thin and tall, soft-spoken and hesitant . . . [with] something sadly touching in his manner." Then twenty-seven, Anthony Perkins had made his movie debut for director George Cukor in *The Actress* (1953). Whether playing a Civil War-era Quaker for director William Wyler in *Friendly Persuasion* (1956) or—less convincingly—baseball star Jimmy Piersall suffering a breakdown in *Fear Strikes Out* (1957), Perkin's callow vulnerability had turned him into a bobby soxer's dreamboat-with-a-brain. Perkins's popularity had even turned the vapid "Moonlight Swim" into a Top-Forty hit.

Conveniently for Hitchcock, Perkins owed Paramount a film under an old contract and could be hired for $40,000. By contrast, signing Cary Grant to star in *North by Northwest* cost that production $450,000 plus 10 percent of the gross over $8 million. The willingness of a late-fifties fan magazine cover boy to play a transvestite—even under the direction of Hitchcock—was admirable. The fifties were conservative years and perhaps few other actors might have taken the risk. Even fewer would have been nearly as "right" for the part. (Only Dean Stockwell strikes one as a viable alternative.) Paul Jasmin, a close pal of Perkins and himself a struggling actor at the time, recalled: "Even though Tony was a friend, what he was doing was a complete mystery, *very hush-hush.* Tony thought he was in the middle of making *the* career move of his life. And he was *right.*"

Yet even the unconventional Perkins, whom teen fans would mob if he dared step from his powder-blue T-bird, suffered misgivings. Perkins commented: "The question was 'Was it a wise thing to rush into in the sixties?' Probably less so than in the eighties, when it seems to me people get away with anything. Look at Vanessa Redgrave in *Second Serve* [in which the actress played a tennis pro who undergoes a sex change], just as an example." Perkins shared his misgivings only with his director. "[Hitchcock] agreed that it was a gamble," the actor said. "He had no idea of the real possible success of the picture, but he suggested that I give it a try anyway."

For the plum role of the blonde, Mary Crane, Hitchcock was anxious to sign the most prominent star appropriate for the part, the better to maximize the shock value of the on-screen killing. The Stefano screenplay describes the character thus: "Her face

. . . betrays a certain inner-tension, worrisome conflicts. She is
. . . an attractive girl nearing the end of her rope." The name
of Eva Marie Saint often cropped up in casting discussions in
the Hitchcock office. The director had grown especially fond of
the lovely, solidly professional leading lady of *North by Northwest*. But perhaps because Hitchcock had taken such pains to
transform Saint's screen image from drab, in *On the Waterfront*,
to sleek, he could not bear to let her backslide. At the behest
of the studio, Hitchcock and his staff viewed footage of every
likely (and unlikely) fair-haired type of the day, including Piper
Laurie, Martha Hyer, Hope Lange, and wholesome Shirley
Jones of *Oklahoma!* (1955) and *Carousel* (1956), who would
soon do an impressive about-face as a trollop in *Elmer Gantry*
(1960). There was even talk, mercifully brief, of MCA client
Lana Turner, suddenly hot again because of the success of a
Douglas Sirk–directed soap opera, *Imitation of Life* (1959), for
Universal-International.

Hitchcock surprised some Hollywood observers by signing
perky, reliable, thirty-two-year-old Janet Leigh to play Mary
Crane. Another client of MCA, Leigh would receive a salary of
$25,000. Despite the efforts she had made under the direction
of Josef von Sternberg, Fred Zinnemann, and Orson Welles,
Leigh had been relegated to turns in costume epics such as
Prince Valiant (1954) or comedies on a par with *The Perfect Fur-
lough* (1958). Still, Leigh was a darling of the fan magazines, a
member of the Peaches-and-Cream brigade with Debbie Reynolds, Doris Day, and June Allyson, who were counterpoints to
sultry mantrap types Elizabeth Taylor and Marilyn Monroe.
Leigh's "storybook" marriage to fifties beefcake prince Tony
("Yondah lies the castle of my foddah") Curtis cemented her
status as Hollywood royalty. Like Janet Leigh, Curtis, another
MCA client and Universal-International contract player, had to

gut it out in such hash as *Kansas Raiders* (1950) and *Son of Ali Baba* (1952) before showing he could be more than just a torso and a smoulder. Hollywood irony: Just as Janet Leigh would begin playing scenes opposite Anthony Perkins in his role as a transvestite for Hitchcock, Tony Curtis would be removing his lipstick, eyeliner, and chemise after playing a drag role for Billy Wilder in *Some Like It Hot* (1959).

"He sent me the novel," Janet Leigh recalled of the beginning of her association with Hitchcock. "With [the book] was a note saying that Mary was not as vital as he intended to have her in the movie. I was intrigued. I felt not only was she vital even in Robert Bloch's novel, but, though you only saw her for a short time in the picture, you don't know *anyone* else but her—except for Norman. He wanted a name actress because of the shock value, but he also wanted someone who could actually *look* like she came from Phoenix. I mean, Lana Turner might *not* be able to look like someone from there. He wanted a vulnerability, a softness. Actually, Mr. Hitchcock needn't have sent me anything. Just the prospect of working with him would have been enough. I've always believed, as it is with the English theater and movies, it doesn't matter how big the part, it's what you make of it. I would see Ralph Richardson doing a minor part and think, if *he* can, I sure as hell can."

Once Hitchcock signed Leigh, he laid down for her the ground rules that so infuriated certain actors. "His camera was absolute," Leigh commented. "Every move was planned before any performer even talked with him. He said, 'Here's your piece of the pie. What you bring to Mary other than what I want is fine. You can do almost anything with Mary and I won't interfere, so long as it's within my concept.' The wardrobe, the suitcase, what I put in the suitcase when I left my job, everything was well-thought-out. He showed me models of the sets—especially the hotel in the opening—and told me exactly how the camera was going to go into the window and follow the characters, all for concise effects."

Hitchcock sold Leigh on the wisdom of her following his carefully choreographed gestures and movements within the camera frame. "Hitchcock's films had so little cutting, he told me, because he had learned the hard way," Leigh said. "Before he had the clout to have his pictures the way he wanted, someone else would cut them their own way; he'd given them too much footage. So he learned to preplan so precisely [so as] *not* to give them extra material, because it was either going to work or not. And if it worked, he didn't want anybody to muck it up."

Contrary to his reputation as a director more comfortable discussing deep-focus than deep motivation, Hitchcock took pains to discuss with Janet Leigh the inner compulsions of Mary Crane. Leigh said, "She was an unspectacular, simple, frustrated person, getting older, seeing herself becoming an old maid, afraid Sam would go off, never having enough money. She was basically a compassionate, honest woman, not a thief. So her momentous, out-of-character decision to commit the robbery showed her passion and terrible frustration. She was a plain, ordinary person that something extraordinary happened to. Most of all, we both wanted to convey that no-place-to-go feeling. He said, 'I will only interfere if you don't come up to where I need you or you go too far.' But there was no conflict in terms of approach to Mary."

But *Psycho* required another blonde, and in that requirement was conflict. To flesh out the role of Lila Crane, the young sister trying to solve the mystery of the vanishing lady, Hitchcock again sought a reliable, affordable actress. According to a character description in the Stefano screenplay, Lila is "an attractive girl with a rather definite manner, a look of purposefulness." Actress Caroline Kearney, a "Doris Day lookalike," had caught the director's eye while playing Wendy Crane in a *Playhouse 90* drama by Arthur Hailey *Airport*) called "Diary of a Nurse" as well as in a Universal horror shocker called *The Thing That Couldn't Die*. Instead of newcomer Kearney, however, Hitchcock cast twenty-nine-year-old, Oklahoma-born Vera Miles. Five years earlier, Miles had similarly intrigued the director when he spotted her on an episode of a TV show, *Medic*.

In September of 1955, Vera Miles was valiantly holding her own against Joan Crawford in *Autumn Leaves*. Hitchcock persuaded the producers to release the actress for four days so that he could direct her in "Revenge," the second episode he was to shoot for airing on *Alfred Hitchcock Presents*. During production, the cool beauty, smarts, and bearing of Miles so captivated Hitchcock that he replaced "Breakdown," the episode originally scheduled to open his debut TV season, with "Revenge." On January 2, 1956, Vera Miles officially began a five-year personal contract under Alfred Hitchcock to star in three films a year. "I feel the same way directing Vera that I did with Grace," crooned a usually more circumspect Hitchcock to a reporter for *Look* magazine. "She has a style, an intelligence, and a quality of understatement." Convinced that he had found in Miles another icebox blonde in the Grace Kelly tradition, Hitchcock ordered costume designer Edith Head and Paramount's platoon of makeup and hair specialists to groom her expensively to his precise specifications. Hitchcock grumbled to Edith Head that Miles was "swamped by color," so he decreed that from then on his protégée should be attired in nothing but black, white, or gray. Upon inspecting Miles's portfolio of publicity photographs, Hitchcock announced to the Paramount publicity department that he was putting a moratorium on any further "cheesecake" shots. Hitchcock and his minions scrutinized and advised Vera Miles upon every public and private move she made—from the company she kept to her commercial tie-in arrangements, such as the one she enjoyed with Lux Soap. Costume designer Rita Riggs observed: "The sort of education one got from Mr. Hitchcock and Miss Head in publicity and the presentation of a new personality, one could not get anywhere else in the world. Although Vera was a lovely girl, she was far too intelligent to be an actress, and too independent to be anyone's Trilby."

To the surprise of few, the relationship between the spunky Miles and her demanding Svengali deteriorated during the making of *The Wrong Man*, which was shot on location in New York and released in 1956. Miles found Hitchcock's attentions toward her stifling and inappropriate. Hitchcock barraged her with flowers, telegrams, and demands for private conferences. Miles found herself constantly in arrears to express her gratitude. "Dear Hitch," began a typical note from Miles, almost three months too late. "It suddenly occurred to me that I didn't thank you for the beautiful flowers you sent me, both when I started *Beau James* and on my birthday. I sincerely appreciate your thoughtfulness and good wishes. Sincerely, Vera."

Matters worsened irrevocably when Miles married Gordon Scott, the new movie Tarzan, during the shooting of *The Wrong Man*. However, Miles's performance as the wife of Henry Fonda in Hitchcock's spare, documentarylike, black-and-white thriller prompted the director to design *Vertigo* as the picture to showcase her as the latest incarnation of the Hitchcock blonde.

By the time the screenplay was ready and James Stewart was signed to squire Miles in the film, the actress enraged Hitchcock by announcing she was pregnant—for the third time. "He was overwhelmed," Miles has said. "He said, 'Don't you know it's bad taste to have more than two?'" Instantly, the director cooled toward Miles. Hitchcock had lavished on his budding star time, money, and, most precious, emotion. Hitchcock associates say that he believed that Miles should have been grateful *and* compliant. Privately, Hitchcock fumed like a rebuffed suitor. Miles observed: "Over the span of years, he's had one type of woman in his films, Ingrid Bergman, Grace Kelly, and so on. Before that, it was Madeleine Carroll. I'm not their type and never had been. I tried to please him but I couldn't. They are all sexy women, but mine is an entirely different approach." Miles remained philosophical about losing the chance for stardom in *Vertigo*. "Hitchcock got his picture," she said. "I got a son."

In the intervening three years, Miles worked well under masterful director John Ford in *The Searchers* but only competently in lesser pictures for lesser directors. During the contretemps over *Vertigo* in November 1957, terse letters had flown back and forth between Miles's agent and the Hitchcock office as to whether the compensation she had already been paid in connection with that film could be applied to any further payment due her under her agreement. However, by September 22, 1959, with Miles still under contract when Hitchcock summoned her for the role in *Psycho*, Miles's agent took a more conciliatory tone in his telegrams: "Be assured of desire to cooperate and intention of accepting your offer." In what could only be read as a comeuppance, Hitchcock tossed his would-be ice goddess a drab, underdeveloped part. To worsen matters, Miles had just had her head shaved for a role in *Five Branded Women* in which she played a Yugoslavian girl punished for consorting with German troops. For *Psycho*, Hitchcock paid off his one-time contender for the throne of "the new Grace Kelly" with $1,750 a week and a dubious wig and wardrobe. "Vera was a pretty headstrong lady," concurs makeup man Jack Barron, who recalled several set-to's between leading lady and director. "She'd do things *her* way and stand up to anybody. Even him."

For the role of Sam Loomis, the heroine's lover, described in the script as "a good-looking, sensual man with warm humorous eyes and a compelling smile," Universal lobbied for contract player John Gavin, a strapping mannequin in the Rock Hudson mold. Hitchcock knew the role was too small to attract a major player, but he stonewalled the studio heads while he, Peggy Robertson, and, sometimes, writer Stefano viewed film on other candidates: Stuart Whitman, Cliff Robertson, Tom Tryon, Leslie Nielsen, Brian Keith, Tom Laughlin, Jack Lord, Rod Taylor (who was to star in *The Birds*), and Robert Loggia (who would play Sam in *Psycho II* in 1983). Again, budget constraints and availability forced Hitchcock to choose Gavin over top-contender Stuart Whitman. An MCA client, Gavin could be borrowed from Universal-International for six weeks at $30,000. "I guess he'll be all right," Hitchcock said with a shrug after watching Gavin's dramaturgic talents taxed by a Ross Hunter tearjerker. Contracts were final for all four leads by November 18. Several Hitchcock associates recall the director's taking wry amusement in the film's highest acting salary: $40,000—the precise amount heroine Mary Crane pilfers from her boss.

Hitchcock ribbed the press by announcing that Judith Anderson and Helen Hayes were the top candidates to play Mother. The quote prompted a deluge of letters and telegrams from senior actresses and their agents desperate to play the role. "Will I be with you this time?" wired actress Norma Varden, unforgettable in *Strangers on a Train* as the flighty Washington dowager nearly throttled by maniacal Bruno Anthony. Wired back Hitchcock, with a touch of malice: "I am afraid not. What a pity!"

In fact, Hitchcock was to employ a small, faceless platoon to capture the many moods of Mother. Margo Epper, a twenty-four-year-old stunt double, was hired for shots of stalking toward the shower curtain with the raised knife. Ann Dore handled shots involving physical contact with the terrified victim. For the over-head shots of Mother sashaying from the bedroom to stab Detective Arbogast or being carried downstairs by Norman, Hitchcock employed Mitzi Koestner, a little person who did stunt and double work and had appeared as a Munchkin in *The Wizard of Oz*. Paul Jasmin, today a fashion photographer and painter who has sold work to such stars as Barbra Streisand and Robert Stack, provided Mother's off-stage voice, while character actress Virginia Gregg dubbed the voice-overs. As Anthony Perkins pointed out, "Everybody had a bit of a crack at it. He [Jasmin] has a line. Virginia certainly has a lot of them. I think another actress has a couple, too." Veteran actress and Emmy-winner Jeanette Nolan is the third voice.

For the supporting cast, Hitchcock acted on two suggestions from screenwriter Stefano. His first recommendation was stage and television actor Martin Balsam for the role of Detective Arbogast, described in the script as possessing "a particularly unfriendly smile." Stefano also recommended Simon Oakland, another stage and TV scene-stealer, to play Dr. Richman, the glib psychiatrist who verbally unravels Norman's psychological peccadillos for the benefit of Mary's sister, Mary's lover Sam, and any audience member rusty on his Freud.

Hitchcock cast his daughter Patricia (*Stage Fright* [1950], *Strangers on a Train* [1951]) in a small role as the heroine's chirpy, poignant office mate, Caroline—uncharitably characterized in the script as "a girl in the last of her teens." Upon learning that his daughter wanted to pursue acting as her profession, Hitchcock had advised: "If you're going to be an actress, be an intelligent one." While Patricia was studying at the Royal Academy of Dramatic Art, Hitchcock cast her in a small role in *Stage Fright*, explaining, "I want to see if she learned anything at the academy and also if it was worth the money." On signing Patricia for

Psycho, Hitchcock half-jibed the press: "After ten years I thought it was time I gave her a job." But the director could hardly be accused of nepotism in the area of salary: Miss Hitchcock was paid $500 per day with a two-day guarantee.

Hitchcock hired reliable supporting players in Frank Albertson as the lecherous oilman Cassidy (although he wanted Alan Reed), John McIntire and Lurene Tuttle (who received $1,250, total) as, respectively, the bucolic sheriff and his wife, Mort Mills as a menacing highway patrolman, and, as a deputy who brings "Norma" Bates blankets in her detention cell, TV star Ted Knight (who was paid $150 per day) making an early film appearance. With his players in place, Hitchcock was nearly ready to begin shooting.

Production Design

Hitchcock believed that canny art direction and set design were crucial to the mood of the picture. When the director's first-choice designers Robert Boyle (*North by Northwest*) and Henry Bumstead (*The Man Who Knew Too Much*) proved to be unavailable, Boyle recommended Joseph Hurley. Hurley was a highly respected, personable production illustrator, and Hitchcock overlooked the fact that he had no previous credits in art direction. "No bad habits to unlearn," Hitchcock confided to his colleagues. The director hired Hurley on November 30, less than a month prior to the scheduled start of principal photography. But the relationship between Hitchcock and Hurley got off to a rocky start when the production designer, somewhat insecure about his first feature assignment, miffed the penny-pinching Hitchcock by requesting to be partnered with production designer Robert Clatworthy (*Touch of Evil*). Hitchcock acquiesced when he realized that *Psycho* would enjoy the services of *two* talented designers for about half the price of Boyle or Bumstead. "Joe and I went to Hitchcock's house in Bel-Air to discuss the film," recalled Clatworthy, a six-time Oscar nominee for art direction who had assisted Robert Boyle on Hitchcock's *Saboteur* (1942). (Joseph Hurley died in 1982, after contributing to such pictures as *Altered States* and *Something Wicked This Way Comes*.) "Even though Hitchcock was an art director himself originally, he spoke only very generally. On the Bates house, he didn't say he wanted any particular look—which was one of the great things about him. He let you present your ideas. I was happy the picture would be in black and white because I always attempted to take out the color, gray it down so it didn't look like a carnival."

With a rapidly approaching production date staring them in the face, Clatworthy and Hurley immediately began to design the Bates house and motel. Contrary to the assertion by some that the *Psycho* house was a standing set at the studio, and to the assertion by novelist James Michener that the residence was based on a "haunted house" built in the early 1800s in Kent, Ohio (a house that served as a center for the radical Students for Democratic Society after the Kent State student killings), the designs of Hurley and Clatworthy were original. Their concepts sprang from solid backgrounds in art theory, history, and canny movie design. "Joe did a lot of illustrations for the movie," Clatworthy said. "It was pretty simple with Hitch, who was a quiet, not particularly exciting man to work with—except that he excited you about his project. If he liked the sketches, that was it. If he didn't, he'd give you very specifically what he wanted changed—just once and that would be *it*. On the house and motel, he didn't say anything much, so we picked a spot kind of off by itself on the back lot and built the thing from the ground up."

Studio crews spent weeks erecting the facades of the house and motel—the former like a skeletal finger pointing skyward, the latter a rangy horizontal—on a hill off "Laramie" Street, named for a Revue sagebrush-and-six-guns series then on NBC. For a modest studio, such set construction smacked of the big time. An apt inspiration for the Bates house may have been the playfully eerie Addams Family residence familiar from the celebrated Charles Addams cartoons in the *New Yorker*. A more direct influence was surely Edward Hopper's *House by the Railroad*, the canvas depicting a melancholy mansard-roofed house, which is in the collection of the Museum of Modern Art in New York. Hurley and Clatworthy's design for Hitchcock was very suggestive of Hopper's creation—from its garret-story, roof-cresting and oculus window, to its cornices and pilasters. One might almost expect to glimpse Mrs. Bates silhouetted in the window of the sloping dormer in Hopper's 1925 painting.

In published dialogues with François Truffaut, Hitchcock characterized the architectural style of the house as "California Gothic, or, when they're particularly awful, they're called 'California Gingerbread'." Construction costs for the Bates manse—the most expensive set of the picture—came to a mere $15,000. Clatworthy and Hurley cannibalized several "stock unit" sections, including a tower from the house used in the James Stewart man-and-his-rabbit comedy *Harvey* (1948), as well as majesterial doors originally from the Crocker House of San Francisco. Costs of refurbishing another standing exterior, the one used for the Fairvale church, came to $1,250.

Robert Clatworthy assessed the interiors required by Hitchcock as "simple" and the bare-bones aspects were reflected in low, below-the-line production costs. Total costs for building and dressing the foyer, hall, a partial kitchen, and stairway of the first floor of the Bates home came to $6,000. Costs for Mother's bedroom and the basement/fruit cellar tallied $1,250 and $2,500, respectively. The Fairvale hardware store and storeroom owned by Sam Loomis cost $3,000. Totals for the corridor and detention room of the "Fairvale County Court House" in which Norman Bates is held: $2,000. Here again, the tight budget was to serve the film splendidly. Clatworthy had demonstrated a "feel" for expressionistically seedy motels and constricted interiors in *Touch of Evil*, another Universal-International picture, and one on which Orson Welles had predated Hitchcock by two years in being an A-movie director working on a B-movie budget. That both master directors tapped the skills and sensibility of Clatworthy may account for some of the visual echoes from Welles's film that resonate in *Psycho*.

Robert Clatworthy recalls Hitchcock's being far more finicky about odd, unsettling details of decor—such as the kitschy sculpture of the hands folded in prayer in Mother's room—than with the structures themselves. Crucial to Hitchcock, too, were the sets for Norman's parlor behind the motel office, the bathroom, and Mother's room. In the screenplay, Stefano writes of the parlor: "It is a room of birds . . . The birds are of many varieties, beautiful, grand, horrible, preying." Equally telling is the description of the motel bathroom, the scene of the greatest horror of the film. Hitchcock disdained the cliché of staging suspense sequences against the usual set pieces of the dark, haunted house. Thus Stefano writes: "The white brightness . . . is almost blinding." Production designer Clatworthy also recalls Hitchcock's enjoining set decorator George Milo to make certain that the bathroom fixtures gleamed. Hitchcock also told Milo: "Let's have lots of mirrors, old boy."

Another aspect of the film's interior design on which Hitchcock insisted initially puzzled Clatworthy. "The Phoenix real estate office was really nothing special," observed the designer.

"But because Janet Leigh was the star of the picture, I tried twice to sell him on the idea of having her desk just outside the boss's office. He never responded. I only found out the morning we were going to shoot that *that's* where his daughter [Patricia] was going to sit. He put Janet way out yonder in Siberia."

Studio construction crews built the interiors of the Bates house on Stage 18-A, as well as on the venerable "Phantom" Stage. The latter soundstage was named for the 1925 Lon Chaney silent version of *The Phantom of the Opera*, one of Universal's prestigious Super-Jewel productions, directed by Rupert Julian. With much fanfare by the studio at the time, the stage had been built to house a replica of the Paris Opera with its underground catacombs and five tiers of balconies. *The Phantom* was to undergo so much cutting before its release that one glimpses little of the set in the movie. No matter. For Hitchcock, the stage was ideal. It could accommodate the director's high angles and basement, stairwell, and fruit cellar set pieces. Besides, think of the *associations*. Several *Psycho* crew members said that Hitchcock took ghoulish delight in having the Bates stairwell built on the exact spot on which the chandelier plunged in *The Phantom of the Opera*.

While his construction crews completed their tasks, Hitchcock and the studio research department ironed out several script problems. On November 23, studio researchers discovered two names similar to "Mary Crane" in the Phoenix, Arizona, phone directory. They advised Hitchcock to choose a new name for his heroine from among "Marjorie, Martha, Marion, Mildred, Muriel, Maxine, Margo, and Marlene." Hitchcock chose "Marion." The legal eagles further suggested that the name of the psychiatrist (to be played by actor Simon Oakland) be altered from "Dr. Simon." Joseph Stefano renamed the character "Dr. Richman." Researchers also suggested that Hitchcock use a "dummy record label" rather than specify Beethoven's *Eroica* in the scene in which Lila Crane searches the room of Norman Bates. Hitchcock declined to do so.

Wardrobe

Dressing *Psycho* became the challenge of Helen Colvig and Rita Riggs. Both were accustomed to working for the Hitchcock TV show, but were novices at feature films. Vincent Dee, their supervisor at Revue, had enjoyed several preliminary meetings with Hitchcock but had unexpectedly required surgery. Recalled Rita Riggs, who worked with Hitchcock on the set and would go on to dress films for such directors as John Huston and Arthur Penn: "We were so excited about the prospect because Mr. Hitchcock had such a *circle* of collaborators around him. In those days, there really was a caste system of film people as opposed to television. But once you were enveloped in Mr. Hitchcock's projects, you were *in*."

Wardrobe supervisor Helen Colvig observed of her Hitchcock assignment: "[Hitchcock] had great fun with his collaborators, way before he even got into working with actors. His joy, and one of his great gifts, was in getting people stirred up about what stirred him. I was kind of shaky, but I'd been told Hitchcock had it in his mind to do it as television—realism, speed, with a documentary feeling around the edges. In our first meeting, his research was so pure, he laid out photographs for every major character. In Phoenix, he'd found a girl like Marion, went into her home, photographed everything from her closet, her bureau drawers, her suitcases."

Rita Riggs, who had "grown comfortable" with the director after costuming his droll introductory appearances on his TV show, marveled at how thoroughly Hitchcock had preplanned a modest-scale film. "The real difference working with Hitchcock and his circle was that you had an entire, cohesive picture laid out before you on storyboards. He truly used storyboards to convey his ideas and desires to all his different craftsmen. You knew *every* angle in the picture, so there was not a lot of time wasted talking an item to death. We also didn't have to waste time worrying about things like shoes, for instance, because we knew he wasn't going to show them in the shot."

Helen Colvig recalled "a long, solid meeting" after which she was left with an unshakable opinion of her director. "Not only did he already see the picture cut and edited, but he could already envision it advertised in the newspapers." According to both costume experts, most of the clothing requirements on *Psycho* were "simple." "Mr. Hitchcock insisted on classicism," explained Riggs. "He said, 'We may laugh at ourselves in ten years, but our fashions will come around again in twenty.' He wouldn't just think of the economic bracket of his characters, but of the line, the momentum of the film itself."

According to Riggs, Janet Leigh's dresses and blouses were purchased off-the-rack from the popular, stylish Beverly Hills store, Jax. That in itself was unheard-of for a major film and a star player of the day. As Helen Colvig put it, "Why make the dress when you can buy it?" Riggs and Colvig hand-picked a medium-blue wool jersey for the actress because, said Riggs, "Mr. Hitchcock was *very* specific about good wool because it takes light so beautifully and photographs a very rich gray."

Both collaborators recall many of Hitchcock's costuming dictates as being far more particular. "He was very specific about what his daughter Patricia wore in the picture," Rita Riggs recalls. "It was a green silk shantung." Another Hitchcock concern was the bra and slip worn by Janet Leigh in the amatory opening scenes in the Phoenix hotel room. "Janet Leigh wanted her lingerie made to order," remembered Helen Colvig. "Mr. Hitchcock said, 'Oh no, my dear. That just won't work for the character. We want that underwear to be identifiable to many women all over the country.' She [Leigh] had a lot of trouble with that, but was satisfied when she got his point of view. He wanted to suck people in so deep, they didn't have time to say, 'Oh, this is just a movie.'" Janet Leigh recalls no such controversy. "I never wanted the lingerie made to order," Leigh observed. "In fact, I suggested the half-bra because it was like what I normally wore."

"A bra and slip—even just showing the midriff section—was very racy then and fairly verboten," Rita Riggs explained. "There was great equivocation about whether Janet would wear a black or white bra and slip in the opening. It went on and on. We had each ready, of course, and not until we were almost ready to shoot did Mr. Hitchcock finally choose white for the opening, black for after she steals the money. It was strictly for character statement. He had an obsession for the 'good' girl or the 'bad' girl."

Another Hitchcock costuming *absolute* centered upon the character of Mother. Although both the novel and the screenplay pinpoint the murder of Mother at age forty, Helen Colvig explained, "He wanted to go right to the image of the sweet little old bent-over lady, so that the public might be fooled. Right from the beginning, he told me he was going to trick the eye by using Anthony Perkins, a few stunt women, as well as a four-foot-tall little person." Small wonder Rita Riggs called mama's dresses "the most important pieces in the picture." She said, "It had to be a print that one would recognize and would transfer from several different-sized figures, moving and static. In silhouette, that print had to look *very* important. We also had a terrible furor trying to get those old ladies' lace-up shoes in enough sizes, including a women's size ten for Tony Perkins!"

Another departure from the standard was the costumes for Vera Miles, Hitchcock's former protégée, once groomed as a successor to Grace Kelly. In *Psycho*, Hitchcock relegated Miles to the lesser of two important female roles. According to Rita Riggs, "Vera was gorgeous, very bright, very independent, and very angry throughout the filming of *Psycho*. Mr. Hitchcock made her look like a dowdy, old-maid schoolteacher although Vera ended up having her things done at Paramount by Edith Head. For most of the film, we saw a lot of the back of her head and she was pretty much stuck in one dress and coat, although they were of a beautiful Rodier fabric in taupe. I have great respect for Miss Head, but I remember thinking 'Gosh, that's a rather dowdy fabric and color.' But it was Mr. Hitchcock's choice. He was very disappointed with Vera, on whom he had invested a lot of time, thought, and emotion in preparing *Vertigo* for her before she got pregnant. That was some of his perversity coming through."

Although Hitchcock had been known to be as finicky about costumes for his male stars as for his female, *Psycho* saw him in a more laissez-faire mode. Noted Helen Colvig: "I recall Hitch saying, 'Either they wear the clothes and do the part the way I want, or they're not going to be in it.' But Tony asked Hitch if he might wear clothes of his choice, like the shirt and certain cut of the sweater that holds [the shirt] there, because he has a long neck. Hitch approved because the look worked for Bates, not just for Tony. He had the whole picture so thoroughly in his hands— every element—that I never worked for anyone who was so easy."

The shower stabbing sequence loomed as a crucial element that was to require maximum coordination on the part of Hitchcock's collaborators. "Hitchcock knew the nude scenes were going to be difficult because he was casting a star," Helen Colvig commented. "In those days, stars tended not to go nude, so he told me they would probably 'double' that—but he still wanted options for costuming and makeup if she was willing to go nude or partially nude."

Makeup

Jack Barron, head of the Universal makeup department, supervised the effects for *Psycho*, and Robert Dawn acted as the on-set artist. Barron, an industry veteran who began as a self-described "makeup flunky" on *Citizen Kane*, was to work on six subsequent Hitchcock projects. "Even on a 'small' picture like *Psycho*," Barron said, "you would be summoned to [Hitchcock's] office expecting a five-minute talk about a specific thing and wind up hearing a discourse on art, current affairs, Hollywood, wine. He loved to talk about having fish flown in from Boston or about his wine cellar that was stocked with rare vintages. The poor man was such a gourmand and couldn't partake because of blood pressure, his weight, or whatever. It was hard to say if he was a lonely man or just wanted to talk about the picture."

During the process of preproduction, Barron was to detect several other idiosyncrasies peculiar to his director. "Hitch wouldn't say much," observed Barron, "but sometimes, you had the feeling he believed you should know *exactly* what he was feeling or thinking. But, a cat can look at a king. Anytime anybody had a question, we asked the king. If you stood up to him and explained your reasons, he would back down. If you didn't, he'd railroad you. For some reason, he had decided he didn't want Mort Mills, who was playing the highway patrolman, to look like himself. He said: 'Change him.' 'How far do you want to go?' I asked. He said: 'Change him *simply*.' So I brought in some mustaches and he immediately pointed one out. Later, he decided against that for the sunglasses, which were not common then. He came up with details that seem tiny but that added a lot to the overall outcome."

Hitchcock also defined his expectations of Barron in the matter of the corpse of Mother to be revealed in the Grand Guignol finale. "'I want this to be a *shocker*,'" Barron recalled Hitchcock insisting. "'This woman has been sitting around a *long* time.' He only wanted to see the skull and dried skin over that, with a steel-gray hairdo parted in the center." Hitchcock had based his concepts on the information he received in response to a memo he sent in early November to the studio research department: "What would be the condition of the corpse of a woman who had been poisoned at age forty—embalmed and buried—then, after two months, disinterred and kept in a residence for ten years?" The details ("mummified . . . [with] brown leatherlike skin over the bones") were provided by an instructor at a Los Angeles college of mortuary science and Hitchcock conveyed them precisely to Jack Barron and Robert Dawn.

When Dawn immediately began sketching prototypes, Hitchcock informed him that they were of no use to him. The director only wanted to view tangible models. "Hitch was a stickler for accuracy," Barron explained. "He didn't want anything just for the sake of shock. At one point, stuff like maggots crawling in and out of the eye sockets was brought up as a notion, but Hitchcock's idea was that the corpse had been there for so long—it wasn't a fresh thing. We did several subtle variations on the head. I mean, what can you *do* with a skull and skin? But Bob was a heck of a good 'rubber' man [a prosthetics man] so he got a real skull, applied rubber to it and colored that." Hitchcock inspected each successive prototype dummy head presented by the makeup men, always requesting to keep the prosthetic device overnight before suggesting refinements. Some believe that the director wanted first to test the model on Alma Hitchcock, whom makeup artist Barron assessed as "a smart, shrewd lady who had a lot of influence over him." Aside from the exacting Mrs. Hitchcock, Janet Leigh was another woman whose reactions mattered to Hitchcock. Leigh recalled: "[Mr. Hitchcock] liked teasing me because I'm a good audience, and he loved scaring me, so he'd experiment with Mother's corpse by using me as a gauge. I'd open my dressing room door and find this horrible creature sitting in my chair. My screams made him decide on his choice of the Madame." The final result was so effective that costumer Rita Riggs admitted: "Having to go down into the set to get that dummy dressed and shoed so gave me the chills, I would actually dress her from behind."

Hitchcock vs. Censors: Round One

On November 18, twelve days before the scheduled start of principal photography, Hitchcock sent the script to the Motion Picture Association of America, the overseeing body of the Hays Office, which was a self-regulatory code of ethics organization created in 1930 by the movie industry, run by former postmaster general Will H. Hays. In 1934, Joseph I. Breen became administrator of the Code that policed many of the very themes and techniques that lay at the heart of Hitchcock. The Code, for instance, stipulated that ". . . the sympathy of the audience should never be thrown to the side of crime, wrongdoing, evil or sin." The Code also insisted that "excessive and lustful kissing, lustful embracing, suggestive postures and gestures, are not to be shown"; but, oddly, that "brutality and possibly gruesomeness . . . be treated *within the careful limits of good taste"* (italics mine). Ironically, many of the powerful and suggestive moments in Hitchcock films gained their force because the Code endorsed the understated style that was a hallmark of the director.

If the Code office threatened to deny a seal of approval to a prospective film, it meant that most theaters would refuse to show it; hence, most producers would think twice about making it. Directors Howard Hughes (*The Outlaw*) and Otto Preminger (*The Moon Is Blue*) had successfully challenged the absolute power of the Hays Office, but problems for Hitchcock with the then-administrator, Geoffrey Shurlock, could spell trouble for *Psycho*.

In 1959, Luigi Luraschi was the Paramount studio liaison with the Code office. Six days after Luraschi had submitted the Hitchcock script to the Shurlock office, Hollywood's watchdogs of morality not only warned Hitchcock that it might be "impossible to issue a certificate on a finished film based on this script," but also virtually predicted a campaign against the film by the influential and even less tolerant National Legion of Decency of the Roman Catholic Church.

Aside from the standard complaints by the Code office about dialogue peppered with uses of "damn," "God," and "hell," the censorship board expressed deeper, more substantive reservations. The censors red-penciled a line of dialogue to be spoken to the heroine by Cassidy, the Texas oilman: "Bed? Only playground that beats Las Vegas." But more serious were charges that the Stefano script was shot through with "[a] very pointed description of an incestuous relationship between Norman and his mother." In Stefano's script, Mother refers to Norman as "ever the sweetheart," and aflame with the "fantasy of making love." Norman himself observes that a son is a poor substitute for "a real lover" and the psychiatrist terms the mother-son relationship "more that of two adolescent lovers." It was also suggested that "the discussion of transvestism . . . be eliminated." In her detention cell, Mother shudders as she recalls Norman, "Always peeping . . . and reading those . . . obscene books and disgusting me with his love."

In a stern rebuke to Hitchcock, Luraschi delivered the message that ". . . if the picture were to contain this kind of a flavor, we would be in serious trouble with the Legion of Decency and also with the various censor boards throughout the international field." Yet Stefano and Hitchcock had deliberately layered-in certain risqué elements as a ruse to divert the censors from more crucial concerns: primarily the action that took place in the shower and bathroom. Luraschi warned Hitchcock: "It will, of course, be necessary to exercise the utmost care in the scenes . . . in the bathtub, and of the effort of Norman to dispose of [Marion's] naked body. These scenes, beginning from the time she steps into the tub, will have to be handled with the utmost discretion and good taste."

In the rebuke, Hitchcock was advised by the censors and the studio "that those scenes dealing with the stabbing of both the girl and the detective be cut and edited in such a manner as to permit smooth elimination of any excess footage involving the knife scenes, since scenes of this type are being drastically cut in the United Kingdom, Australia, and the Scandinavian countries."

Experience had made Hitchcock a master at dealing with censorship problems. In the forties, the screenplays for *Rebecca* and *Suspicion* were laundered to render the motivations of the leading characters less pathological and—purportedly—more palatable to the audience. Censors in the fifties had also forced Hitchcock to tone down racy dialogue and situations in the John Michael Hayes screenplay for *Rear Window*. Similarly, objections to Ernest Lehman's *North by Northwest* screenplay resulted in a less breezily sexy hero and heroine, and a buttoned-down homosexual in Leonard, the assistant to the spy Van Damm, played by Martin Landau. The Production Code office stamped the shooting scripts of *Psycho* with "Approved, subject to seeing the product," an unusual circumstance meant to put Hitchcock and company on notice.

7. SHOOTING

Production #9401, Hitchcock's "30-Day Picture"

On November 11, 1959, Hitchcock captured the first footage for *Psycho*. He borrowed a crew from his previous TV production, #13599, to shoot "photographic tests" of Anthony Perkins. Although the nature of these tests was left unspecified on daily production sheets, it is likely that they may have entailed shots of Perkins as Mother, the only out-of-the-ordinary costume requirement for the actor in the entire picture.

Script supervisor Marshall Schlom, son of RKO B-movie unit producer Herman Schlom, recalled the unceremonious beginning of production. He said, "All of us who regularly did his TV shows went straight from three days of that, then, the next morning, we started the movie with him. We never really got any idea of what was going to happen."

Fourteen days later, Hitchcock and his crew trekked to Fresno and Bakersfield, California, for several days, where they shot footage on Highway 99 that was to be used for the forty-nine process plates necessary for the car trip of the heroine. Hitchcock planned to stylize that sequence heavily, and the plan was to accomplish all of it by the process of rear projection. (By contrast, Hitchcock's previous picture, *North by Northwest*, had required several hundred process shots and his next, *The Birds*, would require 412.) Simultaneously, a second unit spent nearly a week on locations in Phoenix, Arizona. Four of those days were spent on attempts to capture the helicopter shots approaching a hotel window that were to be used in the opening moments of the film. According to a scribble found on a production sheet, Hitchcock was amused by a notion of screenwriter Stefano to sweep the viewer—almost as if he were to become a fly on the wall—into the hotel room window to spy on Sam and Marion, post-tryst.

In a squib that appeared in *Variety* on December 27, 1959, Hitchcock boasted that the film would "open with the longest dolly shot ever attempted by helicopter," a "four-mile scene" that would even top the bravura dolly with which Orson Welles opened *Touch of Evil.* However, the problems of the second-unit crew in capturing the aerial footage were extensive, and most *Psycho* crew members concur that little of Hitchcock's original intention was to come off in the final movie. "That was done before we ever had Tyler mounts or knew much about helicopter shots," observed script supervisor Marshall Schlom.

Psycho, or Production #9401, as the studio referred to it, began principal photography on November 30, 1959, with an estimated thirty-six-day shooting schedule. Hitchcock biographer Donald Spoto has stressed the lengths to which Hitchcock would go in order to keep the nature of his new picture under wraps. Spoto adds, however, that "Wimpy" was used as a substitute moniker for all in-house communications regarding the film. The story perhaps stems from the fact that the name of the second-unit cameraman on the picture, Rex Wimpy, appeared on clapboards and production sheets, and hence in some on-the-set stills for *Psycho*.

Hitchcock, resplendent in his customary Mariani suit, white shirt, and tie, convened his cast for the first day of shooting on Stage 18-A. Every element of the production appeared to be ready. "Mr. Hitchcock said he would never direct a film in which the script wasn't perfect before he started," recalled Schlom. "So we shot a white script, not a 'rainbow' script which had gone through a lot of changes." The director garnered much press by purportedly demanding a closed set for much of the time. Some of that secrecy was due to the unusual plotline, some to the no-nonsense schedule. Aside from Hitchcock's hype to the press about secrecy, many in the cast and crew did not know the ending. "Mr. Hitchcock held up the last few pages of the script—and rightly so," noted wardrobe supervisor Rita Riggs. "When we started to work," observed actress Vera Miles, "we all had to raise our right hands and promise not to divulge one word of the story." "Everything was keyed to that shocking ending," observed actor Paul Jasmin, whose friend Anthony Perkins was to recommend him to Hitchcock for an unusual "voice-over" assignment on the film. "Hitchcock had the whole town talking about this strange, disturbing movie he was making. Everybody wanted to know what he was up to, but he asked all of us not to talk about it."

Even without the extra hush-hush precautions, a Hitchcock set was hardly one on which the idly curious might feel comfortable just dropping by. "*Psycho* was a very reserved set, very formal," according to costumer Rita Riggs. "The male crew *all* wore shirts and ties. Sometimes I even went to work wearing gloves and a handbag. So the pressure to stay off the set was as subliminal as anything else. If a stranger dared to come on, one of the shirt-and-tie brigade might accost him with a firm, polite, 'May we help you?' Mr. Hitchcock never needed to turn his head. He could spot a newcomer out of the corner of his eye." Thus, when Lew Wasserman, the sartorially conservative head of MCA, paid a call on Hitchcock, the dress and demeanor of the crew were up to snuff.

Production began smoothly. A telegram on December 1 from his leading lady surely pleased the old-world, courtly Hitchcock: "Thanks for a nice first day and for the lovely roses. Now I know why it is such a pleasure to work for you. Affectionately, Janet." Two other telegrams perhaps went underappreciated. "Happy *Psycho*, Love, Vera," wired Vera Miles, while producer Herbert Coleman—for whom Hitchcock harbored a grudge for "defecting" from the inner circle—wrote: "All the love in the world with your *Psycho*. Love, Herbie."

The first week of shooting centered primarily on the detainment of Marion by the highway patrolman, her arrival at Bates Motel, and her first encounter with Norman on the motel porch in the rainstorm. Script supervisor Marshall Schlom observed: "The very first day of shooting was on the Golden State Freeway, when she is pulled over by the cop. It was warm. Mr. Hitchcock perspired a lot and did not like the heat or the cold. In fact, he preferred to work on the soundstage, so that day he chose to stay in the car—but always within earshot." Makeup artist Jack Barron noted: "A lot of Hitchcock's scripts were written to accommodate the fact that he liked to start on page one and go right through the script. Of course, if the heroine was driving her car on page ten and again on ninety-two, it would be stupid not to do that at the same time."

Hitchcock also completed a day of "location" shooting more to his liking, since Harry Maher's used car lot at 4270 Lankershim Boulevard was only a stone's throw from Universal in North

Hollywood. Because one sponsor of the Hitchcock TV show was Ford Motor Company, the car lot's usual inventory was displaced in favor of shiny Edsels, Fairlanes, and Mercury models.

Makeup man Jack Barron was not alone in his surprise at seeing cinematographer John Russell lighting the set during the first week of shooting. "I got on the set, looked around and said to John, 'Isn't this color?' He said it wasn't. When I asked Hitch about it, he said, 'But, dear boy, it will have so much more *impact* in black and white.'" Budgetary considerations aside, Hitchcock provided actor Anthony Perkins with another justification: "Hitch talked about being a big fan of *Les Diaboliques*. It was one of the reasons he wanted to make *Psycho* in black and white."

Hitchcock's camera expertise often heightened his expectations of the cinematographer. He and cameraman John Russell had grown accustomed to working together on the Hitchcock TV series. Hitchcock perhaps took it for granted that communication between them would be virtually second-nature. Assistant director Hilton Green observed: "[Hitchcock] never expounded with John or told any cameraman he was wrong. He would tell them what he wanted, ask what lens they would be using. If it wasn't the right one, he'd quietly say, 'What if you did it with such-and-such instead?'"

Marshall Schlom recalled: "Mr. Hitchcock would sit in his chair and, never looking through the camera, say, 'Now I want to do a two-shot, so use a thirty millimeter lens and put the camera right *there*. I think the distance will be ten feet, so you're going to be cutting right in *here* [pointing to a level on the actor's body].' Little photographic problems kept cropping up on *Psycho*. When [Hitchcock] *wasn't* quite sure about the solution, I became a stool-pigeon for him by occasionally looking through the camera just to make certain he was getting what he asked for."

Leonard South, one of Hitchcock's team of feature-film collaborators, recalled the director's phoning him, sounding "very upset." South said, "Hitchcock was a *definite* guy, but not a forceful one. He was too nice to hurt Jack Russell's feelings. He called me, saying, 'Lenny, they bloody well don't understand me,' meaning the people from Universal-Revue who were only used to doing episodic TV. He described a very sophisticated camera move that the crew had wanted to do in a way that he found completely unacceptable. We literally talked the shot through step by step so that he could tell them how to do it properly. Making *Psycho* was a terrible struggle for him, at first."

Marshall Schlom recalled a potentially volatile situation that arose between the director and his TV-oriented cameraman. Because Hitchcock disliked night shooting, he and his crew had reserved for dusk the shots, to be done on the backlot, of Janet Leigh driving toward the motel, as seen from the vantage point of the porch. The director watched coolly from his chair while cinematographer Russell lit the shot and geared up for the artificial rain that the scene required. Schlom observed: "Mr. Hitchcock noticed an arc light backlighting a big oak tree that would show right behind Janet. He asked me, 'Is that arc in the picture?' I quietly got up, stuck my face in the camera, then sat back down: 'Yes, Mr. Hitchcock, it is.' He called over the cameraman and said, 'Jack, is that arc in the picture?' He said, 'No Hitch, the tree's going to cover it.' We shot it. Next day at noon, I went to the dailies and there was the arc in the picture: It looked like a full moon. My head spun. Jack was a friend and I didn't want to get him in trouble.

"My dilemma must have registered in my face because Peggy [Robertson] said, 'What's the problem?' I told her and she said,

'Well, who pays your check? You'll have to tell Mr. Hitchcock.'
I went back to the set and Mr. Hitchcock was talking with
someone. I started to leave and he said, 'Sit down, Marshall.' He
continued talking with the other person and I started to leave
again. *'Marshall? Sit down.'* The other person left and I told Mr.
Hitchcock that the arc was in the picture. He called Jack over. I
was dying. Jack came over and bent down to Mr. Hitchcock, who
said, 'Jack, I just came back from the dailies and I noticed the
arc in the picture.' I'll never forget how he got me off the hook."
Hitchcock and Russell reshot.

Despite the technical glitches, Hitchcock kept the proceed-
ings moving along at a smart pace. "He directed it as if it were
a television show," observed Marshall Schlom. "We did between
fourteen to eighteen setups a day, which, for a major motion
picture director, is a lot. To him it would be a lesser kind of film
than *Vertigo* or *The Man Who Knew Too Much*. In scale, this was
in the same vein as *The Trouble with Harry*. He loved directing
this very good cast in a good script on a small, very manageable
movie. He never went past take three or four because he always
felt the spontaneity would diminish and the scene would take on
a different feeling."

Despite the brisk schedule, Hitchcock was not a man to be
rushed. Makeup artist Jack Barron observed: "I've been on movie
sets for forty-five years, but a Hitchcock set was like no one else's.
People were so taken by him, respected him so. If anyone—electricians, crew, whoever—had something to say, they'd practically
whisper it, out of respect. On a nine o'clock shoot, he'd come
in about eight-thirty. You'd expect him to come in and give the
cameraman the first setup. Not Hitchcock. He'd sit down and
tell stories until he was good and ready, and then say, 'I think
it's time for the first setup.' No one ever dared say, 'Come on,

we have a schedule to keep.' Everybody would think, 'God, we haven't shot anything and here it is ten or eleven A. M.' By the time you went for lunch, he'd have half his day's work done. The whole crew especially loved Thursdays because that was his night to go to Chasen's with 'Mom' [Mrs. Hitchcock]. We knew we'd be home by four o'clock."

Marshall Schlom, who, on completing *Psycho*, would leave Hitchcock to work for such directors as Stanley Kramer and John Huston, observed of Hitchcock's contradictory nature: "There was an aura about [Hitchcock]. He stood there and you didn't want to get too close to him, but he wanted you to. Normally the cameraman and director are locked together, but not with Mr. Hitchcock. John Huston used to come in and shake everybody's hand. 'Did you have a pleasant evening?' he'd say—very gregarious and European. Mr. Hitchcock was very polite to everybody, but he didn't give you the impression he was interested in your private life. And at five-thirty, he would look at his watch and say to Hilton [Green], 'Are we finished?' Hilton would say, 'Yes, Mr. Hitchcock,' and Mr. Hitchcock would announce, 'I think that will be all for today.' Everyone would say goodnight and he'd walk out to his car to be driven home."

From the outset, the warmth and professionalism of Janet Leigh appeared to hearten Hitchcock, just as the dedication with which Anthony Perkins approached his assignment seemed to disarm the director. Wardrobe expert Helen Colvig commented, "Tony was *so* serious about his role. I believe that impressed Mr. Hitchcock and even *touched* him." Perkins has recalled: "Even as the first day proceeded I could see he wanted to know what I thought and what I wanted to do and I was really very surprised by this. I kind of tentatively made some small suggestion about something I might do. He said, 'Do it.'"

A Set Divided

Tempers flared during the filming of the lunch-hour motel liaison of Marion and her lover, Sam. Despite the gamy dialogue and setting, the bra and half-slip worn by the curvaceous Janet Leigh, and the strapping John Gavin baring his torso, Leigh and many crew members claimed that the lack of erotic heat between his co-stars infuriated the director. Hitchcock had no desire to exploit softcore pornography in the scene. Yet he and writer Stefano had carefully designed the scene not only to announce that *Psycho* was a *sixties* picture but also to introduce the voyeuristic theme and film technique that runs through the movie. "One of the reasons for which I wanted to do the scene in that way was that the audiences are changing," the director told François Truffaut. "It seems to me that the straightforward kissing scene would be looked down at by the younger viewers; they'd feel it was silly. I know that they themselves behave as John Gavin and Janet Leigh did."

Previous Hitchcockian benchmarks of cinema eroticism—the longest kiss in the movies in *Notorious* (1946) and the sexy badinage of *Rear Window* (1954) and *To Catch a Thief* (1955)—were to pale beside the opening of *Psycho*. Wardrobe mistress Rita Riggs said, "It seemed so abrupt for two actors to shake hands and jump into bed together. But Mr. Hitchcock loved the perversity of it all and wanted to see what kind of electricity that newness might spark between the two actors." Script supervisor Marshall Schlom elaborated: "He was a little imp. He sat in his chair with a straight, serious face, but that scene was a firecracker, a cause célèbre, and Mr. Hitchcock *knew* it. He felt the hotel scene and the shower scene were the two we had to make sure were right. And since he was getting such flack from the censors, he made sure it was done in good taste."

Never before had actors in a mainstream American film played an erotic duet horizontally, let alone in the seminude. "I was so intrigued by the character and Hitchcock's direction," actress Leigh recalled, "that it didn't dawn on me until I was actually on the set that my being in a half-slip and bra was some big hullabaloo. The set was closed, but the funniest thing was everybody up in the rafters looking down like they thought they really saw something."

"John Gavin had a great look on-screen; unfortunately, he was an awfully cold fish otherwise," a crew member commented of the actor who had been highly touted by talent agent Henry Willson, who had previously landed studio contracts for his stable of such handsome young clients as Rock Hudson, Guy Madison, Rory Calhoun, and Tab Hunter. Hitchcock grew visibly more riled as take after take failed to thaw Gavin's icy reserve. Finally, the director called "Cut" and engaged Janet Leigh in a huddle on the sidelines. "The scene didn't seem to be going as well as Hitch wanted it to," said Janet Leigh, choosing her words carefully. "The scene had to establish the passion of the relationship right from the start, so that Marion's tremendous sacrifice and dangerous act makes sense." In discrete but descriptive terms, Hitchcock requested that Leigh take matters in hand, as it were. Leigh blushed, acquiesced, and Hitchcock got a reasonable facsimile of the required response. But the director's annoyance with John Gavin festered. Privately, Hitchcock referred to the actor as "The Stiff."

Observed Rita Riggs, who went on to do two more Hitchcock pictures after *Psycho*, "I never once heard Mr. Hitchcock raise his voice over the incident, but when we began seeing the dailies, we noticed that we saw a great deal of the back of John Gavin's head." Helen Colvig added: "He was at odds with John. I remember being there when John conveyed through the assistant director that he wanted to come through a door in a certain way. Hitchcock looked askance and told the assistant, 'Don't worry, we'll just cast a shadow over his face. We can knock him out in no time.' I think John was trying really hard to impress Hitch, but he was just irritating him."

"I dislike conflict," Hitchcock once said, "but I won't sacrifice my principles. I draw the line at my work. I loathe people who give less than their full effort. That's deceit . . . I cut such people off."

Co-star Janet Leigh asserted that one mark of Hitchcock's genius was his way of exploiting the passivity of Gavin to good effect. "In a strange way," she said, "it worked for the suspense. Real passion would have justified Marion's theft. But the lack of the complete abandon with Sam might have led some audience members to think, 'I wonder if he really loves her that much?' It made Marion even more sympathetic, which Hitch was very concerned about her being. It also might have titillated the audience a bit into believing that possibly something might develop between Marion and Norman in that very weird but strangely sweet supper scene in the motel den."

Although Hitchcock made no overt display of his displeasure with the casting, few could freeze out someone more totally. Gavin became an outsider while Hitchcock discovered in Leigh and Perkins more convivial players. "Tony was and is a very private person," observed one Hitchcock associate, "but he was very taken with the whole movie, wanted to be part of everything. Hitchcock liked that and helped him a lot. Tony was very serious about the whole thing."

Unlike Janet Leigh, on whom Hitchcock lavished considerable preparation time, Perkins had little or no contact with his director prior to filming. Janet Leigh observed: "Tony was surprised to learn that Hitch and I had meetings prior to filming. But I wonder if it wasn't because he wanted a kind of distance, a not-quite-worldly quality to how Tony played Norman." Perkins admitted, "In *Psycho*, I was confused at first. When we started the picture I had never actually met [Hitchcock] but once [prior to the start of production] and I was very apprehensive about making any statements about what I thought, what I felt about the character and about the different scenes. I got to relaxing more with him and making more and more suggestions and ideas. About four weeks in we were getting along very well but I was still hesitant about bringing him a page of dialogue which was as blackly worked over as this one was. He was in his dressing room reading his air-mailed copy of the *London Times*—which he often does between shots. And I said, 'Mr. Hitchcock, about my speech in tomorrow's scene.' He said, 'Uh, huh' (he's still reading), and I said, 'I've had a few ideas that I thought maybe you might like to listen to.' I was kind of stuttering around. He said, 'All right.' And I started telling him what they were. He said, 'Oh, they're all right.' And I said, 'But, but, but, you might not like them.' He said, 'I'm sure they're all right.' He put the paper down. He said, 'Have you given it a lot of thought? I mean have you really thought it out? Do you really like these changes you've made?' I said, 'Yes, I think they're right.' He said, 'All right, that's the way we'll do it.' I think I worked on it twice as hard that evening and, sure enough, as we went in, he didn't even glance at the original pages. It all sounded right to him."

Perkins developed a powerful affinity not only for the surface behavior of Norman Bates but also for the inner workings. "It was my idea to have Norman nervously chewing candy in the film," Perkins enthused about the character who was to become a national folk antihero. "He would not plot malice against anyone. He has no evil or negative intentions. He has no malice of any kind."

Despite Perkins's obvious dedication to his role in the film, Janet Leigh emerged as Hitchcock's special pet. Between takes, he took constant delight in convulsing her with salty puns, limericks, and off-color jokes. "What he liked to do most," Leigh said, "was to make me blush and that is not a hard thing to do." For all his widely reported disdain for actors, Hitchcock took pains to coax the strongest possible performance from Leigh. Nowhere was this attention more focused than in the many moments that Leigh played without dialogue: Hitchcock's camera seems almost acutely sensitive to the play of emotions on her face. "My part was almost shot alone, in isolation," Leigh emphasized. "I mean, except for the one scene with Gavin, in the office, and the few scenes with Tony, the rest of it was really me, alone. It was very clear with Hitchcock. He said, 'This is the result I want. How you get there is up to you.'"

Although some performers in the film felt their work suffered from the speed and apparent casualness with which Hitchcock shot, Leigh disagreed. "Perhaps none of his other films were shot as fast as *Psycho*," she observed. "But any less-well-prepared director might have taken far more time to shoot *Psycho*. I have a feeling that if one studied the facts and figures on a large-scope Hitchcock picture like, say, *The Man Who Knew Too Much*, he would find that Hitchcock would do it in a much shorter time than most directors. He was so meticulously prepared."

Leigh vividly recalled shooting the scenes in which Marion— about to flee to her lover, her bags packed—drives nervously through downtown Phoenix. In the script, writer Joseph Stefano suggests action and moods:

> We are close on Mary's car, shooting in at her troubled, guilty face. She seems to be driving with that excess of care of one who does not wish to be stopped for a minor traffic irregularity. She stops for a red light at a main intersection. From Mary's viewpoint, we see Lowery and Cassidy crossing the street, passing right in front of Mary's car. Mary freezes.

Leigh explained: "It was a silent shot, obviously, but as I'm driving and having these thoughts, Hitch completely articulated for me what I was thinking. 'Oh-oh,' he'd say, 'there's your boss. He's watching you with a funny look.'" Similarly, Hitchcock articulated for Leigh the off-screen voices of Marion's boss, her co-worker Caroline, and Cassidy, the Texas oilman, each of whom reacts to her disappearance in conversations the character fantasizes as she flees with the stolen money.

Marshall Schlom recalled the director's working "exceptionally closely" with Janet Leigh. "Before every shot, he went to her very quietly and really gave her direction. He also really liked her, so he loved putting her on. He'd whisper something to her out of earshot, she'd giggle and blush, then he'd go back to his chair with the face of an imp. It was a wonderful relationship." Writer Stefano: "As I watched her, I knew she was giving an incredible performance. Hitchcock helped her, but it had to come from inside her."

In the completed scene to which Leigh referred lies part of the justification for the opening shots of the film. As the camera pans a city skyline, the documentary-like titles appear: PHOENIX, ARIZONA . . . FRIDAY, DECEMBER THE ELEVENTH . . . TWO FORTY-THREE P.M. Hitchcock frequently established a precise time and place in the opening shots of his films, but *Psycho* was different. "Hitchcock was mad as hell because he had sent out a second-unit crew to shoot process plates of the city streets," set designer Robert Clatworthy said. "When he saw what they'd shot, he noticed that Christmas decorations were hung over the street. He didn't approve of that at all and said, 'Hmmm. That will take some explaining.' He was always thinking about the audience trying to outsmart him. You can see the decorations in the shots when Janet Leigh's boss walks past her car and peers in the window. There wasn't time to reshoot. So he added the date in the titles at the beginning and hoped some wiseacre wouldn't wonder why there was no other reference to the holidays anywhere else in the picture."

According to many crew members, Hitchcock was extremely class conscious. "Hitchcock was a terrible snob," asserted an actress who was directed by him in two films. "You had to be conversant about fine food, wine, travel. You had to dislike or have low regard for the same people. Sometimes, it was funny. Mostly, it was maddening." Makeup man Jack Barron observed: "He never talked to extras. I remember him asking an assistant to move an entire group of extras because he didn't like the color they were wearing."

As the shooting progressed, Hitchcock consciously helped create of *Psycho* a set divided. As he once admitted to an interviewer, "I felt . . . that the characters in the second part were merely figures." Wardrobe expert Rita Riggs observed: "There were two camps," referring to the schism that Hitchcock tried to maintain between the stars of "Part One" of the film—Janet Leigh and Anthony Perkins—and "Part Two"—Vera Miles and John Gavin. "[Hitchcock] loved that kind of tension. John Huston was the same way. Tony's camp played between takes an extremely erudite game he invented, called 'Essences.' It was a little like 'Twenty Questions.' The person who was 'it' chose a historical or literary character while the others had to guess [the identity] by asking questions like 'If you were a car, would you be a beat-up Pontiac or a Ferrari?' The guessing sometimes went on for days and got so heated that we couldn't wait to finish our work to run back to the game. I think Mr. Hitchcock liked Tony a lot, but he was a very shy, quiet young man. And [many of us] only got to know him because we could see how his mind worked through that wonderful game."

Actress Vera Miles felt the big chill from Hitchcock but acknowledged her role in their estrangement. "I just found it difficult to have someone saying 'Here's what you do,'" she said. "I was stubborn and he wanted someone who could be molded. It wasn't a nasty situation. I would get my barbs and walk away. I didn't do battle. I just said, 'Take it or leave it.' That's how my relationship with Hitchcock ended. There were a few bitter comments from him, but I never retorted in kind. I look back on him very fondly."

The Director Innovates

As much as Hitchcock amused himself with mind games, with feuds, and with the flexing of his directorial muscle, technical challenges were his great delight. For example, in the long day's journey into night that the heroine makes by car, he was determined to avoid cliché. In those days, standard filmmaking procedure for car scenes entailed use of a mock-up "process" body half-car and the rear-projection process. "That's how they do it in the *movies*" was one in the director's arsenal of put-downs. Marshall Schlom explained: "For night-driving scenes, you don't normally use rear projection because, other than the headlights of people behind, it's basically black."

But Hitchcock fixated on finding a means of *visually* conveying that the heroine had lost her way and was turning off the main road. "One day he told the special effects people and the electricians, 'Fellas, this is what we're going to do,'" Marshall related. "With Mr. Hitchcock, it always how '*we're*' going to do, which was wonderful. His idea was ingenious and took no time. He had the crew drape a black velvet backing over the whole rear of the stage behind the mock-up car to make it absolutely black. To [simulate car headlights] behind [Janet Leigh], he had the electricians concoct a three-foot-wide wheel and mounted lights on it. The wheel had a hub in it that could rotate 360 degrees. To convey the illusion that car headlights behind her were going off to camera-right [that is, to the left of Leigh], he had the grips pull the light away from the car body at an angle and control the spin. The lights had little baffles on them, so once they passed camera, they would shut off. Through the car window, it looked as if the car headlights just disappeared to the left or right behind her. As you pulled the wheel away to the rear of the stage, the lights diminished in size until they were thirty or forty feet back from the car."

Delayed by several days of bad weather and concerned about the looming specter of a strike by the Screen Actors Guild, Hitchcock deleted some location shooting as well as elegant camera moves and replaced them with simple, medium shots. During preproduction, Hitchcock asked art director Joseph Hurley to work up moody illustrations of his conception of the Bates swamp scenes. These drawings were used to convey to the crew what the director hoped to find from real-life settings. Suitably desolate locations were found near Travis Air Force Base and at

Grizzly Island, near Fairfield, in northern California, but time and money pressed Hitchcock to substitute "Falls Lake" on the backlot. Similarly, the generic, homespun Main Street on the Universal backlot became the script's "Fairvale" and the studio's main executive office building (which was demolished soon after the shooting) served as a county courthouse. Hitchcock shot these scenes so rapidly that his TV crew detected few differences between the feature film and one of the director's "three-day wonder" TV shows. Screenwriter Joseph Stefano said, "He was working with people who knew him, so there were no displays, no showing off. By this time, Hitchcock didn't have anything to prove to anybody anymore."

Although many of Hitchcock's collaborators were familiar with his work methods, his knowledge of the technical resources of the medium provoked constant wonder. "He really knew lenses," commented set designer Robert Clatworthy, assistant to Robert Boyle on Hitchcock's *Saboteur* (1942) and *Shadow of a Doubt* (1943). "For many years, he carried this little pad with two frames and a pencil. As he'd explain something, say to the cameraman, he'd draw the image of what he wanted from the shot. The cameraman would put a lens on and that's exactly what he'd get."

Despite *Psycho*'s being a "small" picture, Hitchcock exploited a range of techniques that were designed to intensify audience involvement. The director insisted on cameraman John Russell's shooting virtually the entire movie with 50-millimeter lenses. On the 35-millimeter cameras of the day, such lenses gave the closest approximation to human vision technically possible. "He wanted the camera, being the eyes of the audience all the time, to let them [view the action] as if they were seeing it with their own eyes," script supervisor Marshall Schlom explained. Again, Hitchcock reinforced the sensation of voyeurism—of "cruel eyes studying you," as Norman Bates puts it—that permeates the entire film.

No Photographs, Please

As word of the film spread like wildfire through Hollywood, Hitchcock demanded even tighter secrecy from the cast, crew, and publicity flacks. Hitchcock suppressed any synopsis of the plot for public consumption. No other director had done this since Cecil B. DeMille on *The Ten Commandments*. However, as a master of self-promotion, Hitchcock provided "impromptu" photo opportunities at the drop of a clue. Art director Robert Clatworthy recalled: "All through the shooting, Hitchcock kept a director's chair with 'Mrs. Bates' written on the back in prominent view. That was Hitchcock's humor. Mrs. Bates was a real person, by God, so she's got to have a chair." Late one afternoon, Hitchcock plopped into the chair himself—a photo premeditated (and dutifully recorded) as a sop to the studio publicists; later, every key cast member from Martin Balsam to Janet Leigh was also photographed with that chair. Except, of course, for Anthony Perkins.

Paramount grew restive over Hitchcock's insistence on preventing the chief of the studio's still photography department William "Bud" Fraker (who later became the cinematographer of such major films as *Rosemary's Baby* and *Heaven Can Wait*) from shooting any material that might allude too directly to the subject matter or plot surprises. The director tried to fob off the publicity flacks by releasing such innocuous photos as a smiley portrait of Janet Leigh in a striped sweater ("Exactly the kind of attire Mr. Hitchcock did not approve of," costumer Rita Riggs observed). Herb Steinberg, who had joined Paramount in New

York in 1948 and became director of advertising and publicity for the studio, fired off a memo to Hitchcock on December 30. Steinberg wailed about the "static" stills, "which don't give us either the excitement or flavor of what I know you are getting on the screen. I understand your need for secrecy and recognize its value as an exploitation device. I wish, though, that you would allow us to cover everything you shoot, so that we can at least have a record for future use at such time that these secret elements concerning *Psycho* may be released."

Publicist Steinberg proposed a compromise: If Hitchcock would allow the photographer to "shoot as much film as he possibly can," the photographer would hand over his undeveloped film to anyone whom the director might designate until such time that the stills might be released. Hitchcock knew too much about studio photographers and publicists to back down. All of the stills from the picture were designed to be as unrevealing as possible.

For all the apparent precautions about secrecy—Hitchcock had photographs of guards at the door to the soundstages widely distributed to the press—novelist Robert Bloch encountered none of it. "I found myself on the Universal lot on business one day," recalled the writer, several of whose teleplays had been aired on the Hitchcock show by the time *Psycho* was in production. "I walked over to the soundstage where *Psycho* was shooting. In those days they weren't quite so careful about strange and unwanted visitors. I watched Hitchcock direct Tony Perkins walking down along the rows of motel rooms and that was all. I neither introduced myself nor spoke to anyone. Nobody spoke to me."

Screenwriter Joseph Stefano was a regular visitor to the set, at least during the early days of shooting. The Hitchcock ego bloomed whenever he was surrounded by a relative neophyte such as Stefano, eager to learn the moviemaking ropes. But according to some crew members, Hitchcock later regretted his benevolent gesture. Marshall Schlom explained: "In those days, agents and writers were never allowed on sets. I think, out of courtesy, Mr. Hitchcock said [Stefano] could come and watch. Because I held the script in my hand, [Stefano] would watch and listen to his words. He'd whisper to me, 'They changed it.' Well, actors *do* that. Part of my job is knowing when to say something to the director and when not to. But he started to make certain suggestions and criticize a little bit, and I think he was shut up a little bit, too. I *know* he was. Mr. Hitchcock never missed a trick around the set. Those little things got to him. He knew when someone was imposing. He felt that Joe, at times, was imposing and he just didn't allow it to happen."

Veteran vaudevillian, radio and film actress Lurene Tuttle, who played the role of the sheriff's wife ("a small, lively stick of a woman," said the script), had previously starred for Hitchcock in a forties radio adaptation of his great silent, *The Lodger* (1926) (a performance for which Hitchcock complimented the actress with a pat on the derriere). On *Psycho*, Tuttle was disconcerted when the roles played by her and John McIntire were truncated in the editing. She was also concerned that Hitchcock's directorial manner seemed to have changed so much. The actress fretted as Hitchcock watched with apparent boredom her brief rehearsal with McIntire, Vera Miles, and John Gavin: "He trusted actors and didn't give a lot of direction, except to tell me to be sure to stand on my mark. He staged scenes like blueprints. He told me, 'If you move one *inch* either way, you'll be out of my light,' then slumped over in his chair like he'd dozed off. It worried me so that I went to the assistant director and asked, 'Is he sleeping through our scene?' He reassured me, 'That's a good sign. He's designed the scene and your movements so carefully, he knows how it's going to look. He's just enjoying the *sound* of it.'"

Tuttle sufficiently accommodated herself to the unorthodox Hitchcock style to relax. "Working for Hitchcock was like going back to the womb," she said. "I think the four of us felt we were in some kind of safe cocoon." While Hitchcock was clearly fond of the veteran actress, he hardly spared the venom if crossed. "I wasn't hitting my marks right," said Tuttle, recalling a brief scene shot on the "Circle Drive" on the backlot, representing the script's Fairvale Presbyterian church. "He could be witheringly sarcastic. He was neither a sycophant nor a fool. He was very serious the day we shot the scene outside the church. He showed me what he wanted, even *how* I should walk and how fast, but I said, 'Mr. Hitchcock, I do not make big male steps—I make ladies' steps!' He was very angry. I realized, though, if he told me I was standing in the wrong place, it was according to the design he had formulated for the action and his cameras. And you *had* to do it till you got it right."

Hitchcock Amuses Himself

When Hitchcock wasn't snoozing, sequestered in his bungalow with the *London Times*, or holding court with his company, he entertained himself in various trivial pursuits. One of his favorites was deciding exactly where and how he would make his famous cameo appearance in a picture. Although he enjoyed keeping his appearance a secret even from the crew, he occasionally dropped hints. "He wouldn't tell us until the last possible moment," wardrobe mistress Rita Riggs stated. "But he wanted to be in that scene with his daughter. It was his bit of sentimental whimsy." (Others point out that the scene was the first available opportunity for Hitchcock to make his appearance without distracting the audience.)

Hitchcock cast himself as a man standing curbside in a Stetson whom the heroine passes as she hurries back into the real estate office. Of their work together, Patricia Hitchcock has commented, "I've always been in such awe of him, he's such a fine director. It doesn't occur to us on the set that we're father and daughter. Not that he's severe, but always patient and calm. He knows what he wants." Hitchcock *père et fille* brought off the scene smoothly.

During shooting, Hitchcock insisted that his trailer be rigged with an intercontinental telephone hookup. "I wonder what the weather's like in London?" he would ponder aloud between shots, only to waddle into his trailer to find out. "He had really nothing else in this world except food, wine, and fooling around with movies," explained Marshall Schlom. "For tax purposes, he had this ranch up in Los Gatos and grew champagne grapes and lost money. He only drank Montrachet brought in for him from France, which, in the days of two- and three-dollar wines, cost fifteen. We shot *Psycho* just around Christmas and he called Maxim's in Paris saying, 'I want the foie gras.' He had a deal with TWA, which he called 'Teenie-Weenie Airlines.' Maxim's delivered the food to the TWA pilot in Paris who hand-carried it to the Los Angeles Airport to [Hitchcock's] driver, who brought it to the studio. It never went through customs."

At Christmas, Hitchcock bestowed gifts upon only two of his *Psycho* collaborators. Assistant director Hilton Green received one of the first Polaroid cameras. And script supervisor Schlom learned why Hitchcock was so intent upon knowing whether Mrs. Schlom knew the recipe for "lemon curd." Two days before Christmas, Schlom tore off the wrapping from an expensive, out-of-print book that Hitchcock had had shipped especially from New York. But when the intended gift, *The Encyclopedia of Gastronomy*, turned out to be *The Encyclopedia of Astronomy*,

Hitchcock's office went into a quiet uproar. "He personally called New York," Schlom recalled, "and had one of his people locate and hand-carry the correct book overnight. He wanted me to have *that* book on *that* day. That's the kind of person he was."

Inventions and gadgets were another Hitchcock pastime during the shooting of *Psycho*. Marshall Schlom said, "One day he wanted to figure if there was a way of making an electric whisk. We photographed his hand with a mechanical whisk, whisking eggs at a very high rate of speed so that it was projected at very slow motion. He had the special effects man take a Mixmaster and do the same thing, but set the blades on its side trying to make it revolve." Hitchcock seemed to have no intention of doing anything with such inventions. For him, the pleasure was in the working out of the technical details.

On another occasion, Hitchcock mused, "Wouldn't it be wonderful to shoot characters at the Eiffel Tower without ever having to go there?" The director dispatched Schlom on an expensive technical fact-finding mission on state-of-the-art special effects. Nothing that anyone turned up satisfied the director.

Neither, apparently, did the handsome and elaborate St. Charles kitchen that Universal built in the Hitchcock home during the shooting of *Psycho*. When the director found that the kitchen was ³/₈ inch smaller than his specifications, he had it torn out and completely redone—at the studio's expense. Script supervisor Schlom suggested that frustration by the director rather than capriciousness may have been at the heart of the matter. "His wife was a wonderful cook and he had just put in this beautiful kitchen, but he was so heavy, he couldn't get insurance," Schlom explained. "So he was on a diet limited to four ounces of meat a day, with an occasional glass of Dubonnet. He was stricken."

"He could be very funny and self-deprecating," Stefano recalled. "Even though he was still quite heavy, he'd lost a lot of weight. 'My stomach hangs down like an old apron,' he said. Then he told me this wicked story about going to an incredibly lavish dinner at the house of a young director who had tried to impress him. He said, 'The waiter came 'round to refill our wineglasses and he had a napkin around a bottle that wasn't even chilled! What pretension!' He just kept putting these people down unmercifully and I laughed because he was actually *telling* me about it."

Other Hitchcock associates saw the oddities of the director in a benevolent light. "He told me he never had a driving license because he was afraid of getting stopped by the police," recalled Marshall Schlom. "His wife drove. But every year, Ford, one of the sponsors of his show, gave him a new Thunderbird. He'd just give it to his daughter, Pat." On-the-set wardrobe mistress Rita Riggs also saw Hitchcock's foibles in a benevolent light. "He and Alma asked me to dinner at their home one night, which I considered a great privilege," Riggs said, recalling the evening with a grin. "One of my funniest moments in being with Mr. Hitchcock was watching him get into my little Volkswagen bug, filling it up with that wonderful profile that had become so well known. While we drove the freeway to his Bel-Air house, the double-, triple-, and quadruple-takes from other drivers were hilarious."

Riggs saw right through Hitchcock's formality on the set and the intimidating, world-class artworks that hung on the walls of his home. She recalled the "wonderful intimacy" of dining with the director and his wife in their newly remodeled kitchen. "I always thought of him as the prince locked in the frog," Riggs said. "He truly loved beauty so much and set out to create it. I think his perversities and his frustration with his exterior were part of his wonderful creativity. Everyone talks about his pranksterism and practical jokes, but he had a sense of fun about him that I don't think some people picked up on. For instance, one night, I came home to find a carton of wild, French strawberries on my doorstep because we had been talking about them recently. Is that perversity or is that doing something out of sheer enjoyment?"

An apparently unusual aspect to Hitchcock's work method was his entrusting the viewing of dailies to editor George Tomasini and script supervisor Marshall Schlom. "He never went to look at this film," Schlom asserted. "After dailies, George and I had to come back and tell him what we thought was right or wrong. He knew what he had." Tomasini, having worked on *The Wrong Man*, *Vertigo*, and *North by Northwest*, was one of the handful of collaborators in whose taste and instincts Hitchcock placed implicit confidence. That track record notwithstanding, Tomasini was only paid $11,000 to edit *Psycho*.

Schlom recalled the extraordinary pains Hitchcock took to shoot a close-up of Vera Miles reacting to a plain-bound book in Bates's bedroom. As described in the screenplay, the moment is pure gas-lit melodrama. "Lila['s] . . . eyes go wide in shock. And then there is disgust. She slams the book closed, drops it." Schlom observed: "Mr. Hitchcock wanted to *suggest* it was a pornographic book with a slight raise of the eyebrow. It was so important to him, we shot maybe sixteen takes of Vera, which was unusual for him." Hitchcock did little that surprised Miles. "If he told me to jump over the moon," she has said, "I have such confidence in his judgment, I probably would try it." The moment was also remarkable because it was the only time Hitchcock and cameraman John Russell used anything other than the 50-millimeter lens for the movie. "It was a hundred-millimeter lens," said Schlom. "He used to say he saved close-ups for a big emphasis—when he really wanted the audience to *know* something. When George Tomasini and I showed him the edit, he

said, 'Fellas, you've got the wrong take.' We went back to the
Movieola, looked through every take, then put in another one.
'No,' he said, 'still the wrong one.' This went on for three or four
showings—'Wrong again,' he said. Don't you think we had to
print all sixteen takes on one reel and see them on a big screen?
He knew which take was best. He saw what we didn't."

Saul Bass and Screaming in the Shower

In addition to close collaborators Green and Schlom, Hitchcock
valued the innovative eye of graphic designer Saul Bass. "I just
hung around with my papers under my arms," remembered Bass,
whom Hitchcock paid $10,000 for thirteen half-days for thir-
teen consecutive weeks and the screen credit "Pictorial Consultant." Bass said, "When I did some work, I brought it in, showed
it to him, we'd talk and I'd keep walking around and looking.
For me, [*Psycho*] was a little bit like being the tuba player in the
orchestra who only knows *his* part. It's only when he's off for the
day and comes back that he finds out that the piece the orchestra
is playing is *Carmen*."

After his conferences with the director, Bass struck notes that
resonated with Hitchcock. One of the early Bass concepts centered around the final scene that showed Norman Bates in a
detention cell, his persona completely subsumed by Mother's. As
Joseph Stefano described it in the script:

> The walls are white and plain. There is no window. There
> is no furniture except the straight-back chair . . . the room
> has a quality of no-whereness, of calm separation from the
> world.

Said Bass, "I devised a small idea for that, which I call the *Whistler's Mother* thing. In [the painting by James Abbott McNeill Whistler], the mother sits in a rocker and there's a framed painting on the wall. So I set up the thing based on that where Tony Perkins is wrapped in his blanket and there's a wall vent in the ceiling where the frame is in *Whistler's Mother.*" In the shooting, Hitchcock was to eliminate any visual reference to the famed painting.

Two of the most complicated sequences in the film—the shower murder and the killing of Arbogast—involved not only the efforts of Bass, but also of the entire company. Although Hitchcock had in Joseph Hurley one of the finest illustrators in the industry, the director paid Bass $2,000 to render storyboards for the shower scene. "That was a good idea," observed Hurley's collaborator, designer Robert Clatworthy. "Joe could have story-boarded the whole thing, but Saul wouldn't fall into the cliché as we might readily do." The traps were implicit in the sequence: potentially censorable violence, and nudity. Hitchcock told Leonard South, "I'm going to shoot and cut it staccato, so the audience won't know what the hell is going on." Bass responded to Hitchcock's requirements with a montage approach, a barrage of oblique angles, medium shots, and close-ups. Although the scene would contain very little movement and images that, in themselves, might seem banal or benign, the bits of film cut together were meant to create an impression of savage, almost visceral violence. "I had this sort of contention in my head," explained Bass, "a sort of purist notion of making a horrible murder with no blood. It struck me as a nice thing to do."

To accommodate Hitchcock and his crew for rehearsals of the sequence, designers Robert Clatworthy and Joseph Hurley built a mock-up shower. The director auditioned the temporary set during the second week of shooting. "We tested the shower scene by putting up a bathtub and two flat walls on the Phantom Stage," Clatworthy explained. "Joe and I walked onto this big, dark stage during a test and as we got closer, we saw the wardrobe girl wiping off Hitch's blue serge suit with a big towel. Janet was in a bathing suit. Maybe it was because we'd built the thing so quickly, but the paint wasn't completely dry and the shower spray sent it splashing all over the place. Plus, the damn tub didn't drain either. Hitch spotted us. 'Fellows,' he said, 'this is *quite* inadequate. I believe this falls under the heading of the "raised eyebrow" department.'"

For the actual shooting of the sequence, Clatworthy and Hurley built a separate, four-walled unit. Each of the walls was detachable to allow Hitchcock to place his cameras without restriction. In addition, the breakaway construction permitted the director to shoot the shower and tub unit either separately or attached to the larger, full set of the bathroom on Stage 18-A. This set was approximately six feet from the outer tub wall to wall. According to Clatworthy, Hitchcock insisted on "blinding white tiles" and shiny fixtures, a predilection that harked back to earlier scenes in *Murder* (1930) and *Spellbound* (1945).

Previous Hitchcock scenes set in bathrooms had depicted them as places of revelation or of menace. *Psycho* would depart from those. It would break new ground in the suggestion of nudity and in the depiction of outright horror. According to Janet Leigh, Hitchcock had begun preparing her for the sequence in mid-November. "Mr. Hitchcock showed Saul Bass's storyboards to me quite proudly," Leigh said, "telling me in exact detail how he was going to shoot the scene from Saul's plans. The storyboards detailed all the angles, so that I knew the camera would be *there*, then *there*. The camera was at different places all the time." Writer Joseph Stefano recalled an encounter with Hitchcock after a meeting with his leading lady. Stefano noted: "Hitchcock said,

'I'm going to have a problem with Janet. She's very self-conscious about her breasts. She thinks they're too big.' He was aware it was not going to be easy to deal with this woman who was uneasy even standing around on the set in her brassiere. He said, 'We'll try to get it over as fast as possible for her sake.' He wanted no problems or embarrassment for Janet."

Makeup expert Jack Barron noted: "When I first went to Mr. Hitchcock's office to talk about the film, he told me he was going to try and convince Janet to do the sequence in the nude. When it came down to it, she wasn't having any part of it. As time went on, he said he'd try 'for the European version,' but she refused. I asked if I needed to prepare anything, but he said, 'No. We'll cover up as much as we can and we'll never show any actual stabbing. Just bring *plenty* of chocolate syrup for the blood.'" Janet Leigh wonders whether Hitchcock may not have merely been baiting his male collaborators on the aspect of "nudity": "Of course, Mr. Hitchcock *never* asked me to do the scene in the nude because showing nudity on the screen was simply out of the question. Doing the scene actually in the nude would have negated how clever and subtle he was at *suggesting* things."

Supervisor Helen Colvig and on-set costumer Rita Riggs were initially stumped by the dilemmas of simultaneously suggesting nudity, remaining within censorship bounds, and protecting the modesty of a star. "It was hysterical," said Leigh, who pored with Riggs over costumes for strippers in magazines. "They all had feathers, spangles, pinwheels, and birds of paradise. She [Riggs] came up with a brilliant idea, which was to use moleskin, which I had over both breasts and over the vital part—and that's *it*."

"The giggles Janet and I had out of sheer shyness!" recalled Riggs. "It was certainly my first experience with 'nudity' for a movie. I was very aware of not only Janet's but Mr. Hitchcock's shyness, so I approached the job by thinking, 'How would *I* feel?'

The storyboarding, particularly for that sequence, was so innovative, I only had to look at the boards to realize what we *had* to see. And it was clear that we never needed to show the entire body, but, say, a nude back, the tummy area, or breasts almost down to where the nipples begin. I came to think of it as sculpture. If we had to see a part of a breast, say, under the crook of an elbow, I would sculpt moleskin, then glue, cover, and trim away until just the amount of the body that was needed was visible. It was very time-consuming, yes, but most important, it was not to seem invasive to Janet."

As a precautionary measure, Hitchcock hired—at $500, total—Marli Renfro, a red-headed, twenty-three-year-old Manhattan and Las Vegas dancer-model whose proportions (5 feet 4 inches, 36-23-35) approximated Janet Leigh's. "Some directors would announce 'You will do nudity,'" script supervisor Marshall Schlom observed. "But he wasn't about to make Janet uncomfortable or touch anything distasteful on the screen. For him, the shower scene was designed to shock, not titillate." Hitchcock explained to writer Stefano; "'I want someone whose job it is to be naked on a set, so I don't have to worry about covering her.' It was a very smart move on his part." Hitchcock further fanned the curiosity of the press about the scene by reporting that the presence of Miss Renfro was solely "for a rear-view scene of Miss Leigh."

Despite Saul Bass's purist intentions to have a "bloodless murder," the storyboards that he devised for the sequence depict such close-ups as the bloodstained hands of the victim reaching for her punctured neck. After Hitchcock approved the drawings, Bass shot test footage on December 10. "I rented an IMO [an old-style newsreel camera] which had a twenty-five-foot magazine in it," Bass said. "First of all, I wanted to see whether it would work having to cut above the nipple. With the spring loaded, it would run just twenty-five feet before it ran down. I used the stand-in for Janet to shoot it. At the end of the day, I had her stay a little later. We just set up a key light and knocked off twenty-five feet of the stuff and chopped it together to see whether the thing would work. I showed it to Hitch and he thought it looked okay."

Bass explained that the tests for the sequence merely confirmed that his concepts were viable. "The basic point of view of the sequence was based upon a series of repetitive images in which there was a lot of motion but little activity," noted the graphic designer. "After all, all that happens was simply a woman takes a shower, gets hit, and slowly slides down the tub. Instead, [we film] a repetitive series of motions: 'She's taking a shower, taking a shower, taking a shower. She's hit-hit-hit-hit-hit. She slides-slides-slides. She's hit-hit-hit-hit. She slides-slides-slides.' In other words, the movement was very narrow and the amount of activity to get you there was very intense. That was what I brought to Hitchcock. I don't think that shower sequence was a typical Hitchcock sequence, in the normal sense of the word, because he had never used that kind of quick cutting. By modern standards, we don't think that represents staccato cutting because we've gotten so accustomed to flashcuts. But to have, in those days—I don't know what it was, two minutes, three minutes, whatever the sequence ran?—forty or sixty cuts, whatever it might be—was just a very new idea stylistically. As a title person, it was a very natural thing to use that quick-cutting, montage technique to deliver what amounted to an impressionistic, rather than a linear, view of the murder."

According to Hitchcock's breakdown of the Bass storyboards, seventy-eight camera setups would be needed. Many of the shots required the construction of a special scaffold built at the studio mill. An article published in *Variety* at the time scooped several crucial technical aspects of the scene. "Mr. Hitchcock will rehearse with film," journalist James W. Merrick wrote, "staging the scene and photographing it simultaneously from several angles with hand-held IMOs. The results obtained from these light cameras will be assembled, edited, then used as the basis for Mr. Hitchcock's sketches from which he will later photograph the grisly scene with a regular camera."

When the *Variety* reporter asked Hitchcock whether he feared that the sensational aspects of the scene might bring down censorship, the director snapped, "Men *do* kill nude women, you know." The retort recalls the logic of a line of dialogue from the film. When Norman defends Marion by saying, "Mother, she's just a stranger! She's hungry and it's raining out," Mrs. Bates volleys back: "As if men don't desire strangers."

Hitchcock believed he had locked in every predictable element of the sequence before beginning photography on December 18 and continuing from the twenty-first through the twenty-third. Crowds flocked outside Stage 18-A as if it were the studio commissary or the pay window. "I never knew there were so many people at the studio," quipped makeup artist Barron. Hitchcock curbed the rubberneckers—and scored a publicity coup—by installing guards at the doors of the soundstage who were then photographed for publicity-hungry newspapers. "The press and photographers were dying to come on," said Rita Riggs, chuckling. "Mr. Hitchcock fed them precisely what he wanted them to know and they actually felt privileged."

The director baffled his associates, the studio publicity heads, and the chief of the studio still department, Bud Fraker, by permitting the *New York Times*'s Eugene Cook to snoop around the set for a photo essay story. Hitchcock leaked to Cook the news that the character played by Janet Leigh would be murdered in the shower. "I may use a hand-held camera," Hitchcock mused for the press. "I haven't decided yet." The comment is interesting in light of the test footage shot with a newsreel camera by Saul Bass. Yet most *Psycho* crew members consider it as no more than Hitchcock's working the press like a virtuoso. "I can't imagine him thinking about or even liking a hand-held camera," screenwriter Joseph Stefano observed.

From a technical standpoint, the actual shooting of the shower sequence was recalled by assistant director Hilton Green as "nothing extraordinary." He observed: "It was not that difficult because it was laid out. We knew shot for shot and setup for setup where the camera would go ahead of time. It only took time because of the many different angles we had to get. It became the most famous sequence in the picture, but it was not that difficult."

As is often the case with classic movie scenes, the precise details of the shooting of the shower sequence have been obscured by time, selective memory, ego, the haze of legend, and controversy. According to various versions, Anthony Perkins *was* or *was not* involved in the filming. Other stories insist that Janet Leigh *did* or *did not* shoot the sequence in the nude. The shower sequence has been credited to many—from a special film crew imported either from Japan or Germany, to graphic designer Saul Bass entirely. Indeed, during the mid-seventies and continuing today, Bass has startled many by asserting his own *auteurship* of the sequence.

That Hitchcock was parsimonious at doling out credit to others is well established. In his published conversations with François Truffaut, Hitchcock observed of the contributions of Bass, "He did only one scene, but I didn't use his montage. He was supposed to do the titles, but since he was interested in the picture, I let him lay out the sequence of the detective going up the stairs, just before he is stabbed." Hitchcock went on to detail how he was forced to reshoot the Bass scenes. Never in public did Hitchcock acknowledge the involvement of Saul Bass in the shower scene.

Bass, in London to promote his debut feature film, *Phase Four*, in 1973, startled many with revelations about *Psycho* that appeared in the *London Sunday Times*. A reporter for that paper wrote: "He [Bass] was invited by Alfred Hitchcock to design the notorious shower-bath in *Psycho* and wound up directing that too." Reproductions of the Bass storyboards illustrated the piece and the graphic designer was quoted as saying of Hitchcock, "The man's a genius. But why should a genius get away with being so greedy?" According to the *Sunday Times*, Bass went on to say, "When the film came out everyone went wild about the shower-bath murder which I'd done, almost literally shot by shot, from my storyboard. And then Hitchcock had second thoughts."

Over the years, the statements of authorship by Bass, amplified and elaborated for other publications, have been accepted without question by some. In *Halliwell's Film and Video Guide*, an encyclopedic volume of film titles with critical comment, author Leslie Halliwell describes *Psycho* as a "Curious shocker devised by Hitchcock as a tease and received by most critics as an unpleasant horror piece in which the main scene, the shower stabbing, was allegedly directed not by Hitchcock but by Saul Bass." Halliwell, hardly a Hitchcock enthusiast, further cites the directorial credit for *Psycho* as "Alfred Hitchcock (and Saul Bass)."

A *Variety* piece dated June 3, 1981, quotes Bass as having detailed the circumstances of how he came to direct the shower sequence. "I showed it [the test footage shot with the IMO news-reel camera] to Hitch and he very graciously said, you do it. He was on the set. It was really a very generous gesture. It was a thrill for me." Today, Bass, who is internationally known for corporate logos and documentary films, calls the quotes from the *London Sunday Times*, and others of a derogatory nature toward Hitchcock, "totally inaccurate." He details the circumstances of the shooting of the scene by saying, "It came time to shoot it and he benignly waved me on. And that was how it came about."

From a vantage point of thirty years later, Bass observed: "I've directed a feature. It is hell. So complex, wearing, time-consuming. If anybody can help you, you want it. If somebody can relieve you of something, you're grateful. That was the spirit in which [Hitchcock] asked me to *lift* certain things, to concentrate on things he couldn't pay attention to while he was doing everything else."

From the standpoint of many crew members, any confusion as to who directed the scene is groundless. "I was on that set every second," asserted script supervisor Marshall Schlom. "*Nobody* directs Mr. Hitchcock's pictures but Mr. Hitchcock. The set was four 'wild' walls and so tiny, basically no more than the six-foot tub, he could barely get a camera in there. It was a closed set, with a guard at the locked door. There were no visitors. The woman who was Janet Leigh's body, the 'sunbather' or 'nudist,' as Mr. Hitchcock called her, paraded around—which was all new to us. We actually photographed bits and pieces. I don't ever recall seeing a storyboard as we know them today." Wardrobe supervisor Rita Riggs vividly recalled the shooting and the storyboards. As with other crew members, she verified that the shooting was postponed twice: once when Janet Leigh had a headcold and another when the star had her period. "I was involved daily because it was such a critical sequence," Riggs said. "It was shot on a tiny set, with screens all around it. Everyone was extremely protective and tried to treat Janet with as much consideration as possible. The storyboards for that sequence were unbelievable, but Mr. Hitchcock absolutely shot it himself. We shot frame by frame from the storyboards because each of us had to look at them to know exactly what the camera would see. Janet, who was a terrific sport and a wonderful professional throughout, was never nude. After she and I had to get the mole-skin contraption glued on and trimmed, then she'd get into the shower only to have the water wash off the moleskin. As a film-maker, Mr. Hitchcock got impatient several times and would say, 'Oh, *come* now, we've all seen more than that at the beach.' But Janet Leigh was right. As a major star and a beautiful woman with children, why should she expose her whole body? This is a devastating business. People talk."

The wardrobe supervisor admitted that technical bugaboos in shooting the shower scene vexed the usually unflappable director. "Mr. Hitchcock sometimes walked away because he became so exasperated by three hours of running water, nudity, and wipe-offs [of the moleskin covering]. He may have turned over a brief shot or two to an assistant. I remember him sitting there twid-dling his thumbs clockwise or, when particularly exasperated, counterclockwise. I also remember him not trying to generate any giggles to break the tension. Instead, he did a lot of pontifi-cating, which was something he did often to cover his shyness."

Janet Leigh recalls the shooting as if it had been yesterday. "Hitch was very clear about what he wanted from me in the shower scene. He said he wanted me to be sure to show that I was not just getting the dirt off, not an I'm-gonna-wash-that-man-right-out-of-my-hair kind of thing, but cleansing the evil Marion had done and being ready to pay her dues. The shower was a baptism, a taking away of the torment from her mind. Marion became a virgin again. He wanted the audience to feel her peace-fulness, her kind of rebirth, so that the moment of intrusion is even more shocking and tragic."

As Leigh detailed the shooting of the scene, she emphasized,

"Saul Bass was there for the shooting, but he never directed me. Absolutely not. Saul Bass is brilliant, but he couldn't have done the drawings had Mr. Hitchcock not discussed with him what he wanted to get. And you couldn't have filmed the drawings. Why does there always have to be a controversy? When something turns out as well as this [scene] did and has brought attention to all the people involved, you would think that would be a happy memory."

Since the shower murder sequence did not require the services of Anthony Perkins, Hitchcock released him to attend rehearsals in New York for *Greenwillow*, a Frank Loesser–written Broadway musical for which the actor was preparing for a March 8, 1960 opening night. Screenwriter Joseph Stefano roared with laughter as he recalled Hitchcock's discreetly confiding to him that Perkins, whom he thought 'excessively shy around women,' should be spared any unnecessary embarrassment or discomfort. "It just wouldn't be very nice," the director told his screenwriter. Thirty years later, Perkins, on learning of the qualms of his director, observed: "That was sweet of him. Typical of his generosity. Whether imaginary or based on fantasy, still it was awful nice of him to have the idea. I said, 'Look, I've got to take some of these rehearsals,' and, through special graciousness on Hitchcock's part, he said, 'Go ahead, we don't need you for this.' You have only to see the film to see that the silhouette coming in that door has as little resemblance to me as any silhouette could."

Perkins has heard and read the claim of Saul Bass. "To *set up* shot by shot and to *shoot it* are two different worlds apart. He [Bass] may have drawn it shot by shot, but he wasn't on the set. Now, I wasn't *either*, but that's what Hilton [Green] tells me. Now, the [rumors about it having been shot by a] foreign crew? That's crazy. There were no foreign crews in those days coming into Hollywood. Put that one in the circular file. It's a really a good line—*shred* it."

Assistant director Hilton Green characterizes any question of authorship of the scene "ridiculous." "I read [the Bass claim] somewhere," asserted Green. "That really upsets me. That's absolutely ridiculous. Mr. Hitchcock was there every second of the time, I won't even say 'minute.' I will face Saul Bass in person and say I don't know where he came up with that notion that he was there and directed it. Saul Bass might have visited the set once or twice. He did the titles. I share billing with Saul Bass in the credits. But Mr. Hitchcock directed the picture—and that's *including* the shower scene."

"I *know* he shot it," screenwriter Stefano recalled. "Because one of my favorite memories of the whole experience was of Alfred Hitchcock standing there talking seriously about camera angles with a naked model." On-set wardrobe supervisor Rita Riggs elaborated about stand-in Marli Renfro and her director: "Because of makeup, of course, the model could not wear even a robe. But she became so comfortable, I recall her sitting quite nude except for this crazy little patch we always put over the pubic hair, talking with Mr. Hitchcock. I watched Mr. Hitchcock, the model, and the crew one morning standing around having coffee and doughnuts and thought: 'This is surreal.'" When the director placed Renfro in position for her setups, he coolly toted the tape measure from camera to the double's shoulder, while John Russell noted the distance. "I found it no different," quipped Hitchcock, "than if she had been wearing a floor-length Hawaiian muumuu."

For novelist Robert Bloch, the Hitchcock-Bass controversy smacks of the question as to whether it was his original novel or the screenplay by Joseph Stefano that "made" the movie. Bloch, now a veteran of thirty years of dealing with the collaborative art of moviemaking, observed: "Out here, everybody is willing to take bows for success and run like hell from failure. I've heard all the stories about people other than Hitchcock being involved, but there's no corroboration that would lead me to accept it."

Hitchcock rarely described to his interviewers the shooting of the scene except in the glossiest of terms. "It took us seven days to shoot that scene, and there were seventy camera setups for forty-five seconds of footage," the director told François Truffaut. "I used a . . . a naked model who stood in for Janet Leigh. We only showed Miss Leigh's hands, shoulders, and head. All the rest was the stand-in. Naturally, the knife never touched the body; it was all done in the montage. I shot some of it in slow motion so as to cover the breasts. The slow shots were not accelerated later on because they were inserted in the montage so as to give an impression of normal speed."

To writers Ian Cameron and V. F. Perkins, Hitchcock said, "I did photograph a nude girl all the way through. In other words I covered in the shooting every aspect of the killing. Actually some of it was shot in slow motion. I had the camera slow and the girl moving slowly so that I could measure out the movements and the covering of the awkward parts of the body, the arm movement, gesture and so forth." Makeup man Jack Barron shrugs off any question as to the authority or ownership of a Hitchcock set piece: "Hitchcock had such a casual way with directing, it was like he wasn't doing anything. Maybe he'd sit there slumped over, but those eyes never missed *anything*. To me, he wasn't a director's director. I'm not an actor and I don't know how much he'd impart to them, but they'd shoot, he'd say, 'Fine,' and that was that."

As to the controversy about who directed the shower scene, Saul Bass observed: "The interesting question is, So why did I get the credit 'Special Visual Consultant'? Not for the titles. It has to be something more. A great artist makes a film and has a young man come in and do a few things [on it]. And wouldn't you know it, when the film gets reviewed, it's those damn sequences that this kid worked on. It's a little upsetting. But the truth of the matter is, it *was* and *is* Hitch's film. It's all his, no matter what I did."

To simulate the blood Hitchcock required for the shower scene, Jack Barron and Robert Dawn brought their exacting nothing-less-than-state-of-the-art materials. Barron chuckled as he recollected: "Shasta had just come out with chocolate syrup in a plastic squeeze bottle. This was before the days of the 'plastic explosion,' so it was pretty revolutionary. Up to that time in films, we were using Hershey's, but you could do a lot more with a squeeze bottle."

Hitchcock also told several interviewers that he had his makeup and special effects men devise a blood-spurting rubber torso prop that went unused. It makes a good anecdote, but— since Hitchcock preferred understatement and often boasted about never intending to show the blade of the knife puncturing flesh—only an anecdote. Certainly no surviving member of the crew recalled such a prop. "It wasn't his way of doing things," asserts Jack Barron. "He tended to show things after the fact, blood going down the drain and such, not the precise spot where the blood spurted from the body." But when the film was released, sharp-eyed audience-members swore that they saw the knife blade pierce a naked midsection just south of the navel. The frame-by-frame blowup book on *Psycho* by Richard Anobile published in 1974 validated their claim.

Advocates of the contention that someone other than Hitch-cock actually directed the shower scene point to this alleged discrepancy as one of several that point the finger toward Bass or, at least, away from Hitchcock. Janet Leigh, who admitted that hers is definitely the midsection in question, revealed: "No one but Hitchcock directed me in the shower scene. Hitch used a retractable knife. In fact, he held the knife himself because he knew exactly where he wanted that to be for his camera. But his editing brilliance made you sure you saw something else, right?"

Stuntwoman Margo Epper portrayed Mother in the sequence. An amused Anthony Perkins recalled: "The crew always referred to Mother and Norman as *totally* separate people. Mother always has her own 'backstage' persona, as it were. It's not just [acknowledged] that Norman is Mother. It's just not how people want to see it—neither audiences, nor the people who work on the crew." Margo Epper, a veteran at "doubling" stars in dozens of films such as *Camelot* and *Paint Your Wagon*, comes from a three-generation family dynasty of movie stuntpersons. Yet to this day, she displays a certain reluctance and uneasiness in discussing her "strange" experience with Hitchcock. "Hitchcock was an odd person to work for," observed Epper, who was twenty-four when she shot her scenes for *Psycho* in a single day. "We were working on a kind of raised platform. I can remember him standing just below us looking up and saying exactly what to do and how to do it. I was just shown walking with the knife like I was going to stab her. There wasn't really anybody in the shower at the time but he wanted it to be really real, so he'd have you doing the smallest things over and over."

Although Hitchcock would use other doubles to represent Mother in the film, Epper claimed, "When you see her with the knife, that's me." Commented Rita Riggs, who "dressed" Epper for the role, "Margo, because of her horsemanship, is long and lean and had almost a male set of hips. Of all the people possible, she came closest to having Tony's square shoulders and thin hips."

Despite Hitchcock's extensive shooting of Marli Renfro

for certain insert shots, Janet Leigh pointed to the irony that Hitchcock only used shots of the actress herself in the final cut. "That was all me except for when Norman wraps the body in the shower curtain," said Leigh. "Even though you didn't see a close-up of nudity [in that scene], you knew whoever did that had to be nude. I said, 'I'd rather not be nude' and Hitch said, 'There's no reason because you can't tell who it is anyway.'" Makeup man Barron recalled his own and Robert Dawn's disappointment at being replaced by "body makeup women" for the body double scenes Hitchcock shot on December 23.

It is not surprising that Hitchcock would have specific notions as to how the *Psycho* bathroom set should be dressed and photographed. Having once boasted to a baffled interviewer, "Visit a bathroom after I have been there, you would never know I had been there," Hitchcock insisted upon dazzling white porcelain tiles, gleaming fixtures, and an opaque shower curtain. In *Spellbound* (1945), Hitchcock and cinematographer George Barnes had conjured up an eerily disorienting brightness for the bathroom scene in which Gregory Peck hoists a straight razor and heads toward the sleeping Ingrid Bergman. Obtaining a similar effect in *Psycho* created additional headaches for the director and his crew. The high-key lighting created by cinematographer John Russell and the lighting men generated so much reflection that the face of stuntwoman Epper, having been painstakingly backlit to mask her identity, was clearly visible. The problem forced Hitchcock to reshoot Mother's "entry" and stabbing motions. The second time around, makeup man Jack Barron blackened Epper's face. Similarly, another trick of lighting was required to film the compulsive cleaning-up of the bathroom by Norman Bates following the stabbing. "Hitchcock wanted a strong back-light behind Tony to emphasize the strangeness of the scene," explained set designer Clatworthy. "He had the crew cut a hole in the set wall and shone a strong lamp right through it. It made everything look sharper."

Hitchcock challenged cameraman Russell and his production team by devising a point-of-view shot to heighten audience identification with Janet Leigh. He wanted to show water pulsing out of the shower head straight toward the camera. "It was an old-fashioned shower head," noted script supervisor Schlom. "You couldn't control the spray every way you wanted it. Everyone's first and obvious question was, 'If we shoot right at it, how are we going to keep the lens dry?' Mr. Hitchcock said, 'Put the camera *there* with a long lens and block off the inner holes on the shower head so they won't spout water.' By using the longer lens, we could get back a little farther, shoot a little tighter and the water appeared to hit the lens but actually sprayed past it. The guys on the sides got a little soaked but, meanwhile, we got the shot."

Hitchcock became equally excited about working out the complicated mechanics of a camera dolly designed so as to enable him to film the scene as one continuous shot. Just after the stabbing of Marion Crane, the dolly move would open on a screen-filling close-up of the lifeless eye of Janet Leigh, then glide low along the bathroom floor past the toilet, then into the motel room to end on the nightstand and, atop it, the newspaper in which the stolen money is hidden. As the camera held the shot, the open window would disclose Norman running down the stairs from the house toward the motel. Marshall Schlom said, "[Hitchcock] was not like some directors who think, 'Okay, I've dreamed up the most difficult shot. Let's see if the crew can do it.' He simply wanted this particular idea to work and explained to us how it would. It was not trial-and-error. But because it had so many mechanical and technical aspects, making it look like one continuous shot was tough."

In preparation for the shot, Hitchcock had taken Janet Leigh for a fitting for contact lenses. When the ophthalmologist told the director that Leigh might suffer eye damage without at least six weeks to accustom her eyes to the lenses, Hitchcock said, "You'll just have to go it alone, old girl." When cinematographer Russell moved in for the first close-up of Leigh's eye as tightly as safety allowed, Hitchcock was unsatisfied. In postproduction, by use of an optical printer, Hitchcock had the shot of the eye enlarged so that orb appeared to be a perfect "fit" in the bathtub drain as his camera spiraled from the drain. The potent image echoes the credit sequence that Saul Bass designed for *Vertigo*, with its emphasis on a women's eye and hallucinatory, gyrating spirals.

The traveling dolly shot required such split-second cueing of various human, mechanical, and technical elements that Hitchcock needed dozens of retakes. During each attempt, the camera meandered past Janet Leigh—nearly nude—who had to lie slumped on the bathroom floor while holding her breath and a death-stare. As Hitchcock eyed each take, he snapped his fingers to his star to indicate that the camera had moved past her face. Shooting dragged on and on for hours. During an apparently successful take, the shower steam detached the moleskin covering Leigh's breasts. Trying to shake away the memory, Leigh said, "At that point, with that shot, I didn't give a damn."

Because the shower and motel rooms were separate sets and the Bates house was actually on the backlot, the postproduction team was required to optically composite three separate pieces to give Hitchcock his "continuous shot." "He designed the dolly move to come across the door that opens on the motel room," Marshall Schlom explained. "Normally, what you could do is just run the camera past the doorjambs and not notice them. Well, nothing fake in Hitchcock's movies—he wanted everyone in the audience to be in the room *with* [the heroine]. So I timed the dolly and the pan to come across that door. Then he repositioned the camera on the other side of the doorway because he couldn't get the camera through the door. Today, you might be able to do that easily because we have smaller dollies, but in those days, we had these big *machines*.

"He reset the camera from the other side, made the pan and dolly again with exactly the same movement, then went across the door. It was the same exposure in the printer. We blended that and got up to the motel room window, which was actually a screen with projection backing and a projector on the stage throwing an image of Tony running down the stairs. Again, that move to the window had to be perfectly timed because when you come up to it, the plate had to be in motion and when the camera stopped, the door [of the Bates house] had to open and Tony run out. Today, you could do it mechanically with a radio and a voice-cue for the actor to come out the door. We couldn't do that because it was already on film. Nobody but the few of us that worked on it knew it was done with two different shots ending up on a third piece of film."

Hitchcock and Janet Leigh frequently cited the shower sequence as having taken seven days to film. However, the daily production sheets list "INT. BATHROOM—CABIN ONE" as the site for eleven days of shooting, aside from the test footage captured on December 10. Several of the shooting days involved Anthony Perkins and the compulsive cleaning-up after Mother. By the time of the completion of the bathroom scenes, Hitchcock was four days over schedule. But assistant director Hilton Green shrugged and said, "Shooting the shower scene was never seen by us as more than getting the bits and pieces together purely for shock effect. The fragments that we photographed were sort of stored away, but Mr. Hitchcock had a general idea of how he wanted to make the idea progress."

If Hitchcock shot the shower murder and bathroom scenes with an air of "business as usual," some of his collaborators felt otherwise. "There was a *lot* of talk on the lot that, this time, Hitchcock had gone too far," costume supervisor Helen Colvig remembered. "Even the unit manager (Lew Leary) said, 'He'll never get away with this scene.' Frankly, we all thought he'd cut it to just show Mother coming into the bathroom, the knife raising, the blood, the girl falling, and that's it. We thought the bits-and-pieces montage approach lent itself to any censorship or editorial changes he had in mind. It was *so* outrageous for its time."

No member of the Hitchcock team of collaborators could have predicted the impact the sequence was to have in the movie or on movie history. In design and execution, the sequence was a masterstroke. Hitchcock simultaneously succeeded in titillating and shocking the viewer while concealing the nudity of the victim and the true identity of the attacker. Most crucially, the impressionistic montage so stylized and abstracted the action that the sequence was to devastate rather than nauseate the audience. When screenwriter Joseph Stefano was reminded of a statement often quoted by Hitchcock ("I could hear audience's screaming when we planned the scene"), the writer said, "He was lying. He didn't hear screaming. Laughing maybe, not screaming. We had no idea. We thought people would gasp or be silent, but screaming? Never."

Because Hitchcock customarily shot so little extra footage, editing on his pictures was often completed within weeks after the shutdown of production. But the shower sequence was of particular concern to Hitchcock—not to mention to the waiting censors—and he marked it for immediate editing. Script supervisor Marshall Schlom recalled that only he, at the invitation of Hitchcock, joined editor George Tomasini to cut the film. However, Saul Bass asserted, "When we got through shooting the sequence, I edited it with George. In those days, I judged people by what they let me do. The fact that George, with no edginess, was willing to do a rough cut with footage I shot with the IMO, [meant he was] just a nice guy, wonderful and friendly. We did it on a Saturday because he was working over the weekend to get certain stuff ready for Hitch to look at. We finished editing the thing, we showed it to Hitch and he inserted two cuts. One was a spatter of blood on Janet Leigh as she starts to go down while the blows are being struck. The other was a flash-cut of the knife going into her belly. We put the knife against her belly and then pulled it back. I think it was the stand-in."

Hitchcock showed the edited sequence to Mrs. Hitchcock, who had acted as a cutter, screenwriter, and invaluable collaborator on virtually all of her husband's films from the thirties onward. Alma was such a canny and observant filmmaker that on *Vertigo*, for example, she suggested that her husband reedit a scene in which James Stewart runs after a suicidal Kim Novak. The point of the re-edit? To mask the size of the leading lady's feet. On *Psycho*, according to the accounts of several Hitchcock biographers, Alma Hitchcock spotted a glitch that her husband, Bass, Tomasini, and Schlom had missed: Janet Leigh, staring in fixed-eyed close-up on the bathroom floor, gulped. "Actually, it was a blink," recalled Janet Leigh. "[Mrs. Hitchcock] told Hitchcock, she saw me blink in the shot that started close on my eye. The editor and I looked and neither of us saw it. The lady had a very sharp eye." Marshall Schlom said, "There were no KEMMs at the time. Though we must have run that sequence back and forth in the Movieola a couple of hundred times, we completely missed it. So we had to take it out and insert a second cut of the shower head."

Hitchcock developed a fascination for an aural technique to convey the sound a knife makes when jabbing a body. "He told the prop man [Robert Bone] to go out and get a watermelon which we'd stab," recalled Marshall Schlom. "Knowing Hitchcock, the prop man knew he had to come back not only with watermelons of all sizes, but casabas, cantaloupes, and honeydews. Mr. Hitchcock had such a wandering mind that said, 'If this doesn't work, what are we going to use next?' We had to be ready." In a recording studio, prop man Bone auditioned the melons for Hitchcock, who sat listening with his eyes closed. When the demonstration table was littered with shredded fruit, Hitchcock opened his eyes, and intoned simply: "Casaba." The director was satisfied that he and his collaborators had married the precise sound and image for a stylized murder.

Arbogast Meets Mother

Hitchcock had particular fun with the character of the private detective, Milton Arbogast, played by Martin Balsam. The forty-year-old stage and television actor, trained at the Actors Studio, had made his screen debut for Elia Kazan in *On the Waterfront* (1954). A great gift of Balsam's on the stage or screen is the instant impression that he conveys of Everyman. Hitchcock, throughout his career, maintained a healthy irreverence toward the guardians of law and order, and his view of Arbogast—smug, glib, tenacious, slightly dull—is no exception. In film after film, Hitchcock challenges his audiences to cry out "Why don't the hero and heroine go straight to the police?" Because, implies Hitchcock in answer, all that they will find is a universe of Milton Arbogasts. As the director so often put it, "Logic is dull."

Hitchcock was well aware that Martin Balsam was among the two or three best-trained actors in *Psycho*. The director admitted to only perfunctory interest in the characters of Sam and Lila, therefore the conflict between Norman and Arbogast became more crucial. Rehearsing the funny-tense scene where Arbogast interrogates Bates in the motel office, Hitchcock could not have helped but be excited by the electricity between his actors. The suspense master imposed another technical challenge on his collaborators by deciding to shoot the scene more naturalistically than originally had been planned. As had Orson Welles in his radio dramas and in *Citizen Kane*, Hitchcock encouraged Balsam and Perkins to find their own rhythms and subtext, to overlap each other's dialogue. Art director Robert Clatworthy, who watched the shooting, recalled: "The first time they did it, Hitchcock just shot the inquisition in that little office straight through, no cuts. I thought it was marvelous." The crew rewarded the players with a spontaneous outburst of applause. However kinetic the line delivery, Hitchcock wanted more. "It was the first scene Martin and Tony played together," said script supervisor Schlom. "It was a very long scene and Mr. Hitchcock wanted staccato bantering. They did it in one take. At the end of it, this wonderful smile spread across Mr. Hitchcock's face. Despite the comments he made about actors, he appreciated *good* acting, which that certainly was."

Hitchcock got from Balsam and Perkins more than he had bargained for in the scene. But according to Schlom, "The sound man on the movie just went *nuts*. Today, we just 'mike' the actors offstage. Then, that was unheard of. And later, when George Tomasini sat down on the cutting bench, it was a nightmare because the tracks didn't match. Tony and Martin didn't say the same thing at the same time with the same cadence. George, who was one of the best cutters in town, worked three or four days on that to get it mechanically correct. It was masterful."

An added headache for the sound crew in the scene was

Perkins's suggestion to Hitchcock that Norman Bates would chomp Kandy Korn when particularly flustered. As Perkins noted: "I added it a little bit late, so I don't know how clear it is, but I kept nibbling on it through the whole picture. I came to him one morning and asked him and he said, 'Fine, fine.' He didn't even think, he didn't even have to stop to think if it was right or wrong. He had the kind of mind that could instantaneously accept or reject a suggestion." Although the sound men masked the chewing noises, Hitchcock emphasized Perkins's innovation by adding a big close-up, shot from below, of the actor's giraffe-like neck as he nervously gulps the snack food.

The shower murder sequence had proved to be complicated and time-consuming. However, crew members insist that Hitchcock regarded the murder of detective Arbogast on the staircase as more crucial to the picture. The scene certainly presented greater technical challenges. "This was exactly the kind of problem Hitchcock loved to work out with the technical people," recalled directorial assistant Hilton Green. "[Mr. Hitchcock and the crew] started discussions for that scene very early in preproduction. There had been talk about using a crane, but there was no way of getting a crane into a set that you see literally from top to bottom."

Here is how screenwriter Joseph Stefano describes the scene:

INT. FOYER OF BATES HOUSE—NIGHT

> Arbogast gradually eases the door closed, stands against it, waiting. He looks up in the direction of the light, sees no one. The door at the head of the stairs is closed. Arbogast listens, holds his breath, hears what could be human sounds coming from upstairs but realizes these could also be the sounds of an old house after sunset. After a careful wait, he crosses to the stairs, starts up, slowly, guardedly, placing a foot squarely on each step to test it for squeaks or groans

before placing his full weight on it. CAMERA FOLLOWS, remaining on floor level but TRAVELING ALONG the stairway as Arbogast makes his way up.

INT. STAIRWAY AND UPSTAIRS LANDING—EXTREMELY HIGH ANGLE

Same angle as that used at the FADE OUT at the end of Scene #43. We see Arbogast coming up the stairs. And now we see, too, the door of the mother's room, opening, carefully and slowly.

As Arbogast reaches the landing, the door opens and the mother steps out, her hand raised high, the blade of an enormous knife flashing.

C.U.—BIG HEAD OF AN ASTONISHED ARBOGAST

The knife slashes across his cheek and neck. Blood spurts. The sudden attack throws him off balance. He stumbles back and staggers down the whole of the staircase. He frantically gropes for the balustrade as he goes backwards down the stairs. The CAMERA FOLLOWS him all the way down. A wicked knife keeps thrusting itself into the foreground. As he collapses at the bottom, the black head and shoulders of Mrs. Bates plunge into the foreground as the CAMERA MOVES IN to contain the raising [sic] and descending murder weapon.

From the outset, Hitchcock and his team had designed the scene for maximum effect. "The showing of a violent murder at the beginning," the director told Ian Cameron and V. F. Perkins, "was intended purely to instill into the minds of the audience a certain degree of fear of what is to come. Actually in the film, as it goes on, there's less and less violence because it has been transferred to the minds of the audience."

The Arbogast staircase murder had been calculated to shock. Also, it had been designed to camouflage the true "identity" of Mother by featuring a showy, extreme high-angle shot. Originally, Hitchcock had intended to employ the same spectacular angle in three scenes in the narrative. [In the version of *Psycho* released to theaters, Hitchcock also used the high-angle shot to depict Norman's carrying Mother downstairs to the fruit cellar.] Originally, it was to have followed Norman's cleaning up after Marion's murder. In that scene, detailed in three drafts of the screenplay, Norman would have been shown from this bird's-eye view as he ascended the stairs and found bloodstained clothes and shoes in a pile outside Mother's bedroom door. The sequence, cut in editing, was to have ended with a long, silent shot of the Bates house silhouetted against the sky. Then, a slow curl of smoke was to have risen from the chimney.

Saul Bass had scrupulously storyboarded the staircase murder sequence. "This is where Hitch did a reverse on the so-called classic scare or threat scene," the graphic designer explained. I designed and set up the sequence so that when Arbogast went up the stairs, you had close cuts of his hands on the rail, his feet shot through the vertical bars. Because when he was knocked off at the top of the stairs and fell, I wanted his hand to grab onto one of the posts and, as he went down, his hands rip those posts apart."

When Bass showed Hitchcock the storyboards, the director delivered a lecture on the mechanics of a suspense sequence. Bass recalled: "Hitch said, 'No. Wrong point of view. You are telling the audience something might or will happen. He should be going up just like nothing's going to happen. You know, you don't get killed just for walking up the stairs. Rather, he sees a door and says, "Oh, I wonder what's in here." He reaches it and *all hell breaks loose!*' Nobody shot anything until Hitch approved it. So I restoryboarded it just the way we discussed it. I said, 'Why don't we shoot it from above?' Obviously it was right. It worked. But who knows? Maybe what I was [originally] suggesting would have been even better."

"From my point of view," observed script man Marshall Schlom, "Saul Bass's contribution was more in the Arbogast murder than in the shower sequence. The [shower murder] was done purely for shock, but Arbogast's killing was a piece of dramatics, almost a storyline that had to be very carefully followed." Hitchcock scheduled the shooting of the scene for January 14 on the Phantom Stage. For more than a week in advance, painstaking technical rehearsals and preparations were conducted at the end of each shooting day by assistant director Hilton Green, cameraman John Russell, set designer Robert Clatworthy, script supervisor Marshall Schlom, and the stand-in for actor Martin Balsam.

After many trouble-plagued rehearsals, the crew captured on film a successful rehearsal for the complex shot. Hitchcock approved it, and the film was back on schedule. For the sequence, Clatworthy and Hurley had devised a metal bipod run by pulleys that would lift a cinematographer and a relatively lightweight camera to the upper reaches of the soundstage on overhead tracks built to run parallel to the stairs. The system had a glitch: The operator simultaneously had to run the camera *and* manipulate the focus. "That was a very big problem to solve," noted assistant director Green. "[Eventually] it took two camera operators and the assistant cameraman to make the shot with the 'contraption'—that's the only word for it—because the operator had to have someone take over on the panning. We rehearsed and rehearsed the move after Hitchcock went home so there wouldn't be any problems on the day of shooting."

Required before the camera, aside from Martin Balsam, was Mitzi Koestner, the little person doubling for Mother. Anthony

Perkins explained: "The reason she was hired was that Hitch was particularly worried that the audience was going to see through the whole thing. Remember, this scene comes a little more than halfway through the picture. In order to strengthen the illusion, he engaged a woman who was very small and, physically, totally unlike anyone else [who appeared as Mother] in the picture."

On the eve of shooting, from 6:30 to 7:30 P.M., the company conducted another rehearsal. However, the scheduled day of shooting—January 14—brought unforeseen woes. Hitchcock succumbed to a flu bug that had also taken actress Vera Miles and several other company members out of commission during the previous week. Marshall Schlom recalled: "Mr. Hitchcock called Hilton [Green] up at seven-thirty in the morning and said he was ill. He asked me to get on another phone and said, 'Fellas, you know what to do. Go ahead and shoot it.' We did all the pieces that Saul had designed so carefully on storyboard."

"*I* 'directed' that scene," Hilton Green admitted, "but I directed it on the telephone to Hitchcock at his house." Because Hitchcock was uncertain as to how he wanted to cut the scene, Green and the crew shot streamlined versions of Saul Bass's "montage"-style angles (hands on the banister, soles on the carpet). In the absence of Hitchcock, Green and the crew shot the stairway ascent, up to and including the stabbing of Arbogast by Mother. "It worked on the first take," Green said, beaming with relief even today.

When Hitchcock's indisposition lingered into the following day of production, the director shut down the company. To try to make up for being behind schedule, Green and Schlom edited a rough assemblage of the staircase murder sequence from the dailies. Although both collaborators worried when they noticed that the focus of cameraman Russell went awry when Balsam reached the halfway mark on the stairs, neither of them saw the technical glitch as fatal. Schlom commented: "We thought, 'Well, we'll just keep cutting away, so you'll never see it in the finished film.'"

However, when Hitchcock returned to action the following day and viewed the footage in the editing room with Green and Schlom, he knew he had miscalculated. Schlom said, "After the lights went on in the projection room, Mr. Hitchcock went to the front of the house, clasped his hands behind his back and said, 'Fellas, we've made a big mistake. The minute you see the hands on the rail, the feet—you're telegraphing that something's going to happen. Take it all out, except for the monorail shot.' We both asked him, 'What about the little "soft" [out-of-focus] spot?' He said, 'I'll live with that.'"

Hitchcock had not only spurned the Bass concept for the scene but also an alternative proposal put forth by art director Robert Clatworthy. The director listened patiently as Clatworthy described a notion to film the fall of Arbogast from the point of view of the pursuing murderer—or, if one wishes, from the viewpoint of the audience. "I had an idea to put an Arriflex camera in a soft medicine ball with a hole cut for the lens," explained Clatworthy. "We'd start the camera, roll the ball down the stairs with Tony pursuing and stabbing. Hitchcock might have liked the idea even though it might have been time-consuming to shoot, but we had already built the track for the camera, so I was too late anyway."

Instead of either of these proposals, Hitchcock chose the sort of vertiginous, "floating" fall that he had used for the fall of the spies from the Statue of Liberty in *Saboteur* or from Mt. Rushmore in *North by Northwest*. Explained Marshall Schlom: "We took apart the sequence as it had been edited, then put it back together leaving just the one shot of Marty [Balsam] coming upstairs. Then, for when Mom makes the stab, we did that by shooting a moving background plate using the monopod without Marty. Later, we had Marty, sitting in a gimbal, flailing in front of a standard rear-projection screen." Seldom had murder sequences been so difficult for Hitchcock. Few of the crew members knew that the sequence had been redone or were invited to dailies. The moment when Arbogast and Mother meet was to cause a sensation when the *Psycho* team saw it in the rough cut.

Endgame

Falls Lake lay on the Universal-Revue backlot, one of many such large backlot waterways maintained by the studio for films and TV shows. Hitchcock used the lake for the Bates swamp in the scene in which Norman conceals the 1957 Ford Custom 300 containing Marion Crane's corpse and the stolen money. The lake, with its background of nondescript scrub and hills, had been named after the man-made falls that had been built during the days of the studio's founder, Carl Laemmle. Because the site, au naturel, conjured little of the seedy melancholy suggested by Joseph Hurley's sketches, art director Robert Clatworthy suggested dramatizing the bland topography with a painted backing of tall reeds and undergrowth. "Might make all the difference in the world, old boy," Hitchcock responded to Clatworthy. The art director devised an eight-foot-high, twenty-foot-long canvas backing designed to provide for Hitchcock's down-tilting camera a moodier backdrop for the sinking car.

Hitchcock had calculated the scene as an opportunity to wring every possible moment of suspense by showing the car hitting a snag before sinking. The idea was to make each audience member an active conspirator in the agony—and, by implication, the madness—of Norman. To accommodate the director, the prop department devised a mechanical lift. "We built a hydraulic device into the ground very much like an automatic garage door opener," Hilton Green said, explaining the shooting of the scene. "We pushed the car in and the car clamped on as it hit. The device turned and pivoted a little bit, then pulled the car down steadily at a certain tempo, then stopped cold—all mechanically done. You could only do it once, or else you'd have to clean up the whole car and set it up for reshooting the following day. It was done in one take, but it was another scene that took an awful lot of preparation."

On paper, the revelation of the shriveled corpse of Mother in the swivel chair sounded to most of the crew like a milk run. As Joseph Stefano wrote it: "Lila goes to the chair, touches it. The touch disturbs the figure. It starts to turn, slowly, stiffly, a clock-wise movement . . . It is the body of a woman long dead . . . The movement of this stuffed, ill-preserved cadaver, turning as if in response to Lila's call, is actually graceful, ballet-like, and the effect is terrible and obscene." Under Hitchcock, the filming proved to be one of the tougher challenges he threw to his crew.

To heighten the impact of the moment, graphic designer Saul Bass suggested revealing Mother by a naked, hanging light bulb. The device had already jolted audiences in the climatic attic scene in *The Picture of Dorian Gray* (1945), directed by Albert Lewin. "It was a very simple idea," Bass said. "The swinging light caused the light to change on the face and gave it a sort of macabre animation that almost made the face look like it was doing some-thing—laughing, screaming, whatever—when you knew it was dead. It was just macabre, so some excuse had to be found to cause the light to do that." Coming up with a rationale was easy enough: Hitchcock had Vera Miles fling back her arm in panic and her hand swats the light.

"Hitchcock wanted the dummy to turn a certain way and cock a certain way as Vera put her hand on it," Hilton Green explained. "We did it with a camera mount. There was a prop man underneath turning the cranks as a camera operator would do. It took a while before we got it exactly the way Hitchcock was after."

The final production challenge to cause concern within the Hitchcock team was the penultimate scene, known by some on the crew as the-headshrinker-explains-it-all. In this scene, heavy with expository dialogue, the psychiatrist lectures the Fairvale nabobs, Sam, Lila—and the audience—on the skewed psychic psychology of Norman Bates. Hitchcock and his screenwriter knew that the scene, the bane of creative types, was "obligatory": a chance for the audience to catch its collective breath while the "logic" buffs among them got their fill of the facts. Hitchcock planned to do his share to enliven the action with slick camera moves, while stage and movie actor Simon Oakland, as the psychiatrist, did his usual scene stealing.

In preproduction, censors from the Shurlock office had already objected to the use of the term "transvestite," among other complaints, so Hitchcock thought it wise to handle the scene with kid gloves. In the shooting script, the director and screenwriter designed a stylish means of easing into the scene by a long, moving camera track that was to act almost as a "relay race" from the exterior of the state courthouse into the inner sanctum of the cell of "Norma" Bates. Hitchcock's camera was to have followed a TV newscaster (played by actor and real life radio announcer Larry Thor) from the steps of the courthouse crowded with stunned, curious townspeople and reporters eager for news of Bates. Asks the TV Man (as the script identifies him) of a policeman holding back the crowd: "You think they'll take him out that way?" The cop shoots back: "Probably have to. Besides, the taxpayers hate it when something gets slipped out the back on them." The "relay" would then have been picked up by a Coffee Boy (played by Jim Brandt) who trundles a carton of take-out into the office of the chief of police where Sam, Lila, the psychiatrist, and the law await.

As described in the screenplay, Sam would rise, hand Lila her coffee cup, and quip, "It's regular. Okay?" She replies, "I could stand something regular." A few more lines of small talk lead into the psychiatrist's two-page monologue. Hitchcock filmed the opening to the scene as written, then grew concerned that the lead-in slowed down an already lengthy scene. He went back and eliminated the shots of the TV announcer and coffee boy, then filmed actor Simon Oakland (Dr. Richman) entering the office and beginning his talk. "[The scene] was all predicated on how Simon Oakland played the psychiatrist," recalled Marshall Schlom, to whom Hitchcock confided his concerns that the whole picture might spark censorship problems. "It was shot very clinically. Mr. Hitchcock directed Mr. Oakland to say the lines the way he felt they should be told. He printed the first or second take. He yelled cut, went over and shook the actor's hand, saying, 'Thank you very much, Mr. Oakland. You've just saved my picture.'"

Nine days over schedule and having avoided a potentially crippling industry-wide actors' strike, Hitchcock wrapped principal photography on February 1, 1960. To save more time and money before shutting down the film, Hitchcock and his crew shot what was to become one of the most famous advertising trailers in movie history. It had been Hitchcock's custom to mark the completion of production with an expensive, catered "wrap party." For *Psycho*, there was none, nor was there much back-slapping, or promises to keep in touch. After all, the director's favorite performers on the picture—Janet Leigh, Anthony Perkins, and Martin Balsam—had gone on to other projects.

For most of the production crew, another installment of the Hitchcock television show was on tap for the following week. Alfred Hitchcock was delighted to have his "thirty-day picture" back in his hands and in those of the people who, he often said, "Really *make* a picture."

8. POSTPRODUCTION

Retakes, Quibbles, and Indecision

Troubled by his opening shots for the film, Hitchcock, on February 25, ordered a tiny film crew back to Phoenix, Arizona, to reshoot the city skyline. Budgetary and technical limitations of the day made it necessary for Hitchcock to abandon his elaborate "fly on the wall" visual pun in which a helicopter was to have descended over the city and "into" the motel room window. So the director also dropped the notion of the insect that pesters Sam and Marion in the hotel room and let the reference to a fly in the final line of the film ("She wouldn't even harm a fly") stand alone.

Instead, Hitchcock simplified the overview of Phoenix to a panoramic "pan" from left to right, moving progressively closer, toward the hotel window. The new footage was to prove more satisfactory than the first go-around, but the effect never really paid off. In the film, although the two titles ("Friday, December the Eleventh," and "Two Forty-Three P.M.") tend to divert the eye, there are four visible dissolves as the point of view of the camera homes in on the hotel. "We didn't get a very good blend between the original Phoenix shots and the cut to the dolly move into the hotel window, which was done on the soundstage," admitted Marshall Schlom. "There is a definite 'color' change between the shots, even though the movie is in black and white. The camera wasn't quite steady enough, so that when you cut into the facing, you go from 'slightly jiggly' to 'stop,' and from one exposure to another exposure. The whole thing just didn't work." Hitchcock decided not to press; too much time and money had already been wasted on the effect.

While one crew toiled in Phoenix, a second crew in North Hollywood reshot details of the murder of Arbogast to bring the original intentions of Saul Bass in line with Hitchcock's revisions. The crew redid the entrance of actor Balsam into the Bates hall, views of the actor's face and feet heading upstairs [which went unused], inserts of a shadowed, menacing Cupid figure poised with a drawn arrow, and Hitchcockian moving point-of-view shots to put the viewer "with" Arbogast as he climbs the stairs. In addition, Hitchcock reshot for moodier lighting the discovery of Mother by Vera Miles in the basement.

In postproduction, Hitchcock again tapped the expertise of Saul Bass. "We've really got to do something to make the house look forbidding," observed the director to the designer. Hitchcock wanted to parody the conventions of the haunted house genre—stormy nights, rattling windows—by turning the Bates house into one of the giant red herrings of the picture. After all, the horror and tragedy of *Psycho* were of the heart and mind, not of ectoplasm. "I tried the obvious things," explained Bass. "I made a model of the house and tried lighting it various ways, but it all looked fakey. Finally, I found an answer that, like so many of these things, was really wonderful and so dumb and simple, you know? Behind shots of the house, I matted-in a time-lapse, moonlit, cloudy skyscape. The rate of movement was not much above normal because I didn't want the eye to go right *to* it. So when you see the shot, what you look at is the house, but the clouds behind it are moving in a very eerie and abnormal way. I'm not sure that it wasn't even stock footage that I used!"

The Sound of Mother

Hitchcock, having already gone to great visual lengths to ensure the shock ending of *Psycho*, had also employed his wiles to find a "voice" for mother. "Hitch was very eager to play fair, but he also didn't want the audience to see through the whole thing," recalled Anthony Perkins, who discussed with his director the possibility of recording all the lines himself. The idea did not fly, but Perkins persisted. "I still thought it would be clever to have a male voice reading the lines, which is why I suggested Paul Jasmin to Hitch," Perkins said. Jasmin, then twenty-three, a Montana-born budding actor who stormed Hollywood with hopes of becoming the next Montgomery Clift or Gary Cooper, was a natural mimic, a practical joker, and a friend of Perkins.

"I was studying to be an actor," recalled Jasmin, today a successful painter and fashion photographer. "For a joke, I did this old-lady character named 'Eunice Ayers,' a no-bullshit, Marjorie Main kind of gal. Tony [Perkins] and [Broadway and film star] Elaine Stritch used to egg me on, so I'd call up big stars like Rosalind Russell and put her on with this voice for hours. Stanley Kubrick was directing *Spartacus* at Universal at the time and, through a press agent, he heard about our little pranks, loved them, and began to tape the conversations. Then, Tony told Hitchcock about me and gave him some of the tapes."

According to Jasmin, Hitchcock told him that he had decided against using Perkins to record the voice of Mother. Jasmin explained: "Hitchcock had decided that if Tony did the voice right from the beginning, it might give away the whole thing. Then he considered just having a woman do the voice. But that didn't work either because, in the final scene, the voice had to sound at least *something* like Tony. At the summons of Hitchcock, I went out to the soundstage one day. I can't think of another director who was held in such awe. I was *terrified*. Hitchcock was *terrifying*. He was just a god on the set. I did the 'Eunice Ayers' voice for him and he *loved* it. He asked me to go to the sound recording studio and make a tape. After he heard it, he called me back and said, 'Come in and do it.'"

Hitchcock gave Jasmin only the appropriate script pages, the former actor recalled, "Because nobody was allowed to read the final pages. [Hitchcock] really didn't tell you very much and volunteered *nothing*. He just wanted those voices he kept hearing in his head. He sent me to the dubbing room and I just did it scene by scene for an assistant while Hitchcock was on the set shooting. Even just the page or two of dialogue, I had to do again and again. The woman's voice was really shrewish. That's the quality Hitchcock liked."

Hitchcock also required Jasmin's presence on the set for several weeks to feed lines to Perkins. "He had me there for the shots where Tony sinks the car in the swamp and also for when he carries Mother down the stairs," Jasmin explained. "Also, we recorded some lines as if Tony can hear her from the house when the car goes into the swamp. Hitchcock had a notion that, having watched a number of scenes played out, I'd bring something of that atmosphere to the dubbing room when I recorded the lines later. I had no idea what he would or would not eventually use in the movie." (The swamp scene lost its harangue by Mother in the cutting.)

In late January, while Hitchcock shot the climactic monologue of Mother in the detention cell, Jasmin voiced the lines off-camera while Anthony Perkins, wrapped in a blanket, stared eerily into himself and, finally, into the camera. Observed set decorator Robert Clatworthy: "Even watching and listening to the scene as it was shot gave the crew goosebumps. The damn thing was so weird, so uncanny."

In postproduction, Hitchcock revealed another ace up his sleeve regarding the voice of Mother. He hired actresses Jeanette Nolan (Orson Welles's *Macbeth*, 1948) and Virginia Gregg (*Spencer's Mountain*, 1962) to offer greater possibilities for throwing off the audience. Hitchcock personally directed Gregg in a one-day recording session. "Hitchcock rehearsed and coached me very carefully," the actress recalled. "I had thought of Mother as sounding pearly and wheedling, but he had something very fixed in his mind: old, loud, strident, and monstrous. He kept saying, 'Let's make her sound a little more shrewish.' It came so easily that I didn't think he was happy about it and would probably record other people." Gregg admitted that she puzzled over why her director insisted upon Mrs. Bates's sounding more grandmotherly than motherly. "I think that was the sort of voice that Hitchcock was hearing in his head," she reasoned. Gregg subsequently gave voice to Mother in two sequels to *Psycho*.

Emmy-winner Jeanette Nolan, accustomed to five-hour dubbing sessions with Orson Welles on her debut film, *Macbeth*, claimed barely to recall her work on *Psycho*. "I remember my husband [John McIntire, who played Sheriff Chambers in the movie] working on the film more than I remember my own work," the actress said. "I had next to no contact with Mr. Hitchcock. I simply went to the recording studio and looped some of the mother's lines. I also recall doing quite a lot of screaming for the film." The screams were confined to scenes in the shower and in the fruit cellar.

Hitchcock and his sound men, Waldon O. Watson and William Russell, worked their postproduction magic on the voice of Mother. "It wasn't until I saw the movie a second and third time that I understood why I didn't recognize my voice," Paul Jasmin remarked. "But Hitchcock was even more brilliant than I thought. In postproduction, he spliced and blended a mixture of different voices—Virginia, Jeanette, and me—so that what Mother says literally changes from word to word and sentence to sentence. He did that to confuse the audience. I recognize my voice before Tony carries Mother down the stairs. But the very last speech, the monologue, is all a woman; Virginia, with probably a little of Jeanette spliced in."

The director surprised script supervisor Marshall Schlom by inviting him to join George Tomasini in the editing room for the eight weeks it took to assemble the first cut. "George was a very mild person who did not have a huge ego," observed associate Harold Adler, who contributed to the title designs for several Hitchcock pictures including *Vertigo* and *The Birds*. "He used to say that Hitchcock was so well prepared, there was very little film left over to cut." Schlom explained the parameters of the partnership that he enjoyed with Hitchcock and Tomasini, who died in 1964. "It developed into a ritual," Schlom said, grinning at the memory. "First Mr. Hitchcock came in and watched a rough assembly of the film reel, about ten minutes of film, in a 'Stop and Go' room. [A room equipped with a special projector that can stop-frame as well as run the footage backward and forward.] After the lights went up in the small projection room, Mr. Hitchcock would stand before the screen addressing us as if he were the professor and we the students. He'd say, 'Gentlemen, this is what I like and don't like' and then explain exactly what he wanted. Then he'd sit down again and we'd run the film back and forth, which would probably take us an hour and a half to do. He'd say, 'Okay, let's make the changes,' and then go home."

One example of Hitchcock's adding his inimitable touch occurs in the scene in which Marion, packing in her bedroom, keeps shooting glances toward the stolen cash in the envelope on the bed. "When George and I were cutting that scene," recalled Schlom, "the theme was a matter of 'Should she return the money?' or 'Shouldn't she?' We cut, alternating shots of her dressing to leave with shots of the money. [Hitchcock] told us, 'Put in more cuts.' I asked, 'Aren't you hitting the audience over the head?' But it was *his* kind of movie. He said, 'I always want the audience to think what she's thinking. The minute I lose one person, I've lost the entire audience.' And *that*, I understood, is one way he kept audiences at the edge of their seats, straining to get these little bits of information."

During postproduction, however, Hitchcock's imperious and authoritarian demeanor apparently masked uncertainty as to how *Psycho* would fare with the public. The movie had been, after all, funded from his own pocketbook. One clue to the director's state of mind can be found in his indecisive fussing over the closing image of the film. His ambivalence actually led to the movie's being printed and distributed with two slightly different endings. In both versions, the eerie vision of Anthony Perkins grinning into the camera is succeeded by a second shot of the car of the heroine being towed out of the swamp. But in only some prints of the picture is a grinning skull superimposed over Norman's smile. Marshall Schlom explained: "He just wasn't sure which version he wanted to put in the release print—with or without the subliminal cut of Mother's death skull smiling out from Tony's face. I remember Mr. Hitchcock saying, 'It's got to be on and off that [snapping his fingers] quickly. I want the audience to say, 'Did I *see* that?' That sort of technique was different for him because he never tried to play with their heads that way before. He wasn't sure if he was going a little bit too far with that."

The First Screenings

On Tuesday, April 26, 8:00 P.M., in Screening Room 8 at Universal-Revue, Alfred Hitchcock hosted the first rough-cut screening of *Psycho*. Present were such close associates as Hilton Green, George Tomasini, Peggy Robertson, George Milo, Robert Clatworthy, Joseph Hurley, John Russell, Rita Riggs, Helen Colvig, and Jack Barron. Such screenings—an industry ritual—may be the least ideal circumstances under which to see a film. Screening rooms tend to be small and barren; worse, one can become overwhelmed by euphoria, by flop sweat, or by a combination of the two. Often, audience members are too insecure or self-critical to express any reaction at all. Nonetheless, *Psycho* turned some hardened industry-ites to jello. "Even though it was a built-in audience of the crew, it was fun because of the gasps and screams," assistant director Hilton Green enthused. "I loved the way it was put together, the suspense, and *they* loved it." Costume supervisor Helen Colvig said, "When you're on a crew, you tend to pick your contribution to pieces or give yourself plaudits. This was different. Everything to do with Mother and seeing Tony come hurtling down the stairs in a dress just scared the beejeebers out of us." Set designer Robert Clatworthy observed: "What surprised me was it probably looked a little better than we thought it would. It was a helluva picture and turned out to be the *only* picture I've ever been on that I heard people talking about in supermarkets, banks, everywhere."

Screenwriter Stefano suffered more conflicted responses. "It looked awful," he said. "I came out sick. It was long. It had no tension. It looked careless. When we came out, Hitch saw the look on my face. 'A lot of work to do, it's just the rough cut,' he said. He understood I'd only seen one rough cut before. But the movie lacked a lot of stuff, like some of the shots of the stuffed birds on Norman's parlor walls. I was afraid they would maybe decide to leave them out. Hitchcock reassured me that everything would be fine." How could Stefano know what his director had in mind for the *sound* and *music* of *Psycho*?

Sounds and Music

Missing from the rough-cut viewed by Hitchcock and his collaborators on April 26 were essential ingredients of a fully mixed audio track and musical score. No matter how much Hitchcock trusted his composer or sound mixer, he always dictated detailed notes for the dubbing of sound effects and the placement of music. Hitchcock was dogmatic about the dramatic functions of sound and music, and often interwove his suggestions into the screenplay. To François Truffaut, Hitchcock had registered his displeasure with such scores as Miklos Rosza's for *Spellbound* (1945) and Franz Waxman's for *Rebecca* (1940) and *Rear Window* (1954). In fact, the *Psycho* screenplay suggests that Hitchcock was anticipating an experiment at minimizing music, an attempt that was eventually to culminate in *The Birds*, which had no conventional musical score at all. In the description of the opening shots *of Psycho*, which Hitchcock in his notes dubs "Sequence 1," the director writes:

> Traffic noises at their loudest as the Camera is passing over the [venetian] blind, and then diminish once we are inside the Hotel Room.

In Sequence 2, after Marion steals the money and is driving through the city:

> [When] Marion's car comes to a stop at the intersection, we should hear her engine die down to an imperceptible tick over. It is very important to hear her engine sound diminish sharply, because the shot on the screen itself does not clearly show her coming to a stop.

In Sequence 3, Hitchcock writes of Marion's hellish drive that ends at Bates Motel:

> When we reach the night sequence, exaggerate passing car noises when headlights show in her eyes. Make sure that the passing car noises are fairly loud, so that we get the contrast of the silence when she is found by the roadside in the morning . . . Just before the rain starts there should be a rumble of thunder, not too violent, but enough to herald the coming rain. Once the rain starts, there should be a progression of falling rain sound and a slow range of the sound of passing trucks . . . Naturally, wind-shield wipers should be heard all through from the moment she turns them on . . . The rain sounds must be very strong, so that

when the rain stops, we should be strongly aware of the silence and odd dripping noises that follow.

In the screenplay, the description of the scene in which the detective sneaks into the Bates house prescribes the following sound cues:

> Arbogast listens, holds his breath, hears what could be human sounds coming from upstairs but realizes these could also be the sounds of the old house after sunset . . . [He] starts up, slowly, guardedly, placing a foot squarely on each step to test it for squeaks or groans.

For the moment when Arbogast meets his maker, Hitchcock dictates:

> Special note must be taken of the sounds of footsteps on the stairs—because, although we do not see "Mother," we should hear the sounds of her stumbling feet down the stairs in pursuit of Arbogast.

In a scene after Arbogast has been killed, Hitchcock knew what effect a creaky stairway would have on the audience, when:

> As [Lila] climbs [the stairs] she is startled by the creaks and groans of the old wood of the steps. She steps more carefully.

On the shower sequence and its aftermath, Hitchcock's notes to composer Bernard Herrmann and to the sound men Waldon O. Watson and William Russell dated January 8, 1960, are most emphatic. Again, the director seemed intent upon making the impact through image, not music:

> Throughout the killing, there should be the shower noise and the blows of the knife. We should hear the water gurgling down the drain of the bathtub, especially when we go close on it . . . during the murder, the sound of the shower should be continuous and monotonous, only broken by the screams of Marion.

After five consecutive films with composer Bernard Herrmann, Hitchcock deeply respected the contributions of the brilliant, often abrasive New York-born Juilliard graduate. Founder and conductor of a chamber orchestra at age twenty, Herrmann, like Hitchcock, could be a bristly perfectionist, contentious, and a pedant. Although Herrmann was clearly not the sort who easily took direction, the composer was to follow closely Hitchcock's dictates as to the music cues for the opening third of *Psycho*—with a single, unforgettable exception.

"Mr. Hitchcock had a wonderful relationship with Bennie," observed script supervisor Marshall Schlom. "And the way to maintain that was to give Herrmann the latitude to do what he wanted. Mr. Hitchcock only wanted people around him who knew what they were doing." Herrmann, who died in 1975, once told director Brian De Palma, "'I remember sitting in a screening room after seeing the rough cut of *Psycho*. Hitch was nervously pacing back and forth, saying it was awful and that he was going to cut it down for his television show. He was crazy. He didn't know what he had. 'Wait a minute,' I said, 'I have some ideas. How about a score completely for strings? I used to be a violin player, you know . . .' Hitch was crazy then. You know, he made *Psycho* with his own money and he was afraid it was going to be a flop. He didn't even want any music in the shower scene. Can you imagine that?'"

In fact, Hitchcock dictated that he wanted "no music at all through the [motel] sequence" with Marion and Norman. Herrmann so mistrusted the uncharacteristic state into which Hitchcock had worked himself that he ignored a counter-suggestion made by his directorial colleague for *Psycho*: a fidgety, post-bebop jazz score. Screenwriter Stefano, a former musician, recalled Herrmann's telling him, "'I'm going to use only strings.' I thought it was weird. No drums? No rhythm section? At the time, I didn't realize that he had prepared through several movies—*Vertigo* being a good example—for this score. But I felt that Bernard Herrmann was the first person other than Hitchcock and I who dug the movie, the first who said 'Ooops—we've got something else here.'"

For *Psycho*, Bernard Herrmann was to concoct nothing less than a cello and violin masterwork, "black and white" music that throbbed sonorously as often as it gnawed at the nerve endings. The score would prove to be a summation of all of Hermann's previous scores for Hitchcock films, conveying as it did the sense of the abyss that is the human psyche, dread, longing, regret—in short, the wellsprings of the Hitchcock universe. According to Stefano, Hitchcock was particularly amused by Herrmann's "screaming violins," and "gave him more credit than anyone else he ever spoke of." So pleased was the parsimonious director by Herrmann's score that he did the unheard of: He nearly doubled the composer's salary—to $34,501.

Titles

Alfred Hitchcock wanted *Psycho* to look from start to finish like a major feature film made economically. To help accomplish that goal, Saul Bass created one of his prestigious, evocative title sequences. Hitchcock paid Bass $3,000, and production costs for the sequence totaled $21,000. The graphic motifs that Bass suggested were nervous, balletic horizontal and vertical bars that expanded and contracted in mirror-image patterns. In the style of a Rorschach, they simultaneously suggested prison bars, city buildings, and sound waves. "In those days," explained Bass, "I liked strong, clear, structural forms against which to do things. I liked giving more zip to *Psycho* because it was not only the name of the picture but a word that *means* something. I was trying to make it more frenetic and I liked the idea of images suggesting clues coming together. Put these together and now you know something. Put another set of clues together and you know something else. It all adds up to who killed Cock Robin."

According to several former associates of Saul Bass, the graphic designer originally devised the title sequence used for *Psycho* for Otto Preminger's *Anatomy of a Murder* (1959). Apparently, when the volatile, Viennese Preminger reportedly judged the design "child stuff," Bass salted away the concept. Today, Bass contends that the bar motif is the only similarity between the sequence worked up for Preminger and the one used in *Psycho*.

It was the task of Harold Adler, a movie advertising artist and title design letterer, to make the Bass concepts work on film. Adler, an artist for National Screen Service, which specialized in illustrating film credits and movie "trailers," observed: "I don't think [Saul Bass] was too technically involved or oriented at that time. One of the reasons he came to us at National Screen Service was that we tried to contribute to that concept and not let him make any mistakes. The storyboards for the *Psycho* [title sequence] were very complete and precise, which was true of all of Saul's work, but I had to interpret them. They were based on a great deal of movement or parallel bars. The job required [teamwork] and considerable discussion between animation director William Hurtz (*Pinocchio*, *Fantasia*), and cameraman/production man, Paul Stoleroff. It is much less costly to do moves under the camera as opposed to using cel animation. Bill and Paul decided that all the lines that went up and down were to be animated and all the lines that moved side to side would be done under the camera with black bars moving across the screen at random speeds and positions."

Adler, who previously had worked with Bass on the title sequences of *Vertigo* and *North by Northwest* before tackling *Psycho*, explained how it was done: To realize the sequence, the cameraman and animator plotted the action on two separate fields. The cel animation was shot on a twelve-field. The horizontal bars moved across the screen on a twenty-four field. The bars were twice as wide as the artwork drawings on the cels and they all matched on the final result. The field defines what the film will "see" when a "stop-action" animation camera is positioned at a specific distance above the artwork in that field. Because stop-motion cameras photograph one frame at a time, an inanimate object can be moved minutely between exposures. When the film is projected at twenty-four frames per second, the inanimate object appears to move naturally.

The production team for the *Psycho* credit sequence settled on a configuration of over thirty parallel bars for each field. Adler, who handled the horizontal bar movements, explained: "We got six-foot-long aluminum bars and sprayed them black. We worked on a large, white-painted plywood board with push-pins to guide the bars. The bars had to follow a straight line and couldn't wiggle. Paul [Stoleroff] and I manually pushed in each bar at predetermined distances for each exposure. The bars came in at different positions and speeds. Each bar was precisely timed by numbers of frames per second, called 'counts.' Each bar had to be pushed in and shot separately. Once a bar had gone across the screen, it was tied down. There were lots of retakes because they'd come in crooked or something."

So much for graphic motifs; the title lettering still had to be done. Up until about the sixties, nearly all movie titles were hand-lettered with a brush. Typography did not have the theatrical pizzazz that film titles and trailers called for. Harold Adler, like other artists in the field, customarily laid out his title concepts in chalk on black poster board. Finished concepts were executed in white paint on the black poster board. Adler observed: "On a lot of pictures, Saul [Bass] liked to use small and sometimes thin type like he used in advertising. But working in film is a different medium from print. You're reducing images to three-quarters of a inch and you have a reproduction problem. I did the title, *Psycho*, in Venus Bold Extended [a popular typeface style of the day] and got two reverse photostats made. I cut one of the photostats into three horizontal parts. I moved the top section [of the title letters] in one direction and shot it at a certain speed, moved the bottom in another direction at another speed, and the middle part at another speed. So you were really getting three images, each one a third of the height of the lettering, coming in at different speeds. For the last frame, we popped on the word *Psycho*, which was the intact photostat by itself. For the other big titles, like 'Directed by Alfred Hitchcock,' I used News Gothic Bold typeface and we did the same three-cut technique as for the title of the movie." Observed Adler of his experiences with Hitchcock on *Psycho*: "We made it work. Oh, God, I would have hated to work in the Hitchcock office. It was so strait-laced and formal when he was present. Mr. Hitchcock was the most articulate person I ever met. And he always had specific ideas of what he wanted. I was amazed to see that his library in his large office contained more art books and current magazines on graphics than I owned. He would specify specific new type styles that he had seen advertised in *Graphis*, a magazine mostly graphic artists would get."

Hitchcock Braves Another Screening

During completion of the impressive contributions by Bernard Herrmann and Saul Bass, Hitchcock and editor George Tomasini sharpened the pace of the picture with minor trims. The collaborators cut unnecessary interchanges between Marion and Sam (in the hotel room), between Marion and Cassidy (the oilman who sexually harasses her), and between Sam and Lila. Also edited were shots of Marion hurrying from the hotel after her rendezvous with Sam, and of exteriors as she drives away from her house with the stolen money. By late spring, Hitchcock could feel more confident in the tighter 111-minute answer print that was now enhanced by a powerful musical score. Although he had been troubled by the mixed response to the first screening of the picture, Hitchcock knew that *Psycho* was in far better shape for its second. He invited to this screening the head of MCA, Lew Wasserman; novelist Robert Bloch; Bernard Herrmann; Janet Leigh and Tony Curtis, (Leigh's husband at the time); Hilton Green; Marshall Schlom; and most of the technical crew and their spouses. Even for Green, who had seen and liked the earlier cut, the movie was a revelation. "When the music came in," Green said, "it just knocked people out of their seats." Elaborated Schlom: "I was sitting in the back row with my wife, Mr. and Mrs. Hitchcock, and Hilton and his wife. It wasn't the shower sequence the wives and girlfriends were buzzing about. Everybody was saying, 'Wait till you see Marty [Balsam] getting killed.' But only Mr. Hitchcock, Hilton, and I knew that the form of the Arbogast scene had been changed [from the original Saul Bass montage]. So when Marty started up the stairs, and the camera pulled back, Mother's knife came in and Bernie Herrmann's music started shrieking, everybody came off their seats a good six inches! When even the fellows who photographed it were taken, we knew we were successful!"

Janet Leigh admitted, "Even though I knew what was going to come, I screamed. And even though I knew I was sitting there in that screening quite alive and well, it was a very emotional thing to see your own demise." Novelist Robert Bloch retains a clear recollection of Leigh and Hitchcock at the screening. "I sat in the front row of this dingy, drab, claustrophobic screening room," Bloch said. "When the screening was over, I vividly recall Hitchcock asking Janet Leigh what she thought of it. She said, 'When that knife went into me on the screen, I could feel it!' Hitchcock said, 'My dear, the knife *never* went into you.' She realized, and consequently so did I, that that was truly the case." (Or so Hitchcock wanted everyone to believe.) Leigh recalled: "What I said was, 'I *believed* that the knife went into me.' It was that real, that horrifying, though, of course, it *couldn't* to any extent because you could not show penetration."

Outside the screening room, Hitchcock and Bloch made their introductions, but when the director asked the novelist for his reactions, Bloch found himself at something of a loss. Just as screenwriter Stefano had expressed conflicting reactions to a screening of *Psycho*, so did Bloch to his screening. Bloch said, "I told him, 'I'll be frank. It's either going to be your biggest success or your biggest flop.' And that was precisely how I felt. Nobody could tell at that juncture how the public would react to something that graphic. My only real cavil was the psychological explanation. It could have been done in about one-third of the time, been perfectly clear to audiences, and given final momentum to the finale."

Bloch, an avowed Bernard Herrmann admirer ever since hearing the score for the William Dieterle-directed *The Devil and Daniel Webster* (1941), recalled that he was relieved that the composer never sought out his opinion of the *Psycho* score. "I simply didn't know how to take it," Bloch said. "It was quite innovative, discordant—not the sort of thing one usually expected to accompany that kind of motion picture. It threw me for a loop. I was not quite prepared for such *screeching.*"

Screenwriter Stefano viewed the revised cut of the picture at another screening. "It was much closer to what ultimately came out," Stefano observed. "I thought, 'That's a good picture,' but that's about all I felt." The writer found himself unable to reconcile the cutting of dialogue and images he felt would have encouraged audiences to feel the emotional impact of Marion's murder.. According to Stefano, Hitchcock had trimmed the very image that had most potently realized the poignancy of that death: a sustained, overhead shot of the lifeless body of Janet Leigh sprawled over the bathtub, her buttocks exposed.

"It was a perfectly heartbreaking shot that came right before the close-up of Janet's eyes," Stefano said, and even after thirty years he recalled the shot with brimming eyes. "That one shot really brought home the tragedy of a lost life. I have never seen anything more painful than to see that beauty murdered. It was so poetic and so hurtful." Hitchcock enraged Stefano by admitting he had axed the shot to appease the censors. The writer remembered arguing, "If you had cut it because you didn't want to arouse painful emotions—fine. But to cut it because the girl's buttocks were exposed? As if there were actually something sexual about it!"

In spite of his words, Stefano *did* also reproach Hitchcock for avoiding deep emotion. The unease Hitchcock appeared to feel toward letting *Psycho* be anything more than a straight-out shocker hit Stefano hard. According to the writer, at the first sign that the characters or situation might carry emotional weight, Hitchcock ridiculed or cut it. It was as if the financial and critical trouncing of the deeply felt *Vertigo* had scarred Hitchcock irrevocably when it came to self-exposure. "Any time I had tried to get across a few seconds of silent memory for a lost life, it got cut," Stefano complained. "He had also made some cuts for time toward the end of the movie that I felt bad about. It was a scene with Sam and Lila, the only point in the movie where you got the sense Sam was aware of the loss of this woman he had loved."

Hitchcock also showed the film to Saul Bass. The graphic designer said, "Frankly I was amazed that the shower sequence had the effect it did. I thought it was a very tight and effective little murder, but I didn't fully understand the impact it was going to have, how truly shocking the whole thing was."

Director vs. Censors, Round Two

Armed with a film that was nearly ready to face the world, Hitchcock further played with the press by announcing, on May 4, that his upcoming film had to do with "metaphysical sex." On the same day, he prepared to renew his battle with the censors, expecting the best but fearing the worst. Janet Leigh delighted in recalling: "He told me how he had planned all along to manipulate the censors by deliberately putting in things so bizarre, he could come back to them and say, 'Tsk-tsk. All right, I'll take *that* out, but you've got to give me this.' He bargained with them like the master he was."

Script supervisor Marshall Schlom acknowledged that Hitchcock practically rubbed his hands together in anticipation of springing the traps he had laid for the Shurlock office censors throughout the shooting. "In the shower scene, Mr. Hitchcock wanted to *suggest*, not show, the nudity," said Schlom of the key scene for which the censors were waiting. "But if you stop-frame and magnify it, there are definitely a couple of frames showing a bare breast and nipple." The censor board liaison for Paramount, Luigi Luraschi, took the film to the seven censors and waited for a reply. As expected, the board went berserk over the shower murder and requested that the scene be sent back to them for closer scrutiny. Luraschi complied and the verdict was returned: Three censors saw nudity; two did not. Memo from the Shurlock office to the Hitchcock office: "Please take out the nudity."

Marshall Schlom recalled, the following day, Hitchcock—murmuring his contrition and his intent to comply with the wishes of the Shurlock office—merely repacked the film. Without editing so much as a frame, he shipped it back to the censors. Now the three board members who *had* seen nudity the previous day did *not* and the two who did not now *did*. Much to the bemusement of Hitchcock and his staff, the shenanigans over who saw what dragged on for well over a week.

Marshall Schlom recalled: "Finally Mr. Hitchcock said, 'I will take out the nudity if you will allow me to keep the two people in bed in the opening.' They said, 'No.' He countered by saying, 'All right. If you leave the shower sequence as is, I will reshoot the opening, but I want you people on the set to tell me how you will pass it just watching it.' We scheduled a reshoot, but they never showed up, so we never shot it. And they finally agreed they didn't see the nudity in the shower sequence which, of course, was there all the time." As a sop to the Shurlock office, Hitchcock made minor cuts in dialogue, which brought down the running time of *Psycho* to 109 minutes.

9. PUBLICITY

The Care And Handling of *Psycho*

Having handily outwitted the censors, Hitchcock was free to turn his attentions to outsmarting the moviegoing public. By this time he was satisfied that he had realized his goals: He had made a picture unlike anything he had previously done and he had brought it in at a price. He was also soon to learn he had made a picture unlike anyone had ever seen. But how best to sell *Psycho* as a new kind of Hitchcock—one that went way beyond his usual "polite" thrills? First, Hitchcock concentrated not on the stars of the picture but on the title itself. Having taken a particular fancy to the title design for the book jacket by artist Tony Palladino, Hitchcock contacted the advertising agency, McCann-Erickson, to arrange a deal. "[Hitchcock] called me one day," artist Palladino said, "telling me it was a smashing design and that he thought it would be perfect for the ads for this film. He wanted the lettering to dominate the newspaper and poster advertising, with just a few photographs of the main actors. I found it exciting learning how absolutely pragmatic he was. He preplanned so carefully, he could skim off the fat. I really got the sense he respected creative accomplishment in others." Palladino received $5,000 for a complete buy-out of his concept, hardly a paltry sum when one considers that novelist Robert Bloch had received little more for the rights to the original book!

That mission accomplished, Hitchcock turned to another critical component of marketing. Script supervisor Schlom explained: "He worried that once the first audiences saw the movie, they'd tell the ending and that would kill the picture." In order to combat that probability and to enhance the aura of mystery surrounding the film, Hitchcock chose not to show the film in advance to critics or opinion-makers, a move that flew in the face of what is perceived as industry tradition and privilege. Hitchcock deflected the angry questions of some reporters by saying, "I would like the screening at dead of night in a deserted barn. Preferably a barn with owls." MCA president Lew Wasserman reportedly advised Hitchcock to book *Psycho* nationally in thousands of theaters directly following the prerelease engagement in two New York theaters on June 16. If word-of-mouth buried the picture, it was reasoned, the Hitchcock name would at least lure in the faithful for a week or two. Produced on such a tight budget, the picture might even stand a chance of breaking even. When a man of Wasserman's business acumen offered advice, men like Hitchcock took heed. Wasserman, a former agent of MCA, had rocked the movie business when he negotiated a profit-sharing deal for his client James Stewart on a Universal-International western, *Winchester '73* (1950), directed by Anthony Mann. The takings made Stewart a millionaire. Hitchcock bought Wasserman's strategy for booking *Psycho* and rode it to the last penny.

A screening of the film for executives at Paramount—studio chief Y. Frank Freeman among them—did not shake their view that the film was a decidedly minor, forgettable, even disreputable Hitchcock effort. They assumed *Psycho* would vanish quickly anyway, so they put no obstacles in the way of the director's policy of no screenings or preview showings. But what they did not know was that Hitchcock had in mind a publicity blitz that would rank as one of the most smoothly engineered of all time. Lacking a presold story, showy production values, or surefire box-office stars, Hitchcock maximized his three most exploitable commodities: the title, the shock climax, and his own persona as a roly-poly ringmaster of a macabre circus of horrors.

Hitchcock, Paramount publicity director Herb Steinberg, and several officers of the Paramount sales and publicity department decided to adhere to the decision to open the picture in a single prerelease engagement in a theater in New York. There, they would test an unusual ad campaign and audience admissions policy that—if successful—would be enforced throughout the country. Every newspaper and magazine ad would stress that "No one . . . BUT NO ONE . . . will be admitted to the theater after the start of each performance of *Psycho*." Other advertising campaigns for earlier movies had offered such warnings. In 1958, even Paramount's advertising manual for Hitchcock's *Vertigo*, for example, suggested issuing those hoary reproofs: "Don't tell the secret of *Vertigo*" and "No one will be seated during the last ten minutes of *Vertigo*." But for *Psycho*, Hitchcock and Paramount were to top not only their own ballyhoo gimmicks but also those used for such films as *Les Diaboliques*. With the blessing of Paramount's worldwide sales strategist George Weltner and executives Y. Frank Freeman and Barney Balaban, Hitchcock not only advised but also *insisted* that theater owners follow his decree against admitting patrons once the picture began; finally, he demanded the *enforcing* of his decree as a contractual prerequisite for any theater exhibitor who booked the film. In a bulletin to exhibitors, Hitchcock wrote, "I believe this is a vital step in creating the aura of mysterious importance this unusual motion picture so richly deserves."

Ticket buyers were accustomed to casually dropping in and out in the days when movie houses opened at 10:00 A.M. and double-features, short subjects, and previews of coming attractions ran continuously through late evening. Owners of several major theater chains feared that patrons would rebel at being told when and how they could view a movie—even by the mighty Hitchcock. Some chains rumbled about boycotts. Hitchcock stood fast. "I walk up and down here like Felix the Cat," the director told a reporter in his Paramount offices, "trying to dream up new plot ideas. I'm playing my game with the public—trying to outwit them. All that my writer and I do in scheming surprises can be destroyed by letting the viewer walk in during the middle of the picture."

To rationalize further to movie exhibitors the offbeat admission policy, Hitchcock and Paramount mailed to them two elaborate (and irresistibly hokey) sales manuals. Each book ran longer than twenty pages and Hitchcock personally detailed the whys and wherefores of his publicity gimmicks. Each also explained exactly how to enhance the aura of the film as a suspense "Event." Such Hollywood showmanship and hucksterism had been routine for major releases of the thirties and forties. By the fifties, with the inroads into movie patronage made by TV, this brand of all-the-stops-out exploitation was more commonly employed on 3-D pictures, widescreen Cinemascope spectacles, or fast-buck sex and horror "quickies."

In one of these manuals, "The Care and Handling of *Psycho*," Hitchcock is thus quoted alongside a reprint of the on-the-set article that had appeared in the *New York Times*:

> As you read the copy . . . please note that my own firm but non-belligerent stand on the top secrecy policy was recognized in the editorial cooperation of the mighty *Times* itself. I might add that this same pictorialized pastiche must certainly have piqued the curiosity of millions coast-to-coast.

For *Psycho*, Hitchcock and Paramount deemed no advertising ploy beneath them. Publicity materials included tips for hiring Pinkerton guards to enforce the admission policies. "This man of the law will not only handle lines and crowds admirably," advised Hitchcock, "but can also help your cashier explain our policy when doors are closed. Our experience has taught us that such explanations bring refund requests down to a bare minimum." The kits also boasted order forms for large lobby clocks to remind audiences of the starting times for the movie and also five-foot-high cardboard standees of Hitchcock's likeness to be used in conjunction with recorded messages to incoming and outgoing audiences. In one, the director said:

> How do you do, ladies and gentlemen. I must apologize for inconveniencing you this way. However, this queuing up and standing about is good for you. It will make you appreciate the seats inside. It will also make you appreciate *Psycho*. You see, *Psycho* is most enjoyable when viewed beginning at the beginning and proceeding to the end. I realize this is a revolutionary concept, but we have

discovered that *Psycho* is unlike most motion pictures, and does not improve when run backwards.

Theater owners were advised to mount speakers along the outside walls to broadcast other such recorded messages from Hitchcock:

The manager of this theater has been instructed, at the risk of his life, not to admit to the theater any persons after the picture starts. Any spurious attempts to enter by side doors, fire escapes, or ventilating shafts will be met by force. I have been told this is the first time such remarkable measures have been necessary . . . but then this is the first time they've ever seen a picture like *Psycho*.

Hitchcock even lectured theater managers across the nation on how to *show* the film:

Experience in all our opening engagements has shown us that it enhances the dignity and importance of *Psycho* to close your house curtains over the screen after the end-titles of the picture, and keep the theater dark for ½ minute. During these 30 seconds of stygian blackness, the suspense of *Psycho* is indelibly engraved in the mind of the audience, later to be discussed among gaping friends and relations. You will then bring up house lights of a greenish hue, and shine spotlights of this ominous hue across the faces of your departing patrons. Never, never, never will I permit *Psycho* to be followed immediately by a short subject or newsreel.

Alfred Hitchcock made certain that the print ads and lobby poster advertising did not repeat mistakes of the past. A proponent of the old Hollywood axiom, "If the picture flops, blame the ad campaign," Hitchcock had been made aware that many had judged as too "arty" the advertising campaign for his previous Paramount release, Vertigo. Posters and print ads for that film had featured evocatively stylized Saul Bass art suggesting a man and woman trapped in a vortex. The coffeehouse crowd got it; puzzled mainstream audiences stayed away. Hitchcock also took a cue from the differences between the European release posters for *Les Diaboliques* (disturbing graphic motifs suggesting elongated hands, murky waters, two figures lowering a wicker trunk by ropes) and the streamlined, hard-sell American ads (a photo of a terrified Vera Clouzot in a nightgown).

Anxious for *Psycho* advertising to avoid any possible ambiguity, Hitchcock had authorized photographer William "Bud" Fraker to capture a series of publicity shots of Janet Leigh standing and reclining, clad in a white bra and half-slip, and of John Gavin, semi-crouched and stripped to the waist; the shots, printed in tabloidlike half-tone and monochromed in bold yellow and orange-red, served as the "key art" for the ads. These photographs, besides being unambiguous, were to shatter taboos by becoming the first blatantly "suggestive" photographic images ever to advertise a mainstream Hollywood feature. To these were added publicity portraits of Vera Miles (stifling a scream as her hands clutch her face) and Anthony Perkins (doing likewise).

In the advertisements, Hitchcock also broke precedent with what had become another standard Hollywood practice: the re-use in advertising posters of the Saul Bass title designs used in the credit sequence. Commented title-letterer Harold Adler: "Saul liked to use very tall, thin type that looked very stylish in print but was not bold and sometimes hard to read." Hitchcock opted instead to employ in the posters and ads the title concept by Tony Palladino that had been effective on the cover of the original novel—bold, shattered letters. The cut-and-paste, tab-loid look of the posters and print ads was much in keeping with the jagged, jarring nature of the movie itself.

Yet perhaps Hitchcock's single most potent publicity gimmick was the three preview trailers for the film. They were produced at a total cost of $9,619.09, and one of them has become legendary. The trailers were shot by cinematographer and special effects expert Rex Wimpy over three days at the tail end of production: for about three hours on January 28, for five hours on January 29, and finally—using one of the leading ladies—on February 1. About one month prior to the openings of the film, Paramount released two of the three—the two being brief "teaser" trailers—to theaters nationwide. The first reinforced Hitchcock's policy that "No one but no one will be admitted to the theater after *Psycho* begins," while the second pushed secrecy. "Please don't tell the ending," Hitchcock scolded. "It's the only one we have." By far the most innovative was the third trailer—Hitchcock's six-minute tour of the Bates house and motel.

In the tradition of David O. Selznick's preview-of-coming-attractions trailer for *Gone With the Wind* and the Orson Welles trailer for *Citizen Kane*, Hitchcock wanted the public to glimpse no actual footage from *Psycho* in the previews. Such a ploy was not new to Hitchcock trailers. For his first Technicolor film, *Rope* (1948), he had also concocted an offbeat trailer that features a character who is murdered *before* the action of the film begins. Hitchcock assigned the writing of the trailer script for *Psycho* to James Allardice, one of his contract writers. Allardice, a play-wright (*At War With the Army*) and Emmy-winner (*The George Gobel Show*), generally scripted Hitchcock's lugubrious, sponsor-baiting lead-ins to *Alfred Hitchcock Presents*. Allardice devised a tongue-in-cheek script that cast Hitchcock as equal parts geek-show carnival barker and House of Horrors tour-guide. "Here we have a quiet little motel . . ." says the Master, shot from a bird's-eye angle as he stands before the motel set. "Tucked away off the main highway and, as you can see, perfectly harmless-looking, whereas it has now become known as the scene of the crime."

As the camera glides down for a close-up of Hitchcock, he explains:

> This motel also has, as an adjunct, an old house, which is, if I may say so, a little more sinister-looking, less innocent than the motel itself.

With the house now looming behind him, Hitchcock continues to lay it on:

> . . . And in this house the most dire, horrible events took place. I think we can go inside, because the place is up for sale. Although I don't know who's going to buy it now.
>
> In that window in the second floor, the one in front, that's where the woman was first seen. Let's go inside.

At the lower stair landing, Hitch halts:

> You see, even in daylight, this place looks a bit sinister. It was at the top of these stairs that the second murder took place. She came out of the door there and met the victim at the top. Of course, in a flash there was the knife, and in no time—

Hitchcock's fingers spiral and his features register mild disgust:

> . . . the victim tumbled and fell with a horrible crash, I think the back broke immediately, and hit the floor. It's difficult

to describe how the twisting of the [his fingers twitch] of the . . . well, I won't dwell on it. Come upstairs.

On the stair landing, Hitchcock prattles on:

Of course the victim, or should I say the victims, hadn't any idea of the kind of people they'd be confronted with in this house. Especially the woman. She was the weirdest and the most . . . well, let's go into her bedroom.

Hitchcock wanders into Mother's bedroom and points out features of interests:

Here's the woman's room, still beautifully preserved. And the imprint of her body on the bed where she used to lie. I think some of her clothes are still in the wardrobe. [He looks and shakes his head.] Bathroom.

This was the son's room, but we won't go in there because his favorite spot was the little parlor behind the office in the motel. Let's go down there.

Hitchcock leads the viewer into the parlor behind the motel office:

This young man, you had to feel sorry for him. After all, being dominated by an almost maniacal woman was enough to drive anyone to the extreme of, oh, well, let's go in.

The tour guide wanders about the parlor, indicating:

I suppose you'd call this his hideaway. His hobby was taxidermy. A crow here, an owl there. An important scene took place in this room. There was a private supper here. By the way, this picture [pointing to the painting on the wall] has great significance because . . . let's go along into cabin number one. I want to show you something there.

Hitchcock approves of the stark white bathroom of cabin one:

All tidied up. The bathroom. Oh, they've cleaned all this up now. Big difference. You should have seen the blood. The whole, the whole place was, well, it's too horrible to describe. Dreadful. And I tell you, a very important clue was found here. [He points to the toilet] Down there. Well, the murderer, you see, crept in here very silently—of course, the shower was on, there was no sound, and uh . . .

Shooting a look toward the opaque shower curtain, Hitchcock reaches out and tears it aside. A blonde in the stall screams and the screeching violins of Bernard Herrmann's score shred the air. The shrieking woman is Janet Leigh, right? Look closer. The blonde is none other than Hitchcock contractee Vera Miles in a wig.

The screen goes black and, over music *not* from the Bernard Herrmann score, a narrator says, "The picture you must see from the beginning—or not at all!"

As is the case with the movie itself, the trailer is a gigantic hoax, a gleefully macabre con game. In retrospect, the promotional reel might seem audacious for the amount of plot information Hitchcock divulges. However, the narration adheres to a basic Hitchcockian tenet of suspense: *Tell* the audience something awful is going to happen—in the bathroom, say—then let them work themselves into a lather anticipating the pay-off. A more surprising and revealing aspect to the trailer: How "on-the-nose" is the monologue written for Hitchcock by James Allardice. What Hitchcock *says* almost suggests the director's fear that prospective viewers needed to be prodded into seeing the house as "sinister" or Norman as someone "you had to feel sorry for." The trailer takes the bully approach, but overall it adroitly strews clues that lead nowhere, and protects the surprise that it is Janet Leigh, the biggest star, who comes to harm in the shower.

On completing the trailers, Hitchcock personally recorded close to a dozen radio commercials. "It is not true, as has been suggested," he intoned in one of these, "that *Psycho* frightens the moviegoer speechless. I understand a number of men sent their wives there in the hope that this was true." With the completion of his promotional tools, Hitchcock and Paramount closed the budget books on the film. Total production costs came to $806,947.55. By comparison, a Hitchcock half-hour television show of the day cost $129,000 an episode. In 1989, the cost of an average hour of prime-time television hovered at about $1 million; the budget for an average feature was about $16 million.

Just ahead of the release of the movie, Fawcett World Library reprinted *Psycho* in paperback, with a new cover design that stressed the film tie-in ("Alfred Hitchcock's most chilling movie from the novel by Robert Bloch"), cast credits, and two photographs of Janet Leigh. In addition, the ever-hammy Hitchcock posed for photographer Gordon Parks in a *Life magazine* spread to publicize the movie "about murder in a motel and an amateur taxidermist's strange way of showing filial love." Parks embedded the face of Hitchcock in the center of a huge, malevolent flower, his fist strangling a rose.

The more the director toyed with the press about his forty-seventh release, the more scribes descended on the actors to prise out information. "*Psycho* is the weirdy of all times," Vera Miles told gossiper Louella Parsons. "Of all Hitchcock thrillers, this is the one that will get people right out of their chairs. I'd like to tell you the plot, but when we started to work we all had to raise our right hands and promise not to divulge one word of the story." Lurene Tuttle, who appeared in the supporting role of the wife of the sheriff, angered the Hitchcock office by divulging to a local columnist that Anthony Perkins "dressed up as his own mother" in the film.

Knowing he had a final duty in launching his off-center film, the director and his wife, Alma, embarked on a halfhearted vacation-cum-promotional junket in advance of the opening of *Psycho* on June 16 at the DeMille and Baronet theaters in New York. From June 8 through June 21, Hitchcock would try to scare up business in New York, Boston, Philadelphia, and Chicago. On September 13, if the movie appeared to warrant the effort, the couple would fly to Europe to promote *Psycho* in London, Munich, Berlin, Frankfurt, and Paris. Neither Alma nor Alfred Hitchcock knew it at the time, but these trips and the film that they were to promote would forever alter their professional lives.

10. THE RELEASE

The World Goes *Psycho*

Psycho opened during the summer of a boom-time America. The population stood at just over 180 million and the median income at $5,700. 1960 seemed a year of optimism for most white Americans, but discord and upheaval thrummed just beneath the country's chrome-and-vinyl surface. While Broadway theatergoers caught the show from center orchestra seats at $8.60, kidnapper-rapist Caryl Chessmann had been put to death in the gas chamber at San Quentin on May 2. It was the year when the marriage of those sweethearts of TV, Lucy and Desi, came apart at the seams. The average secretary—like Marion Crane—earned about $75 a week, and could sip a five-cent glass of Coke and hum along to such jukebox hits as "Theme from 'A Summer Place,'" "Teen Angel," "Put Your Head on My Shoulder," or "Everybody's Somebody's Fool." Adolf Eichmann stood trial in Israel as a ruthless exterminator of Jews. Ted Williams retired from the Red Sox after slamming his 521st homer, and the "King of the Movies," Clark Gable, died weeks after making *The Misfits* with Marilyn Monroe. Elvis, another show business king, returned from the army after a two-year hitch.

Audiences flocked to movies starring box-office favorites Doris Day, Rock Hudson, Cary Grant, Elizabeth Taylor, Debbie Reynolds, Tony Curtis, Sandra Dee, Frank Sinatra, Jack Lemmon, and John Wayne. It was a time when a Chevrolet Bel-Air cost $2,818 and ads urged us to "Move on Up to Schlitz," or posed the burning question: "Is it true blondes have more fun?" America's favorite mom, Jane Wyatt, won an Emmy for *Father Knows Best*, and our favorite G-man, Robert Stack, won his for *The Untouchables*.

Psycho was sprung upon a moviegoing public who might feel naughty or adventurous enough to stray to an occasional *La Dolce Vita* or *The Virgin Spring*. But a swell time at the movies for most Americans ran more along the lines of *Exodus*, *From the Terrace*, *Journey to the Center of the Earth*, or *Sunrise at Campobello*. Families gathered around televisions tuned to *I Love Lucy*, *Bachelor Father*, *The Flintstones*, *Hawaiian Eye*, and *This is Your Life*. No wonder Paramount and Hitchcock were slightly anxious when when the National Legion of Decency of the Roman Catholic Church gave *Psycho* a "B" rating: "Morally objectionable in part for all." There were rumblings about further sanctions, but they came to nothing.

By the late eighties, *Psycho* had been endorsed by such diverse critics as film theorist Robin Wood, who called it "one of the key works of our age," and director Peter Bogdanovich, who termed it "probably the most visual, most cinematic picture [Hitchcock] ever made." Critic Peter Cowie calls it "not only Hitchcock's greatest film; it is the most intelligent and disturbing horror film ever made." But this praise came twenty years after the movie's debut. When it opened on June 16, 1960, *Psycho* won only mid-dling-to-hostile reaction from New York critics. In spite of that, the response of the public to the movie surprised everyone. From the first day, lines began forming on Broadway just after 8:00 A.M. and did not let up until the late night show. Who would have expected it? The manicured nails of Paramount executives scratched their heads in wonder: Is the response a midsummer *fluke*, peculiar only to heat-crazed New Yorkers? From the earliest indicators, Hitchcock's publicity stunts were going over like gang-busters. Ticket holders standing in line grilled the patrons who poured out of the theater laughing, outraged, shaken: "What's the ending?" The answer came back from most: "You've gotta see it for yourself!" Customers *were not* revealing Hitchcock's trick conclusion.

"I recall it opened on Sunday in New York," said Marshall Schlom, for whom life had returned to business-as-usual, working on a Hitchcock TV show directly after completing *Psycho*. (June 16, 1960 was in fact a Thursday). "The next morning, we got these stories from theater owners who were calling the distribu-tion exchanges telling them about people going berserk in the audience, running up and down the aisles. It was mayhem. They had to call the cops." At 9:00 A.M., a telegram arrived from Lew Wasserman: "What will you do for an encore?"

Only when *Psycho* shattered attendance records and unleashed further pandemonium upon its June 22 openings at the Para-mount Theater in Boston, the Arcadia in Philadelphia, and the Woods Theater in Chicago did Hitchcock and Paramount grasp that the picture was rapidly growing into an audience phenom-enon. "Must report three faintings at Paramount Theater and expect many more among trade when weeks' [box-office] figure published," cabled a Boston exhibitor. "Paramount didn't think they had anything special," screenwriter Joseph Stefano said.

"Once they found out they did, they and Hitchcock poured lots more money into promotion."

On the heels of his East Coast promotional tour, Hitchcock consulted with the Paramount sales and promotion staff in California. For months, the walls of the Hitchcock production offices in the Producer's Building at the studio rumbled like an earthquake epicenter. Nationwide bulletins poured in about state police who had to be called in to untangle drive-in theater gridlock, and about quick-thinking concessionaires who used golf carts to sell snacks to patrons waiting in their cars. A frantic theater manager called Paramount from Chicago: *Psycho* ticket holders caught in line in a downpour were threatening to dismantle the Woods Theater unless the manager let them inside. Finally, Hitchcock intercepted the calls. "Buy them umbrellas," advised the director as glibly as Marie Antoinette, and buy them umbrellas the manager did. The act and the quote won Hitchcock reams of free publicity when they made front-page news in the morning edition.

No amount of optimism or carefully orchestrated hucksterism could have prepared anyone—least of all Alfred Hitchcock—for the firestorm the film was creating. Certainly no one could have predicted how powerfully *Psycho* tapped into the American subconscious. Faintings. Walk-outs. Repeat visits. Boycotts. Angry phone calls and letters. Talk of banning the film rang from church pulpits and psychiatrists' offices. Never before had any director so worked the emotions of the audience like stops on an organ console. Only the American public first knew what a monster Hitchcock had spawned. "The atmosphere surrounding *Psycho* was deeply charged with apprehension," wrote film theorist William Pechter, describing how it felt to watch the film with an audience of the day. "Something awful is always about to happen. One could sense that the audience was constantly aware of this; indeed, it had the solidarity of a convention assembled on the common understanding of some unspoken *entente terrible;* it was, in the fullest sense, an audience; not merely the random gathering of discrete individuals attendant at most plays and movies."

Star Janet Leigh graciously avoided any public showing of *Psycho* because she believed her mere presence would dispel the impact of the movie on others. "A theater manager told me about a little boy who went to the first showing the first day it opened," said Leigh, whose enormous popularity with audiences at the time created crowds wherever she went. "They emptied the theater and the little boy went back to every show that day. He kept running up and down the aisles yelling, 'Oh my gosh, oh my gosh—wait till you see what's going to happen!'"

Joseph Stefano and his wife invited a group of their friends to a theater on the day *Psycho* opened in Los Angeles. "As the movie went on," the writer said with a laugh, "I saw people grabbing each other, howling, screaming, reacting like six-year-olds at a Saturday matinee. I couldn't believe what was happening. I found it hard to reconcile our movie with how the audience was reacting. I *never* thought it was a movie that would make people scream. When Marion Crane was in the shower and audiences saw the woman coming toward her, I thought they'd shudder and go 'How awful,' but I never thought they'd be so vocal. And neither did Hitchcock. When the shower sequence was over, paralysis set in. Nobody knew quite what to do."

Anthony Perkins also asserts that audience response to the humor in *Psycho* caught Hitchcock short. "It's not scrupulously clear," Perkins said, "what Hitchcock's specific and precise intentions were for the tone of the film. But, after hearing audiences around the country *roar,* Hitchcock—perhaps reluctantly—acknowledged that it was OK to laugh at the film and that, perhaps, it was a comedy after all. He *didn't* realize how funny audiences would find the movie, generally. More importantly, I don't think he was prepared for the amount and intensity of the on-the-spot laughs that he got from first-run audiences around the world. He was confused, at first, incredulous second, and despondent third."

To Perkins, Hitchcock confided, "I've always been able to predict the audience's reaction. Here, I haven't been able to." With his movie provoking unexpectedly vocal screams and laughter, Hitchcock petitioned studio head Lew Wasserman to let him "remix" the film to keep those reactions from running rough-shod over the dialogue. Referring to the scene that immediately followed Norman's sinking Marion's car in the swamp, Anthony Perkins recalled, "The entire scene in the hardware store [in which a woman is buying rat poison and Lila visits Sam] was practically inaudible because of the leftover howls from the previous scene. Lew Wasserman talked Hitch out of putting more volume into some of the scenes, saying 'You can't do that. We've already made our prints.'"

Alfred Hitchcock undertook a full-scale publicity tour for *Psycho* only when he was convinced that he had a freak block-buster on his hands. "Generally, once he finished a publicity tour," Marshall Schlom explained, "Mr. Hitchcock was quite anxious to get moving into preproduction for his next film or working with a new writer. *Psycho* stopped everything else cold." Relentlessly and adroitly, the director continued to promote the movie around the world. Wherever the movie played, the scene was the same: long lines, audiences on the knife-edge of screams and laughter, and Hitchcock stoking his newly minted legend as a master of shock.

To the picture's domestic success—$9.5 million revenue from its first thirteen thousand theatrical engagements—was added another $6 million in international grosses. Only *Ben-Hur* made more money in America. But the location shooting, expensive cast, mammoth sets, and $15 million budget of that William Wyler epic meant it had cost about sixteen times what *Psycho* had. Hitchcock expected that his fellow filmmakers might acknowledge his achievement. "He gloried in economy," cameraman Leonard South observed. "He made *Psycho* out of nothing and that's what appealed to him."

As for the first wave of mixed critical response to *Psycho*, Hitchcock had learned to take the "wait and see" attitude. Such previous Hitchcock films as *Foreign Correspondent, Shadow of a Doubt, Notorious, North by Northwest,* and *Vertigo*—today acknowledged as superior entries—had also won varied critical response at the time of their release. The "turnaround" phenomena that had occurred with several of his movies prompted the director to observe, "My movies go from failures to masterpieces, without ever being successes!" Such a reversal of critical opinion had never allowed Hitchcock to balm his ego with regard to such efforts as *Jamaica Inn, The Paradine Case,* or *Stage Fright.* Still, the director seemed to trust that *Psycho* would meet a happier end.

Screenwriter Joseph Stefano said: "Hitch was annoyed [that *Psycho*] had gotten some bad reviews based, he felt, on the fact he hadn't let the critics see it in advance. In fact, one critic actually told me that's why he panned the movie." John Russell Taylor, film critic for the *London Times* from the early sixties through 1973, observed: "Many of the critics were alienated by being required to see the film with an ordinary audience, and being refused admission if they arrived late." In 1978, Kenneth Tynan wrote in the *London Observer:* "Hitchcock's major sin was to have antagonized the critics before they ever saw the picture. He had urged them by letter not to divulge the ending, and he had announced that nobody would be admitted to the cinema once the film had begun. Thus they went to the press show already huffy and affronted; and what they reviewed was not so much the film itself as the effect of its publicity on their egos."

Janet Leigh, accustomed to more often being underestimated than attacked by critics, defended the Hitchcock screening strategy: "To have a few critics looking at the film in a screening room would have been a mistake." Undoubtedly. Yet beyond any annoyance that critics might have felt toward Hitchcock's promotional stunts, nothing the director had previously made had prepared critics or audiences for the black comedy or hair-raising Gothic horror of *Psycho*.

"A blot on an honorable career," wrote Bosley Crowther of the *New York Times*, who complained that *Psycho* was ". . . slowly paced for Mr. Hitchcock and given over to a lot of detail." However, Crowther led a contingent of critics who would later revise their opinions. He ranked the movie on his ten best list of 1960 and, in 1965, praised Roman Polanski's *Repulsion* as "a psychological thriller in the classic style of *Psycho*.'" Critic Wanda Hale, in a four-star review in the *New York Daily News*, found the film more to her liking: "The suspense builds up slowly but surely to an almost unbearable pitch of excitement. Anthony Perkins's performance is the best of his career—Janet Leigh has never been better."

Esquire critic Dwight MacDonald thought *Psycho* "merely one of those television shows padded out to two hours by adding pointless subplots and realistic detail" and believed it "a reflection of a most unpleasant mind, a mean, sly, sadistic little mind." On the other hand, Andrew Sarris in the *Village Voice* judged *Psycho* as "[the] first American movie since *Touch of Evil* to stand in the same creative rank as the great European films." Paul F. Buckley of the *New York Herald Tribune* found it "rather difficult to be amused at the forms insanity may take," but added that the movie "keeps your attention like a snake charmer." Justin Gilbert of the *New York Daily Mirror* thought the film was "played out perfectly," the performances "excellent." "This one is forked lightning," Gilbert wrote, calling it "a scary startler, shake 'n' shock brand." The *Time* reviewer was persuaded that he had seen ". . . one of the messiest, most nauseating murders ever filmed. At close range, the camera watches every twitch, gurgle, convulsion and hemorrhage in the process by which a living human becomes a corpse." The following year, the same magazine ranked William Castle's *Homicidal*—a hilariously hambone, poor man's *Psycho*—on its top ten. By 1966, *Time* had revised its opinion and now described *Psycho* as "superlative" and "masterly."

When *Psycho* stormed through Europe and South America in September and October, critical opinion was also divided. Across two continents and over three months, Hitchcock, along with Paramount vice-president Jerry Pickman and advertising and publicity chief Martin Davis, touted his new nerve-jangler. The first stop on the publicity tour was England, where he told an English journalist, "People are going to be shocked when they see my new picture. There are some horrible goings on. It isn't anything like my other films. People are always saying I fall back on the old theme—the average man caught up in bizarre situations. This will show them."

Before British censors rated the film with an "X" Certificate, they sliced a shot of Anthony Perkins studying his bloodstained hands in the bathroom. Also deleted were six frames of Mother's taking a knife to Detective Arbogast at the foot of the stairs. [Audiences in some American cities, thanks to cuts demanded by the National Legion of Decency, never saw those shots either]. Perhaps, as some have observed, the judgment of some critics toward Hitchcock's film may have been skewed not only because they had been invited to a showing with the paying public but also because they had to wade through thirty-five minutes of short subjects and preview trailers. "One of the most vile and disgusting films ever made," wrote one critic. The scribe for *Sight and Sound* declared, "*Psycho* comes nearer to attaining an exhilarating balance between content and style than anything Hitchcock has done in years," but called it "a very minor work." V. F. Perkins in *Oxford Opinion*, perhaps to chide his colleague, prescribed a second viewing: "The first time it is only a splendid entertainment, a 'very minor film' in fact. But when one can no longer be distracted from the characters by an irrelevant 'mystery' *Psycho* becomes immeasurably rewarding as well as much more thrilling." The same critic particularly singled out as "spectacularly brilliant" the acting of Janet Leigh, Anthony Perkins, and Martin Balsam and the "layers of tension" Hitchcock was able to tease out of their scenes together. "Even Tennessee Williams is here outclassed," wrote the critic, "in the business of demonstrating the presence of something unspoken." V. F. Perkins concluded that the subject matter of the movie was "fit only for a tragedian. And that is what Hitchcock finally shows himself to be."

The critic for the *Daily Express* headlined his review "Murder in the Bathtub and Boredom in the Stalls" and wrote, "It is sad to see a really big man make a fool of himself." Another reviewer observed: "When the thrill king starts dredging this kind of cesspool, it's time for him to abdicate." The review from the delightfully acidic C.A. Lejeune promised not to give away the ending "for the simple reason that I grew so sick and tired of the whole beastly business that I didn't stop to see it. Your edict may keep me out of the theater, my dear Hitchcock, but I'm hanged if it will keep me in." Wrote a critic for *Cahiers du Cinéma*, "This film is constructed like Dante's *Inferno*, in concentric circles that get narrower and narrower and deeper and deeper. Every scene is a lesson in direction by its precision, its sharpness, its efficacy, but also its beauty. Perhaps Hitchcock half-abandons himself in this film; or why, between the images of *Psycho*, did I believe that I overheard the secrets of a man of sixty?"

Undoubtedly to the relief of Hitchcock, surprisingly few critics—even the French—commented upon the obvious debt that *Psycho* owed to *Les Diaboliques*. The director tended to claim haughty indifference toward the work of his American contemporaries. Apparently, he felt freer in adapting the best moves of a European contemporary. Similarities between *Les Diaboliques* and *Psycho* range from surface matters—black-and-white cinematography; the grubby milieu of rented rooms and humdrum jobs; the merciless, despairing tone and careworn characters; the matching hairdos of Janet Leigh and Simone Signoret—to thematic, visual, and structural motifs. For example, like heroines Nicole Horner and Christina Delasalle in *Les Diaboliques*, the desperate, impulsive Marion Crane precipitates her mistaking someone else's cash as a way out of her "private trap." In the "second act" of both films, a soiled, Everyman-type detective—Inspector Fichet (Charles Vanel) in the earlier film, Milton Arbogast (Martin Balsam) in the later—arrives to bedevil the lead characters. Like Clouzot with his corpse in the bathtub, Hitchcock stages his central, horrific murder set piece in a shower. The scheming heroines in *Les Diaboliques* conceal a corpse in a fetid swimming pool; *Psycho* provides Norman Bates with a hungry, convenient swamp. *Les Diaboliques* features big close-ups of a gulping Adam's apple (in the latter movie, Norman swallows the Kandy Korn when Arbogast interrogates him) and also of a bathtub drain. And clearly, the raison d'être of both films appears to be the surprise, "twist" finale.

Even the pronouncements that Hitchcock and Clouzot made about their films sound a similar note. "I sought," Clouzot observed, "only to amuse myself and the little child who sleeps in all our hearts—the child who hides her head under the bed-covers and begs, 'Daddy, Daddy, frighten me.'" Hitchcock said: "*Psycho* is a film that was made with quite a sense of amusement on my part. To me, it's a fun picture . . . It's rather like taking [the audience] through the haunted house at the fairground or the roller-coaster."

Drawing such comparisons between films and their makers would have required that mainstream critics look more analyti-cally than was the style of the day at "genre" or mass entertainment films. It would also have required that critics take with a grain of salt the public pronouncements such entertainers as Hitchcock made about their work. As critic Robin Wood observed of Hitch-cock's jolly, intellectually elusive public persona in 1965: "Never trust the artist, trust the tale." Wood remarked of Hitchcock's press statements about the "fun" aspects of *Psycho*: "This, need-less to say, must not affect one's estimate of the film itself. For the maker of *Psycho* to regard it as a 'fun' picture can be taken as his means of preserving his sanity; for the critic to do so—and to give it his approval on these grounds—is quite unpardonable. Hitchcock . . . is a much greater artist than he knows."

Yet at the time of the release of *Psycho*, deep-focus critical exam-inations of popular "entertainment" movies had not yet come into vogue. In the early sixties, critic Andrew Sarris adapted and imported to America the *politique des auteurs*, or auteur theory, first espoused in Paris by François Truffaut in 1954. Truffaut and such other contributors to *Cahiers du Cinéma* as Eric Rohmer and Claude Chabrol—each of whom would soon become film-makers themselves—viewed the director as the "author" of the film. True auteur status was conferred only upon the director whose filmmaking style, strong personality, and preoccupations stamped movie after movie. Thus, *Cahiers* critics and their acolytes mined such films as Hitchcock's *The Wrong Man*, John Ford's *The Searchers*, or Howard Hawks's *Rio Bravo* for nuance, theme, symbolism, and subtext as carefully as other critics might examine the offerings of Michelangelo Antonioni, Ingmar Bergman, Federico Fellini, or Alain Resnais. As Vincent Canby summed it up in the *New York Times*, "In the *Cahiers* credo, if an apple could inspire a great painting, a murder mystery—a *Laura* or *Psycho* or *The Lady from Shanghai*—could be a great film."

In 1957, Rohmer and Chabrol published in France the first book-length study of Alfred Hitchcock. The soon-to-be directors examined Hitchcock's first forty-four films, with special attention to his Catholicism and on such recurring motifs as the "transfer of guilt" between an "innocent" hero and a "less innocent" anti-hero or heroine. With the subsequent publication in 1966 by Truffaut of his book-length conversations with Hitchcock, the Master of Suspense could hope for no more culturally impeccable a trio of champions. Truffaut, who had made a striking transition from theorist to director, was already acclaimed as a leader of the French "New Wave" for such films as *The 400 Blows* and *Jules and Jim*. Truffaut had also helped make it possible for Jean-Luc Godard to do *Breathless*, another milestone of the new filmmaking movement. Such other films as *Hiroshima, Mon Amour* and *The Lovers*, from *Cahiers du Cinéma*-influenced directors, made the "New Wave" filmmakers the toasts of the festival circuit. Truffaut argued persuasively for taking Hitchcock seriously as an artist. By the time of the publication *Hitchcock/Truffaut*, *Psycho* had been declared a work of art by many observers and Hitchcock a cult figurehead. Truffaut left to such other critics as Peter Bogdanovich, John Russell Taylor, and Robin Wood the task of elevating Hitchcock to an icon.

Yet in 1960, most of the worldwide pop-cultural and critical enshrinement for the movie and its director still lay several years ahead. For the time being, however, Hitchcock might balm any pain he felt from the stings of the critics with thoughts of the extraordinary box-office takings. In Colombia, where the movie was called *Psicosis*, records toppled as they did throughout South America, Portugal, Italy, Germany, India, and China. In Paris, where it was called *Psychose*, the movie earned $34,000 in five days, prompting a jubilant exhibitor to cable Paramount that it "far exceed[ed] anything we have ever seen."

With the mixed notices for Hitchcock came an almost uni-lateral dismissal of the source novel by Robert Bloch. Many observers judged the book vastly inferior to the screenplay by Joseph Stefano. Observed Bloch, who continues to take exception to the charges decades later: "Most film 'historians,' particularly the British, wrote that *Psycho* was a short story in a cult maga-zine or that Hitchcock took this little thing and blew it up into something bigger. The inference being that he introduced all the things that seemed to make the film work—killing the heroine early in the story, killing her off in the shower, taxidermy—when, of course, they're all in the book."

What appeared to offend Bloch even more was his perception that screenwriter Stefano had done little to discourage the belief that *he* was the author of *Psycho*. In *Who's Who in America*, the biographical entry for Mr. Stefano lists him as author of the "orig-inal screenplay" for *Psycho*, as well as of *The Naked Edge* (1961), a thriller directed by Michael Anderson and starring Gary Cooper and Deborah Kerr. The latter is actually based on *First Train to Babylon* by Max Erlich. *The Naked Edge* was also promoted with the line "Only the man who wrote *Psycho* could write *The Naked Edge*." In 1969, Universal advertised *Eye of the Cat*, based on a Stefano screenplay, with a similar tag line.

Although Hitchcock could never be accused of magnanimity in the matter of credit, there is some suggestion that he shared the umbrage felt by Bloch. The director told interviewer Charles Higham, "The screenplay writer contributed dialogue mostly, no ideas." Robert Bloch said, "That Hitch himself began to give me credit for the thing was kind. Had I [written] the script, I would have known I couldn't have had a Rod Steiger-type up there on the screen. That would have been about as 'surprising' as having Flora Robson puttering around and revealing her—gasp!—as the killer in the final reel. To put in a red herring by making Norman a younger, more personable man was visually correct and worked perfectly. I started the novel with Norman without going to an interlude between the heroine and her boyfriend. He also expanded the trip to the motel and introduced the possible pursuer in the form of the state trooper. Other than that, he stuck very, very closely to the novel. It's all there, right down to the final sentence, 'I wouldn't even harm a fly.'"

World audiences saw slightly different versions of the picture, depending upon local censors. On November 21, censors in Singapore shortened the stabbing of Detective Arbogast and excised the second shot of the mummified corpse of Mrs. Bates. British censors, having already eliminated the shots of Norman staring at his bloodstained hands while cleaning up after the murder of Marion, made further cuts in dialogue. Despite these variations, *Psycho* continued to pack theaters throughout the summer and into the fall of 1960. Repeat business was strong. In the parlance of the industry, the picture had "legs." On his return from Europe, Hitchcock received from Paramount a check for the first-quarter returns: $2.5 million. Hitchcock dutifully filed and categorized the more coherent or amusing of the thousands of letters he received about the movie. Among the letters were several from critic Bosley Crowther of the *New York Times*, who had originally called the movie "a blot" on Hitchcock's career. As *Psycho* developed into a cultural phenomenon, Crowther revised his judgment in print and called Hitchcock's movie a worthy successor to Fritz Lang's *M* (1931) and to Henri-Georges Clouzot's *Les Diaboliques*. By the time of Crowther's August 28, 1960, piece in the *Times*, the critic raised his voice with those defending *Psycho* against censorship and outright banning. Surely Hitchcock might have savored the irony.

Other "fan" letters might have cut Hitchcock—the compleat detail man—to the quick. Multiple complaints from ophthalmologists pointed out a technical gaffe: In the extreme close-up of Janet Leigh after the violent stabbing, the pupils of her eyes should have been *dilated*, not contracted. "A simple drop of belladonna would have handled it," chided one doctor. The director made restitution for his error in *Frenzy* (1972) in the insistent, freeze-frame close-up of actress Barbara Leigh-Hunt, who played the victim of rape and strangulation by a psychotic fruit seller. Her pupils were dilated in the proper manner of poststrangulation.

Hitchcock also saved many laudatory fan letters, but the wrathful letters outnumbered those. One woman wrote, "I don't give a Goddam whether you continue to make movies like *Psycho* because, believe me, I will not be viewing them." A favorite of the director was the offended Canadian classical music fan who voiced an objection to the close-up of Beethoven's *Eroica* during the scene in which Vera Miles searches the bedroom of Norman Bates. He called it "a direct insult to the composer and a very poor attempt to prove that his music is good for lunatics only."

Naturally, the notoriety surrounding *Psycho* only served to ensure its high status among the most seen and written-about movies of 1960. "At the time we were making *Psycho*," assistant director Hilton Green admitted, "I don't think any of the crew felt we were making anything but a good movie. At the time it came out, it was not a critical blockbuster. But it just *gained* and *gained* over time." Hitchcock cameraman Leonard South claimed that, originally, *Psycho* "embarrassed" the director. "'Here's this bloody piece of crap,'" the director told South, "'and the money doesn't stop coming in.'" Similarly, writer Joseph Stefano recalled a luncheon meeting with Hitchcock shortly after the opening of the movie. "I walked in, seeing Hitch for the first time since all the rumpus and commotion started. He gave me this completely baffled look and just shrugged his shoulders." Costumer Rita Riggs, whom Hitchcock would hire for his next two pictures, said, "Mr. Hitchcock was *stunned* that this simple, black-and-white picture made so much money. I remember him saying, 'Now I have to hurry up and do another picture because of taxes!'"

Not all of the critical and public scrutiny under which *Psycho* put Hitchcock was welcomed. Since the thirties, the director had been accustomed to banking on his own quotability. Yet never before had his press statements been sifted by sociologists and psychologists for hidden meaning and implication. And never before had Hitchcock been publicly taken to task for the moral vision that one of his films allegedly expressed. *Psycho* began to be cited in discussions of serious and frivolous phenomena: the rise in crime; the decline in sales of opaque shower curtains; the alarming upswing in violence, particularly toward women; the downturn in motel stays. In interviews, Hitchcock hid behind the breezy speeches and patter that James Allardice wrote for him. Hitchcock willingly wore the mask of a maker of "*fun* pictures." It seemed the director would not—or could not—respond to such charges any other way.

A nineteen-year-old man, Leroy Pinkowski, drew a life sentence for the "thrill slaying" stabbing of a fourteen-year-old. Pinkowski allegedly admitted that he had seen *Psycho* several times and that it had influenced him. When police convicted twenty-nine-year-old Henry Adolph Busch of slaying three elderly women, he also allegedly cited the Hitchcock movie as his inspiration. Reporters pressed Hitchcock for a statement. "These boys have killed before," the director responded, inaccurately in the case of one of the young men. "I want to know what movie they saw those times, or did they do it after drinking chocolate milk?"

For *Redbook* magazine, Hitchcock agreed to talk with psychiatrist Dr. Fredric Wertham, an author and outspoken critic of media violence. The published account of their dialogue suggests that Hitchcock was not about to be pinned down. Wertham, after admitting that he had not seen *Psycho*, tried several times to get the director to admit that the violence in the film was "A little stronger than you would have put in formerly—say ten or fifteen years ago?" Hitchcock replied, "I have *always* felt that you should do the minimum on the screen to get the maximum audience effect. Sometimes it is necessary to go into some element of violence, but I only do it if I have a strong reason." Wertham persisted: "But wasn't this violence stronger than your usual dose?" Eventually, Hitchcock conceded: "It was." "More?" asked Wertham. "More," Hitchcock replied. So it went for Wertham, and one suspects that it was, for him, much like dealing with a particularly defensive patient.

The psychiatrist may have hoped to elicit from Hitchcock at least an artistic, if not moral, justification for that violence. Yet one is left with the clear impression that Hitchcock might justify the bloodletting in *Psycho* similarly to the way in which he had justified to François Truffaut the risqué opening scenes. "Audiences," Hitchcock said, "are changing. I think that nowadays you have to show them the way they themselves behave most of the time." Thus, the filmmaker implied that he was a reporter, not a shaper, of human behavior.

In other magazines and forums, Hitchcock also played the role of glib entertainer. Penelope Houston, author of "The Figure in the Carpet," a major assessment of Hitchcock in *Sight and Sound*, asked Hitchcock, "What is the deepest logic of your films?" and he answered: "To put the audience through it." To the man whose daughter would not bathe after seeing *Les Diaboliques* or shower since *Psycho*, Hitchcock suggested: "Dry cleaning." Such statements and others like them only fueled the argument of those who contended that *Psycho* was the creation of a cynical, irresponsible filmmaker whose sole allegiance was to the box office. One had only to *see Psycho* truly—or almost any other Hitchcock work—to discover what the director was actually "about." Beneath the shock and suspense tactics lies a reservoir of profound understanding of the fragility of life. Lurking beneath the adventure and thrills is Hitchcock's outrage toward the cruelty we inflict upon each other in the name of love.

Should Hitchcock have spelled out his philosophy and thematic concerns or should he simply have hoped that audiences and critics would discover those for themselves? One could argue either way. "I'm more interested in the technique of storytelling by means of film rather than in what the film contains," he said, disclaiming any intellectual content in his films. But Hitchcock the interviewee often struck one as more facile than erudite, more cleverly concealing than revelatory. Further, as a moviemaker, he impressed one as more informed by craft, passion, and intuition than by erudition. In any event, Hitchcock seemed content to utter things like, "I could never have made a film like *Psycho* without a sense of humor." He let his films do the real talking.

From *Psycho* onward, Hitchcock would be interviewed and profiled as never before. The movie that solidified his status as one of Hollywood's most imitated, envied, and powerful directors also caused him to be studied, psychoanalyzed, tried, and judged from the armchair. There are indications that the international hullabaloo over *Psycho* disoriented the delicate internal clockwork that ran Hitchcock's world. "He had been a man without much ego," observed cameraman Leonard South, who had known the director since 1950. "He only knew that he was successful, that he could put on film the things that his mind could dream up." Writer Joseph Stefano commented: "*Psycho* had much more of an effect on Hitchcock than Hitchcock had on it. A man goes for years and years feeling he's not properly appreciated—although he's loved, respected, well-paid—but deep down, he feels that nobody *really* knows how good he is. Suddenly, with this strange little picture, there begins all this rumbling about his work, about *who* he *is*. 'They' began to say, 'You were right. You really *are* good!' Hitchcock went to pieces. I think it just blew his mind. He got his dream and it only made him more frightened. Who knows? Maybe he didn't think he was all that good."

No matter how Hitchcock assessed his own work, slowly but surely after *Psycho*, the moviemaking and journalistic worlds would begin *telling* him just how good he was. Hitchcock career retrospectives at major museums throughout the world became commonplace. Much of that to-do rapidly accelerated after the embracing of *Psycho* by the *Cahiers* critics. "If there is anyone who loves to hear the art of the director extolled," wrote Vincent Canby describing the auteurist adulation of Hitchcock, Howard Hawks, and others in the *New York Times*, "it is the director. [Admirers of Hawks and Hitchcock] suffered through *I was a Male War Bride* [Hawks, 1949] and *The Farmer's Wife* [Hitchcock, 1928], and the directors submitted equally uncomfortably to hours of exhaustive interviews by erudite French historians." Hitchcock may have tried to mask his ambivalent responses to the attention that *Psycho* had brought on. Yet some within the Hitchcock camp believed that a new self-consciousness had already begun to creep in.

Talking to an interviewer from *TV Guide* about a review in *The New Yorker* that described an aspect of *Psycho* as "unconscious,"

Hitchcock railed, "The stupid idiots! As if I don't *know* what I'm doing. My technique is serious. I am *consciously* aware of what I am doing in *all* my work." Stefano asserted: "I think [Hitchcock] was appalled and a little *insulted* by having made such a low-budget movie and getting a response such as he'd never gotten before, even when he'd spent all that money and done such lavish things. It was like serving people extraordinary feasts time after time, then serving hot dogs and they say, 'This is the best thing I've ever tasted!' What happened to all those great meals I've served?"

Several Hitchcock associates suggest that *Psycho*, besides increasing Hitchcock's self-awareness, also may have heightened his uncertainty as to his next, best career move. One collaborator speculated that Hitchcock may have poured Herculean effort into promoting *Psycho* to delay his having to search for a follow up (though his efforts also brought added revenue to the film). Yet postponing that inevitability might have taken a toll on Hitchcock, as well. "He was a *picture-maker*," script supervisor Marshall Schlom said. "And when he wasn't doing that, he felt that he was not functioning."

A Hitchcock associate described how he once found the director deep in conversation with the head of a marketing research firm. Hitchcock wanted precise data from the researcher as to *why Psycho* was such a hit. The colleague said, "The implication seemed that Hitchcock wanted to crack the spine of the movie, boil it all down to a formula to find out how he might do it again. That was completely alien to the old boy I had known." However, perhaps truer to the old boy was the fact that Hitchcock dropped the whole notion once he found out what such research would cost him.

For a time, however, he may have tried to mask to the world outside and perhaps even to himself, the sea-change. Yet indications of changes in Hitchcock were to surface as time went by. In an unusually generous and expansive mood, Hitchcock sent writer-critic Anthony Boucher a case of fine champagne. As if to explain himself, he wired the writer whose "Criminals-At-Large" column in the Sunday *New York Times* the director and his staff scoured weekly: "You see, I bought the rights to *Psycho* after reading your review." In what may have been another flirtation with largesse, Hitchcock debated with his financial advisers the possibility of distributing among his crew a percentage of the windfall profits from the film; director Cecil B. DeMille had done this when *The Ten Commandments* (1956) had made over $80 million in receipts. However, Hitchcock ultimately spurned the idea, prompting a disgruntled associate to observe, "Tax consequences, not generosity, had everything to do with the decision. He made so much money, he had to shelter it somehow." Rumors persist that instead, Hitchcock cut in MCA president Lew Wasserman for a percentage—to show his gratitude for Wasserman's promotional and booking suggestions that had helped mine gold from *Psycho*, and to shelter his personal profits.

In Hollywood, few things turn a detractor into a sycophant faster than big box office. Such a veteran of the business as Hitchcock could not help but be aware of that fact of life. Throughout his life, the director appeared to pride himself on remaining aloof from industry opinion. "[Mrs. Hitchcock] and I entertain rarely, rarely go out," Hitchcock occasionally told interviewers. "I have a few friends, businessmen mostly." Yet as Hitchcock associates like Joseph Stefano have pointed out, the moviemaker appeared to crave acclaim from peers, even if he might have mistrusted it. Hitchcock certainly monitored the shifting opinion of *Psycho* within the moviemaking community. One dramatic sign of a reversal came when, in a yearly poll of British critics, *Psycho* tied for first place with *The Angry Silence*. The movie collected similar honors that followed great box-office receipts. Above everything, Hitchcock had his eye on Hollywood's best revenge: the Oscar.

Hitchcock and The Oscars: "Always A Bridesmaid?"

If *Psycho* were to win Alfred Hitchcock an Academy Award for best director, the victory would be all the sweeter. Hitchcock told interviewers that he was most proud of three of his films: *Shadow of a Doubt*, *Notorious*, and *The Trouble with Harry*. Yet there are those who believe that Hitchcock hoped to win an Oscar for his directing of *Psycho*—as much for intrinsic merit as for his lifetime of filmmaking. Would an Oscar help compensate Hitchcock for 1940, when *Rebecca* had won for best film but John Ford had been named best director for *The Grapes of Wrath?* Would it make up for Hitchcock's going home empty-handed after nominations for *Lifeboat* (1943), *Spellbound* (1945), and *Rear Window* (1954)? "He really wanted the Oscar," Joseph Stefano said. "He'd been nominated and lost many times before. He wanted that vote of confidence from the industry."

Hitchcock was fully aware that Oscars could sometimes have less to do with moviemaking artistry than with popularity, intimidation, or politicking. By Hollywood standards, Hitchcock was adept at none of those. "He was uncommonly shy and ill at ease around people and at functions," cinematographer Leonard South said. "So many people mistook that for aloofness or rudeness. 'Oh,' they thought, 'he's a snooty Englishman.'" Most recently, Hitchcock believed that MGM had underplayed his own *North by Northwest* (1959) for another, more expensive production in its promotion within the trade for Oscar nominations. "I was told to expect no nominations for my picture," he told an interviewer years later, "because they wanted to promote *Ben-Hur*." MGM's stately, culturally reputable biblical epic directed by William Wyler won twelve nominations. Hitchcock's romantic spy thriller won only three. "Always a bridesmaid," Hitchcock dead-panned for the press. But one suspects that his disappointment, and rancor, were no bluff.

Hitchcock found cause for celebration from the Oscar nominations for spring of 1961. Nominated with him for best director were Jack Cardiff (*Sons and Lovers*), Jules Dassin (*Never on Sunday*), Billy Wilder (*The Apartment*), and Fred Zinnemann *The Sundowners*). When Janet Leigh was nominated for best supporting actress, she told the press, "I think I have just as good a chance as any of the other girls," the "girls" being Glynis Johns (*The Sundowners*), Shirley Jones (*Elmer Gantry*), Shirley Knight (*The Dark at the Top of the Stairs*), and Mary Ure (*Sons and Lovers*). Competing with the cinematography of John Russell were Joseph LaShelle (*The Apartment*), Charles B. Lang, Jr. (*The Facts of Life*), Ernest Laszlo (*Inherit the Wind*), and Freddie Francis (*Sons and Lovers*). Psycho art and set directors Robert Clatworthy, Joseph Hurley, and George Milo won their nomination alongside Alexander Trauner and Edward G. Boyle for *The Apartment*, Joseph McMillan Johnson, Kenneth A. Reid, and Ross Dowd for *The Facts of Life*, Tom Morahan and Lionel Couch for *Sons and Lovers*, and Hal Pereira, Walter Tyler, Sam Comer, and Arthur Krams for *Visit to a Small Planet*.

Among the dozens of congratulatory wires that Hitchcock received was one from Janet Leigh and Tony Curtis: "If this is what it's like to be *Psycho*, like to be like this all the time. Congratulations on your nomination and good luck." Wired screenwriter Ernest Lehman, who had been nominated the previous year for *North by Northwest*: "I was pleased to read of your Academy Award nomination. Congratulations, and all that sort of thing. I hope you are well and happy." Anthony Perkins cabled: "So happy for you. Hope it goes all the way." Hitchcock wired Perkins, who had been snubbed for a deserved nomination: "I am ashamed of your fellow actors." Had Hitchcock been in a commiserating frame of mind, he might also have consoled composer Bernard Herrmann for being passed over for his electrifying score. Whatever Hitchcock's motivations were at the time, he did forward a fan letter to Herrmann. The response of the composer may come as close to revealing his ambivalence toward writing for films as any statement a biographer is likely to find:

> Composing music for films (and television) is in many ways a very unrewarding artistic endeavor. So often one's efforts are scarcely even noticed, not because the music is unworthy, nor that the picture may be more or less successful, but because it is frequently just taken for granted.

On April 17, 1961, at Santa Monica Civic Auditorium, Alma and Alfred Hitchcock made a relatively rare appearance at the 33rd Academy Awards ceremony, rubbing elbows with bejeweled, hopeful, edgy nominees, invitees, and guests. Cyd Charisse (whom MGM recommended to Hitchcock for the female lead in *North by Northwest*) and her husband, Tony Martin, announced Freddie Francis—not John Russell—as the winner for best cinematographer for *Sons and Lovers*. Next, Tina Louise and Tony Randall handed out an art direction Oscar to the designers of *The Apartment*, not of *Psycho*. After Hugh Griffith called out the name Shirley Jones, not Janet Leigh, for best supporting actress, one sole award possibility for *Psycho* remained. Gina Lollobrigida sexily murmured, "The winner is Billy Wilder for *The Apartment*!" Again, Hitchcock was edged out. "I don't think [Hitchcock] felt that his work was ever really appreciated to the point where he felt it should be," Joseph Stefano observed. "I don't think he ever really understood why he had never won an Oscar. He thought the industry looked down their noses at him. In the midst of so much, he was unhappy."

11. AFTERGLOW AND AFTERMATH

Unhappy though he may have been, the pragmatic Hitchcock could take comfort in *Psycho*'s having earned $15 million domestically by the end of its first year of release. Many Hitchcock associates contend that the director personally realized well in excess of $15 million from the movie. This was in an era when the average movie ticket cost seventy cents. While the movie was the hottest thing on several continents, Lew Wasserman aggressively wooed—and signed—Hitchcock to a production deal with Universal-International. Cameraman South observed: "Knowing Universal, Wasserman, and that clan, Hitch wanted everything in writing that he had full, complete say-so as to everything he made." The negotiations dragged on, but finally, lawyers for both parties struck a production agreement for five Hitchcock films, with options for more. As part of his studio deal, Hitchcock moved his "filmmaking" family into a lavish private compound situated close to the main studio gate. The enclave encompassed a capacious suite of offices filled with antiques; rooms for editing, art, costumes, and conferences; a twenty-seat screening room; a kitchenette and private dining room; and a soundstage directly across the street. For Hitchcock, it represented the realization of a career-long goal. Such key members of Hitchcock's technical team as cameramen Robert Burks and Leonard South, art directors Robert Boyle and Henry Bumstead, editor George Tomasini, and costume designer Edith Head were close at hand for consultation.

In 1962, as part of his arrangement with the studio, Hitchcock swapped for about 150,000 shares of MCA stock all rights to *Psycho* and to his TV anthology series. In one fell swoop, the transaction made him the third largest shareholder in the company, a multimillionaire, and his own boss. Yet in the realm where art and commerce meet, Hitchcock and Universal were better matched fiscally than artistically. "Hitch was a rare combination of true artist, technician, and businessman," Leonard South said. "[Lew] Wasserman was basically an agent who became a good friend. I think Wasserman always had the idea that there was more money to be made out of this man." As agent Michael Ludmer observed: "The question arises 'Why is there no indisputably great late-period Hitchcock movie?' And the answers to that question are very complicated."

Once the public hysteria over *Psycho* had subsided, the question that Lew Wasserman had posed to Hitchcock ("What will you do for an encore?") hung in the air. Members of the Hitchcock professional family assumed (indeed, *hoped*) that the director's triumph in the horror genre would end his flirtation with that form. Before, during, and after his negotiations with Wasserman and Universal-International, the director appeared unable to decide upon *any* follow-up project. Hitchcock had thought of making for 20th Century-Fox a movie version of *Piege pour un Homme Seul,* a play by Robert Thomas about a woman who returns from a mysterious disappearance to find her husband insisting she is not his wife. He also poured considerable effort into a project from a novel by Paul Stanton, *Village of Stars*, a sort of *The High and the Mighty* set aboard a plane carrying an A-bomb. Hitchcock told columnists that the piece appealed to him for its topicality and also for its opportunity to wring suspense out of a confined space, a la *Lifeboat*, *Rope*, and *Rear Window*. After dropping both of these projects, the director developed a doomsday fantasy from Daphne du Maurier's short story, "The Birds" and then a movie to be taken from the wistful Sir James Barrie play about a melancholy ghost named "Mary Rose." Also under discussion was a film adaptation of a Winston Graham novel, *Marnie*, about a sexually troubled kleptomaniac.

In the end, Hitchcock settled on *Marnie*. The choice delighted screenwriter Joseph Stefano, with whom Hitchcock had exercised an option for two additional assignments during the shooting of *Psycho*. Believing that Hitchcock again wanted to try something entirely new, Stefano had hoped to interest him in collaborating on a romantic supernatural thriller, a la *The Uninvited* (1943). At least *Marnie*, Stefano believed, was very much "mainstream Hitchcock material." The writer explained: "For a long time, I felt that doing *Psycho* was the biggest career mistake I ever made. I wanted to be associated with a real Hitchcock picture. Hitch was thrilled because Grace Kelly had agreed to star in *Marnie*. He said, 'They [Kelly and Prince Rainier] need the money,' and told me, 'Now this is a different thing from *Psycho* because we're going to change the story quite a bit.' What fascinated Hitch about it was a strange trio: the woman, the husband who makes her go to a psychiatrist, and the psychiatrist who finds himself more and more romantically involved with the woman. The fifty-page treatment was exciting. It *worked*. I thought it was going to be a wonderful movie. But by the time I finished it, Grace Kelly had changed her mind. Hitchcock said, 'Apparently, she got the money from some other sources.' To him, Kelly had tricked him and he would not forgive her. I was shattered."

Instead, Hitchcock turned to the eerie du Maurier horror fantasy, "The Birds." Although Stefano felt nothing but "enormous fondness and gratitude" toward Hitchcock, the project held no appeal to the writer, who viewed it as another horror movie. Stefano declined the screenwriting job. Whether or not the director was conscious of it at the time, his choice of material signaled to some close associates that he was throwing down the gauntlet. Others wondered whether he might be throwing in the towel. Many believed he was listening much too closely to the advice of Lew Wasserman. Different as it might have been from *Psycho*, *The Birds* was another offbeat shocker. The production proved to be extremely complex. Not only did Hitchcock undertake major special effects to depict the bird attacks but also once again attempted to play starmaker, this time to a completely inexperienced actress, former model Tippi Hedren. "Hitch loved to challenge himself," Leonard South said. "Creating a new star was the one thing he hadn't done." Despite Hitchcock's disappointment with Vera Miles in the fifties, an associate believed that Hitchcock's quest to find a "new Grace Kelly" was revived by *Psycho*. "Hitchcock was the real star of *Psycho* and he knew it," the colleague said. "It was as if he now believed that anything he touched—a novice performer, a not-good-enough project—he could turn into gold. It may have been understandable after the success of *Psycho*, but his judgment was badly clouded."

The Birds, coming three years after *Psycho*, virtually guaranteed Hitchcock and Universal reams of publicity and financial success. Yet even the release and advertising campaign for the film suggested that the director had taken to heart his lionization by intellectual critics. At the invitation of Robert Favre Le

Bret, Hitchcock debuted *The Birds* and Tippi Hedren to the world critics and press gathered at the Cannes Film Festival. In a newspaper ad for the film, Hitchcock proclaimed: "I have, in my time, produced many films whose major intent was to mystify and astonish their viewers. Inasmuch as such stories often brought much pleasure, they fulfilled their requirements. This time, however, I have introduced serious purpose beneath the pleasure. There is a terrifying meaning lurking right underneath the surface shock and suspense of *The Birds*. When you discover it, your pleasure will be more than doubled." Serious purpose? Meaning? Had Hitchcock finally decided to declare himself an artist, to put to rest his public persona as merely a maker of "fun pictures"?

Some critics made extravagant claims for the allegorical and symbolic content that they perceived in *The Birds*. Hitchcock's rather remarkable film may even support some of their theories. But other observers took Hitchcock to task for what they saw as a pretentious, "New Wave"-style ending that left ambiguous not only the cause of the bird attacks but also the fate of the leading characters. "The Master," wrote a critic for *Time*, "has traded in his uncomplicated tenets of terror for a new outlook that is vaguely *nouvelle vague*."

Robert Bloch commented: "After these great paeans of praise from the French, *The Birds* was to be Hitchcock's career apotheosis—the film for which he would be remembered. I don't think the film today is regarded in that light. I don't think Hitch was satisfied with it and several times went back to what he thought of as a formula: more familiar kinds of material and stars who were hot properties. To me that signified that he didn't have much faith in the stories themselves."

It was during the production of *The Birds* that Universal first began to play watchdog over Hitchcock. Leonard South recalled,

"A studio guy showed up on location in San Francisco asking such questions as, 'Do you think you're going to be out of here by Friday?'" Hitch said, "When Friday comes, if we're ready to come back to the studio, that's what we'll do." Hitch called him "the hatchet man." There was *never* any of that from Paramount, where [studio head] Y. Frank Freeman showed Hitch the greatest respect. [Paramount] was a much, much better operation for Hitch."

Matters were slowly to worsen between Hitchcock and the company. About midway through production on *The Birds*, Hitchcock again contacted Joseph Stefano about reviving *Marnie* as a starring vehicle for his protégée Tippi Hedren. Stefano declined with regret because of his commitment as producer of the acclaimed science fiction TV series, *The Outer Limits*. "That did not go down at all well with him," Stefano recalled. "The next thing I know, my agent told me that Hitchcock wants to loan me out to Columbia. I said, 'Tell him, let's just forget about [the commitment] until he wants me to do another picture. He doesn't have to pay me.'" But to Hitchcock, it appeared, a commitment was a commitment. Since he didn't want to pay Stefano for *not* doing another picture, why not make money on him?

Hitchcock next developed *Marnie* with Evan Hunter, screenwriter of *The Birds*. Later, he devised a completely different approach with playwright Jay Presson Allen. Stefano was stung by the lost opportunity to collaborate again with Hitchcock. The writer observed: "I don't think he ever recovered from *Psycho*. But when we made it, Hitchcock was just trying to make a good movie. He seemed past the stage of needing to prove anything to anyone. I wish he'd called me and said, 'Let's do another picture for a million dollars.' It would have been a killer, but he never needed or wanted to do that kind of thing again."

Much went awry for Hitchcock on *Marnie* (1964), a film that today divides even his admirers. The movie was the first for Geoffrey-Stanley Productions, named sentimentally by Hitchcock after a pair of Yorkshire terriers owned by him and his wife. "Hitch was absolutely partial to dogs," Leonard South recalled, "and often brought Geoffrey and Stanley to work with him. He was keeping an eye on them playing outside his office one day when, right under his eyes, suddenly a truck backed over Geoffrey and killed him. Such a sensitive man as Hitch was—well, he wasn't right for weeks and weeks." That loss, compounded by the critical and financial flop of *Marnie*, was topped by the apathy of the public toward Tippi Hedren—despite the actress's coming through for her mentor with a remarkably moving and sensitive performance. The sixty-five-year-old director suffered a crisis of confidence.

And with that crisis spiraled the interventions of Universal. Hitchcock hoped to revive the Sir James Barrie Scottish ghost story from a Jay Presson Allen screenplay, probably to star Tippi Hedren. Universal executives urged Hitchcock not to make it; some say they prevented him from making it. Either way, he complied. The director next tried to interest such writers as novelist Vladimir Nabokov (*Lolita, Pale Fire*) as screenwriter for what he called a "downbeat, realistic spy thriller that debunks the James Bond idea." The studio insisted that Hitchcock take a less gloomy approach to that material in *Torn Curtain*, and that he utilize the expensive—and inappropriate—services of Paul Newman and Julie Andrews. But when it came to spending money on creative elements more important to Hitchcock than star players, Universal bosses drew the line. Cameraman Leonard South observed: "The studio wanted big stars in it, but [Hitchcock] and Paul Newman did not get along well at all. Hitch wanted to do things right on that picture, shoot it in West Germany.

Instead, Universal had a German crew shoot crappy background plates. Then, [Hitchcock] had a falling-out with Bernard Herrmann because Universal wanted a more upbeat score. Hitch lost all interest in the picture." Recalling the "set piece" scene of the film—the long, slow killing in a kitchen by a spy and a hausfrau—Joseph Stefano said, "It saddened me. Hitchcock was now playing to his audience." Indeed, *Torn Curtain* found its audience, albeit one increasingly impatient with Hitchcock for not giving them something as riveting as *Psycho*.

The Universal executives imposed on Hitchcock *Topaz*, a Leon Uris best-seller about a spy scandal in the French government. Rushed into a globe-hopping production without a screenworthy script, Hitchcock tried to impart finesse and dash to what was otherwise an utter shambles. Shown in London and previewed in America with several different endings, *Topaz* was a financial failure and nearly Hitchcock's Waterloo.

Ironically, while newer Hitchcock efforts were striking out with fans and critics, the reputation of *Psycho* grew. The movie had become a staple on the revival-theater-and-campus circuit. By the early seventies, ten scholarly book-length studies of Hitchcock had been published, in addition to hundreds of articles from all over the world that featured *Psycho* as a key work in his career. In 1977 the movie appeared on the American Film Institute's poll as one of the "Greatest Films of All Time," as it already had on the polls of such journals as *Sight and Sound*. Universal made an additional $5 million from the first of several theatrical rereleases in 1965 *before* the parent company, MCA, had licensed *Psycho* for a network and syndicated television showings and for home videotape and disc sales. The *New York Post* declared *Psycho* the most profitable black-and-white film in the annals of cinema since D. W. Griffith's silent classic, *The Birth of a Nation* (1915).

Just after the slaying of the daughter of senatorial candidate

Charles Percy in Chicago in 1966, CBS canceled a scheduled national airing *of Psycho*, even though network censors had spliced nine minutes of footage from the running time. To date, the film has never been shown on national television. In the early seventies, composer Bernard Herrmann conducted the London Philharmonic Orchestra for a recording of a condensed version of his score for the film. Herrmann wrote in the liner notes for that album: "I felt that I was able to complement the black and white photography of the film with a black and white sound. I believe this is the only time in films that a purely string orchestra has been used." On October 2, 1975, Herrmann conducted the National Philharmonic Orchestra in a recording of the entire score.

Considering Hitchcock's preference for working with familiar casts and crews, it may at first seem curious that few alumnae of *Psycho* were summoned for an encore. Newspapers reported that Anthony Perkins and Hitchcock had signed a two-picture deal. Perkins was said to be intent on interesting Hitchcock in something called *The Man Who Lost His Head*, but nothing came of it. Similarly, in the mid-sixties, Hitchcock summoned writer Robert Bloch to hatch a successor to *Psycho*. Bloch met Hitchcock to discuss the director's notion to graft elements of the real-life murder cases of seductive British murderers Haigh and Christie of the forties onto an original suspense narrative that might form a long-hoped-for "prequel" to the classic *Shadow of a Doubt* (1942). Bloch—by that time the recipient of an Edgar Award from The Mystery Writers of America for *Psycho*, and a prolific screenwriter—found himself unable to agree to the terms of Hitchcock's contract. The arrangement proposed by Hitchcock meant that Bloch was to be paid only when and if he were to come up with an approach that pleased the director. Bloch moved on. No one dared reject Hitchcock. When the writer's name came across Hitchcock's desk on a short list of writers for a later project, the director wrote next to it: "Too many pictures for William Castle"—a reference to the director for whom Bloch had written *Strait-Jacket*, a low-budget shocker featuring Joan Crawford as an apparent axe-murderess.

Janet Leigh, who today routinely turns over crank mail and death threats to the FBI after local station TV showings of *Psycho*, claimed to understand why she did not work again for Hitchcock. "I would have *loved* to have worked for him again," she admitted. "But I understand why not. Marion was a one-time role. She made such an imprint, Hitchcock could not bring her back to life. And *Psycho* was a once-only film."

Certainly it was a once-only Hitchcock film for most of the technical crew. "*Psycho* was an experiment in solving movie-type problems with television solutions," observed a member of the director's feature-film team. "Hitchcock was unhappy with a lot of those TV guys and had no further use for them, *except* on his TV show."

In the remaining years of creativity that Hitchcock enjoyed after *Psycho*, he completed six pictures and planned at least half a dozen more, the final project being a never-filmed spy-romance set in New York and Finland—*The Short Night*. Yet the notoriety of his "thirty-day picture" dogged and overshadowed every project that the Master of Suspense undertook until his death in 1980. In the nearly thirty years since the release of *Psycho*, the picture slipped beyond mere popularity and into the annals of pop culture. As Peter Bogdanovich has pointed out, largely due to *Psycho*, audiences accustomed themselves to arriving at the start of a film. With *Psycho*, the barriers of big-screen shock and violence had been blown wide. After the Hitchcock film, the biggest star in the cast could die on-screen *before* the end of the movie. In 1981, a British group called Landscape had a hit record called "Norman Bates" and the video presented comic Pamela Stephenson as Marion Crane. In *Carrie* (1976), director Brian De Palma named the high school attended by the heroine "Bates High School." Hitchcock's film has spawned Bates Motel T-shirts and shower curtains. The shower scene has been parodied by such filmmakers as Mel Brooks in *High Anxiety* and reworked by Brian De Palma in *Dressed to Kill* and by Roman Polanski in *Frantic*. Even preadolescent kids are familiar with the "screeching violins" of Bernard Herrmann's theme music, courtesy of local station television reruns of *Psycho* and "homages" to the composer's work in numerous film scores, such as *Carrie, Dressed to Kill, A Nightmare on Elm Street,* and *Fatal Attraction*. Universal produced and Richard Franklin directed *Psycho II*, not related to the novel of the same name by Robert Bloch. Earlier, Franklin had directed *Roadgames* starring Jamie Lee Curtis, daughter of Janet Leigh, as "Hitch." Anthony Perkins directed *Psycho III*. The studio also produced an unsold television pilot, "Bates Motel." On the Universal Studios Tour—on which the *Psycho* mansion is a key attraction—guides announce that plans are afoot for *Psycho IV* to star Perkins, perhaps from a screenplay by Joseph Stefano. In the 1989 edition of his *TV Movies and Video Guide*, critic Leonard Maltin wrote of the most recent sequel, "Goodnight, Norman."

Hitchcock once characterized *Psycho* as "One of the most cinematic movies I've made and there you get a clear example of the use of film to cause an audience to respond emotionally." Yet the hundreds of successors to *Psycho* only serve to display how scrupulous and restrained a filmmaker Hitchcock had been. If any energy remains in the *Psycho* formula—The Crackpot With the Knife, The Blonde, The Weird House, The Serpentine Plot—too few of Hitchcock's followers and imitators have had what it takes to tap it.

During the sixties and seventies, Hitchcock grew more infirm with arthritis and heart problems and his competitors became legion. He seemed to become more frenzied in his search for outstanding material. In early 1964, when Hitchcock wrote and telephoned novelist Vladimir Nabokov with proposals for two movie screenplays, he described his "desperation for a story" as "immediate and urgent." Nabokov counterproposed an idea about a spy, which Hitchcock rejected as too like a 1955 movie called *The Man Who Never Was*. A scheduled meeting between the two never took place. "The main problem for Hitch after *Psycho*," asserted Michael Ludmer, who functioned as an inhouse story finder and unofficial literary agent, "was that the material just wasn't there. Fewer novelists and playwrights of the calibre of [Hitchcock collaborators] Thornton Wilder, Maxwell Anderson, or Robert Sherwood, existed. Hitch's access to them, indeed, the access of all Hollywood to them, had changed. Top writers would not be interested in coming to Los Angeles for six to ten weeks to work on material that was not their own. So the Paddy Chayevskys were pleased as punch to hear from Hitchcock, but they'd look at that material and say, 'I'd love to work for you, but not on this.'"

Hitchcock watched as a parade of directors stepped forward to "do a Hitchcock." Some of them publicly acknowledged their debt to the Master, others did not. Perhaps it was only fitting that the British-based Hammer Films (the success of which had been a prod to Hitchcock for making *Psycho*) embarked on a series of *Psycho*-like shockers, including *Scream of Fear* (1960), *Maniac* (1962), *Paranoiac* (1962), *Nightmare* (1963), and *Die! Die! My Darling!*, *Hysteria*, and *Crescendo* (all 1964). The influence of *Psycho* is apparent on efforts from William Castle (*Homicidal*, 1961; *Strait-Jacket*, 1964), Robert Aldrich (*Whatever Happened to Baby Jane?*, 1962; *Hush, Hush, Sweet Charlotte*,

1964), Michael Powell (*Peeping Tom*, 1962), Francis Ford Coppola (*Dementia-13*, 1963), Roman Polanski (*Repulsion*, 1965), George Romero (*Night of the Living Dead*, 1968), Noel Black (*Pretty Poison*, 1968), Roy Boulting (*Twisted Nerve*, 1968), Herbert Kastle (*The Honeymoon Killers*, 1970), Bob Clark and Alan Ormsby (*Deranged*, 1974, based on the story of Ed Gein), Tobe Hooper (*The Texas Chainsaw Massacre*, 1974, also inspired in part by Gein), and Brian De Palma (*Sisters*, 1973; *Dressed to Kill*, 1980). Before *Psycho*, would audiences have been as well prepared for the mood swings and blood-letting of Arthur Penn's *Bonnie and Clyde* (1967) or Sam Peckinpah's *The Wild Bunch* (1969)?

Yet surely, any malicious merriment Hitchcock might have enjoyed at the shortcomings of his directorial colleagues must have palled as he realized that he could not top *Psycho* either. Running for cover, the director tried to reclaim audiences who clamored for another killer-on-the-loose thriller. During the mid-sixties, Hitchcock interviewed or hired a phalanx of writers, from Benn Levy (*Murder!*, 1930) to Broadway playwright Hugh Wheeler, from novelist Howard Fast to playwrights Lillian Hellman and Edward Albee, to devise a script based on the real-life case of Englishman Neville Heath, a baby-faced seducer-murderer with a compulsion to carve up the bodies of young women. Story conferences and script drafts alike came to a dead-end when Hitchcock asked the rhetorical question: "Is this too much like *Psycho*?" *Frenzy* (1972), his only other late-period psycho-shocker, was an attempt to apply old-style film craft to a latter-day tale of a Jack the Ripper–type at large in swinging London. Many critics consider it the best film of Hitchcock's final decade, but some audiences and critics felt let down.

Endless TV showings, imitations, and parodies have dulled the cutting edge of *Psycho*, particularly to a generation that may mistake spurting blood bags, flash editing, and cranked-up soundtracks for real thrills. By contrast to the *Friday the 13th* or *Nightmare on Elm Street* series and their hellspawn, the fuss made over Hitchcock may seem as incomprehensible today as an old TV show or silent movie. Today's children of Jason and Freddie may puzzle over why 1960 audiences screamed bloody murder over Norman. But should they be so lucky, perhaps a nineties-style Hitchcock counterpart might creep up on them unawares and scare the beejesus out of moviegoing America all over again.

When director François Truffaut tried to pry out of Hitchcock comments on the experimental and artistic nature of *Psycho*, Hitchcock admitted: "I can't get a real appreciation of the picture in the terms we're using now." Rather, observed the director, "*Psycho*, more than any of my other pictures, is a film that belongs to filmmakers, to you and me." For the cinematic and literary successors to Hitchcock, the legacy is awesome. Novelist Stephen King (*Carrie*, *The Shining*), who ranks *Psycho* as one of "the scariest films ever made," marks it as a touchstone for bringing the archetypal Jekyll-and-Hyde figure into the modern vernacular. "*Psycho* is effective because it brings the werewolf myth home," King has written. "It is not outside evil, predestination; the fault lies not in our stars but in ourselves. We know that Norman is only outwardly the Werewolf when he's wearing Mom's duds and speaking in Mom's voice; but we have the uneasy suspicion that he's the Werewolf *all* the time."

Director Brian De Palma (*Carrie*, *Body Double*), one of the most technically accomplished of his generation, has appropriated plot-lines and much surface technique from Hitchcock. In 1980, De Palma said, "Dealing with Hitchcock is like dealing with Bach—he wrote every tune that was ever done. Hitchcock thought up practically every cinematic idea that has been used and probably will be used in this form."

Few films since *Psycho* have seeped as much as it did into the dark imagination and consciousness of the public. Merits or demerits of the *Psycho* successors aside, that select circle must include *Rosemary's Baby, Night of the Living Dead, The Exorcist, Halloween, Dressed to Kill, Mulholland Drive, Seven, The Skin I Live In, Black Swan* and *House at The End of the Street*, among many others. The timing of the release of the Polanski and Romero movies could not have been more perfect. America was reeling from the horrors of a televised jungle war, rioting in the streets, campus turmoil, the duplicity of Lyndon Johnson and Richard Nixon, and the murders of Martin Luther King, Jr., and Robert Kennedy. A movie theater seat seemed as good a vantage point as any from which to view the apocalypse. Americans experienced the horror with a media-hip irony and detachment. Television had only made that attitude possible. The events of the era made it, for some, a survival tool.

In *The Exorcist*, director William Friedkin went straight for the jugular. In its sequences that document the casual horrors and insensitivity of the medical profession in diagnosing the ills of a little girl, the movie is riveting. From there on in, it's strictly an affair for the special effects team—much upchucking of pea soup, levitations, and twist-o-matic heads. Unlike many shockers that are popular with teenagers and the action crowd, *The Exorcist* (like the William Peter Blatty best-seller on which it was based) struck a nerve with audiences of *all* ages.

Director Adrian Lyne was acutely aware of the shadow of Hitchcock looming over *Fatal Attraction*. Like Polanski in *Repulsion*, Lyne kept the audience on tenterhooks by reversing the psycho-knifing-the-blonde cliché with the blonde being the psycho who wields the knife. "Hitchcock was obviously so brilliant," Lyne observed. "A genius. At the time *Psycho* came out, the shower scene was revolutionary. It was and *is* so impressive, the quick cuts, the bits and pieces. But today, compared to the rest of the film, that scene looks strangely naive. What *is* absolutely wonderful about the scene is the sound of the knife."

But audience response to early rough-cut previews of his own *Fatal Attraction* (1987) made Lyne realize that any thriller must stand comparison to Hitchcock. In the script and film as originally shot, the ravaged Alix (Glenn Close) stabs herself to death like Madame Butterfly, tricking her one-night-stand lover (Michael Douglas) into marking the knife with his fingerprints. When blood-thirsty preview audiences demanded a more violent showdown, director Lyne regrouped his cast to stage a bathroom sequence reminiscent not only of Hitchcock but also of *Les Diaboliques*. "Although the comparison [to those films] was always there," said Lyne, "I was anxious to avoid a repeat of the Hitchcock scene and was trying to avoid the knife-wielding sort of wacko. Both Glenn and I were reluctant to do it. In the end, I said to her, 'Rather than hold the knife in a threatening way, perhaps you could let it dangle by your side—sort of twitch with it, almost like you're scratching yourself.' Anybody who could do that without feeling it was capable of *anything*. Like Hitchcock, we were setting up a generic sort of jeopardy that carried through the rest of the sequence. In retrospect, the new ending is better than the original one."

Lyne attributed to believable characters the phenomenal box-office records of *Psycho* and *Fatal Attraction*. He said, "The fact that Hitchcock's main star was killed so early in *Psycho* was brilliant thinking. Almost everyone who saw my film put themselves in the shoes of the lover, the wife, the husband—sometimes all three. It was very real to them. A movie is much more difficult for the audience to dismiss if they can identify intimately with the problems of the characters in it."

In the nearly thirty years since the theatrical release of Psycho, the picture attained the status of an international pop culture icon. In 1960, when Alfred Hitchcock assessed *Psycho* for one of the umpteen reporters on his publicity tour, he observed: "It's a pretty good film. But, more important, it's the first shocker I've ever made. The pictures I've done before were thrillers. This one *literally* shocks you." The fact is, the most famous and one of the most emulated of all Hitchcock films—for all its immediate power over audiences and its long-range impact upon international cinema—uprooted and altered no one more irrevocably than the director himself.

PSYCHO CAST AND CREDITS

1960. A Paramount Release. Cast: Anthony Perkins (Norman Bates), Vera Miles (Lila Crane), John Gavin (Sam Loomis). Co-starring Martin Balsam (Milton Arbogast) and John McIntire (Sheriff Chambers). With Simon Oakland (Dr. Richmond), Vaughn Taylor (Mr. Lowery), Frank Albertson (Cassidy), Lurene Tuttle (Mrs. Chambers), Pat Hitchcock (Caroline), John Anderson ("California Charlie"), Mort Mills (Highway Patrolman), and Janet Leigh (as Marion Crane). Stand-ins: Margo Epper, June Gleason, Myra Jones, Paul Matthews, Frank Vinci, John Drake, Ann Dore. Director of Photography: John L. Russell, A.S.C. Art Direction: Joseph Hurley and Robert Clatworthy. Set Decorator: George Milo. Unit Manager: Lew Leary. Title Design: Saul Bass. Editor: George Tomasini, A.C.E. Costume Supervisor: Helen Colvig. Wardrobe: Rita Riggs. Makeup Supervision: Jack Barron and Robert Dawn. Hairstylist: Florence Bush. Special Effects: Clarence Champagne. Sound Recording: Waldon O. Watson and William Russell. Assistant Director: Hilton A. Green. Pictorial Consultant: Saul Bass. Music: Bernard Herrmann. Director: Alfred Hitchcock. Running Time: 109 minutes.

AND AFTER *PSYCHO*

FRANK ALBERTSON (actor, "Tom Cassidy"), whose career includes appearances in such films as *Alice Adams* (1935) and *Bachelor Mother* (1939), later regularly appeared on TV series including *Alfred Hitchcock Presents, Bringing Up Buddy, The Real McCoys* and in the feature films *Girl on the Run* (1961), *Don't Knock the Twist* (1962), *Johnny Cool* and *Bye Bye Birdie* (1963). He died at age fifty-five in 1964.

JAMES ALLARDICE (writer of trailer, publicity), a former Yale playwriting student, caught the attention of MCA and Paramount in 1949 when he was hired to adapt his comedy *At War with the Army* for Dean Martin and Jerry Lewis. A top TV comedy writer and Emmy-winner when MCA aligned him with Hitchcock, Allardice scripted Hitchcock's merrily macabre situations and monologues that bookended the director's television shows for ten years. Allardice also wrote the droll speeches Hitchcock gave before the National Press Club and other organizations. Actor-producer Norman Lloyd observed of the death of Allardice in 1965, "I always felt that when Hitch said he didn't want to go on with the series any longer it was because he knew there would never be another Jimmy Allardice."

MARTIN BALSAM (actor, "Milton Arbogast") continued to steal scenes in such movies as *Breakfast at Tiffany's* (1961), *Seven Days in May* (1964), *A Thousand Clowns* (Oscar for Best Supporting Actor, 1965), *Catch-22*, *Little Big Man* (1970), *Murder on the Orient Express* (1974), *All the President's Men* (1976), *The Goodbye People* (1984), *Death Wish 3* (1985) and, throughout his later career, in such TV series as *Maude*, *Quincy M.E.*, and *Archie Bunker's Place*. He worked again with Hitchcock when he "co-starred" with Tippi Hedren during the screen test that led to the inexperienced actress' starring in *The Birds*. Martin Balsam died in 1996.

SAUL BASS (titles, pictorial consultant) contributed remarkable and widely imitated title sequences to such films as *Spartacus* and *Ocean's Eleven* (1960), *West Side Story* (1961), *A Walk on the Wild Side* (1962), *It's a Mad, Mad, Mad, Mad World* (1963), *Bunny Lake Is Missing* (1965), and *Seconds* and *Grand Prix* (1966). He produced and directed TV commercials, shorts, and documentaries, including *The Searching Eye* (1963), *From Here to There* (1964), *Why Man Creates* (1968), and a feature film, *Phase IV* (1974). He created influential "key art" for dozens of poster campaigns, including *Exodus* (1960), *Advise and Consent* (1962), *Nine Hours to Rama* and *The Cardinal* (1963), *The Fixer* (1968), *The Human Factor* (1979), *Alien* (1979), *The Shining* (1980), *Talk Radio* (1988), *Big* (1988), *Goodfellas* (1990), *Cape Fear* (1991), *The Age of Innocence* (1993) and *Casino* (1995). He died in 1996.

ROBERT BLOCH (novelist) wrote over a thousand short stories, over a dozen novels, teleplays for such shows as *Darkroom*, and screenplays for such films as *Strait-Jacket* and *The Nightwalker* (1964), *The House That Dripped Blood* (1971), and *Tales From the*

Crypt (1972), the latter based on the gory E.C. Comics. A disciple and correspondent of horror master writer H.P. Lovecraft, Bloch lived to see his reputation grow steadily over the years. After the enormous success of *Psycho*, Hitchcock wanted Bloch to develop an original thriller but the two could never come to financial terms. Bloch's iconic characters and situations formed the basis for three *Psycho* sequels and several TV series. He died in 1994.

JAMES P. CAVANAGH (screenwriter) had written teleplays for the Hitchcock series before tackling the first attempts to adapt Robert Bloch's novel *Psycho* into a screenplay. The teleplays include "The Hidden Thing," "The Creeper," "Fog Closing In," "None Are So Blind," "The End of Indian Summer," "One More Mile To Go," "Sylvia," "Arthur," and "Mother, May I Go Out To Swim?" Hitchcock rejected Cavanagh's *Psycho* script, but Cavanagh continued to work for the director's TV series ("Coming, Mama," "A Jury of Her Peers," "Where Beauty Lies") before his death in 1971 at age forty-nine.

ROBERT CLATWORTHY (art direction) lent his expertise to such films as *The Parent Trap* (1961), *That Touch of Mink* (1962), *Inside Daisy Clover* (1965), *Ship of Fools* (1965), *Guess Who's Coming To Dinner* (1967), *Cactus Flower* (1969), *The Secret of Santa Vittoria* (1969), *Butterflies Are Free* (1972), *Report to the Commissioner* (1974), *From Noon 'Till Three* (1976), *Carwash* (1976), and *Another Man, Another Chance* (1977). For TV, he worked on the series *Rawhide* and *Twilight Zone*. In 1989, art director Anton Furst and director Tim Burton, who collaborated on *Batman*, called Clatworthy and Joseph Hurley's *Psycho* motel and Victorian house the best movie "special effect" ever created. He died in 1992.

HERBERT COLEMAN (assistant director) had been associated with Hitchcock since becoming his assistant director on *Rear Window* and associate on every Hitchcock project prior to *Psycho*, the project on which Coleman departed. He later worked on many TV productions, including as producer of *Checkmate* and *Whispering Smith* and he often seemed on the verge of directing and producing feature films. He rejoined Hitchcock in 1964 as producer of with 16 episodes of *The Alfred Hitchcock Hour* and continued as associate producer through the troubled production of Hitchcock's production of *Topaz*, released in 1969. He died in 2001.

JOHN GAVIN (actor, Sam Loomis) became president of the Screen Actors Guild from 1971 to 1973. Later, he was appointed ambassador to Mexico by President Ronald Reagan, another former Guild president and conservative Republican. Before turning to politics, the actor's credits included *Back Street* (1961), *Midnight Lace* (1960), *Romanoff and Juliet* (1961), *Tammy Tell Me True* (1961), the TV series *Destry Rides Again* (1964), *Thoroughly Modern Millie* (1967), and TV mini-series *Rich Man, Poor Man* (1976). Mr. Gavin, who rarely publicly discussed working with Hitchcock, spoke about *Psycho* to his co-star Janet Leigh for her 1995 book on *Psycho*.

HILTON GREEN (assistant director), Hitchcock's assistant director of 41 episodes of *Alfred Hitchcock Presents*, also did the same for *Marnie* and on episodes of *Coronado 9*, *McHale's Navy* and *Ironside*. He produced *Psycho II* (1983), *Psycho III* (1986), *Psycho IV: The Beginning* (1990), *Sixteen Candles* (1984), *Encino Man* (1992) and *Home Alone 3* (1997).

VIRGINIA GREGG, who provided the voice of Mother in the first three *Psycho* films, appeared in *All the Fine Young*

Cannibals (1960), *House of Women*, *Spencer's Mountain* (1962) and numerous guest appearances in TV series and made-for-TV movies. She died in 1986.

BERNARD HERRMANN (composer) acted as sound consultant to Hitchcock on *The Birds* (1963) and composer for *Marnie* (1964). Hitchcock forever alienated Herrmann by replacing the musician's score for *Torn Curtain* (1966) with one by John Addison. Among the composer's later credits: *The Bride Wore Black* (1967), *Twisted Nerve* (1969), *The Battle of Neretva* (1971), *Sisters* (1973), and *Taxi Driver* and *Obsession* both released the year following his death in 1975.

PATRICIA HITCHCOCK (actor, Caroline) appeared in the TV version of Dorothy Parker's "Ladies of the Corridor" with Cloris Leachman and Barbara Baxley, shown on PBS, and in a TV movie version of *Six Characters in Search of an Author*. Her last film was *Skateboard* in 1978. In 1984, she endowed the Margaret Herrick Library of the Academy of Motion Picture Arts and Sciences with her father's career papers, photographs, memos, and production files.

JOSEPH HURLEY (art direction) was a visual consultant on *The Reivers* (1969) and production illustrator on *Chinatown* (1974), *The China Syndrome* (1979), *The Postman Always Rings Twice* (1981) and *The Best Little Whorehouse in Texas* (1982). He was the production illustrator to designer Richard MacDonald on both *Altered States* (1980) and *Something Wicked This Way Comes* (1983). He died in 1982.

PAUL JASMIN (voice of Mother), today a respected photographer, fashion designer and painter, has done "key art" for movie posters for such films as *American Gigolo* (1980), *An Officer and a Gentleman* (1982), and *Permanent Record* (1988). His fashion photography has appeared in such magazines as *Vogue* and *Interview* and his canvases hang in the homes of Barbra Streisand, Sofia Coppola and Marisa Berenson. His books include *Hollywood Cowboy: Paul Jasmin* (2002), *Lost Angeles* (2008) and *California Dreaming* (2011). A close friend of Anthony Perkins for over two decades, Mr. Jasmin also appeared in roles in *Midnight Cowboy* (1969), *Looker* (1981), *Adaptation* (2002) and *Marie Antoinette* (2006).

JANET LEIGH (actor, Marion Crane) went on to appear in such projects as *The Manchurian Candidate* (1962), *Bye Bye Birdie* (1963), *Boardwalk*, *The Fog* (1979) and a brief appearance in *Halloween H20: 20 Years Later* (1998). In 1982, she published a successful autobiography, *There Really Was a Hollywood*, a 1995 book on *Psycho*, a 1996 novel *House of Destiny* and a Hollywood-set novel, *The Dream Factory*, in 2002. Her daughters with actor Tony Curtis, Jamie Lee Curtis and Kelly Lee Curtis, are also actors. Janet Leigh died in 2004.

LUIGI LURASCHI (studio censorship board liaison) left Hollywood in 1960 to work in Italy for Dino DeLaurentiis. He was a consultant to Paramount Pictures in Europe. He died in Paris, France in 2002.

VERA MILES (actor, Lila Crane) worked again for Alfred Hitchcock in "Incident at a Corner," a one-hour teleplay broadcast on *Ford Startime*, for John Ford in the feature film *The Man Who Shot Liberty Valance* (1962), and for Don Siegel in *The Hanged Man* (1964). She appeared in *The Spirit Is Willing*

(1967), *One Little Indian* (1973), *The Castaway Cowboy* (1974), and *Psycho II* (1983), directed by Richard Franklin. In 1989, she starred in a stage production, *The Immigrant*, in Southern California.

MORT MILLS (actor, Highway Patrolman) played another memorable scene for Hitchcock as the farmer who aids Paul Newman in *Torn Curtain* (1966). He had appeared for Orson Welles in *Touch of Evil* (1958) and, later, in *Twenty Plus Two* (1961), *The Quick Gun* (1964), *The Name of the Game Is Kill* (1968) and in guest roles on numerous TV series until his death in 1993.

JEANETTE NOLAN (actor; voice of Mother, screams) appeared in such films as *Two Rode Together* (1961), *The Man Who Shot Liberty Valance* (1962), *My Blood Runs Cold* (1965), TV shows such as *Lassie: The New Beginning*; and such series as *The Richard Boone Show* (1963), *The Virginian* (1967) and dozens of other right into the late 1980s. She has provided character voices for such animated features as *The Rescuers* (1977), *The Fox and the Hound* (1981). Her final feature film role was in *The Horse Whisperer* (1998), released the same year as her death.

SIMON OAKLAND (actor, Dr. Richmond) appeared in *The Rise and Fall of Legs Diamond* (1960), *West Side Story* (1961), *Follow That Dream* (1962), *The Satan Bug* (1965), *Tony Rome* and *The Sand Pebbles* (1967), *Bullitt* (1968), *On a Clear Day You Can See Forever* (1970), and the TV series, *The Night Stalker*, *Toma*, *Baa Baa Black Sheep*, *Charlie's Angels*, *Vegas*, *Chips*, and four episodes of *Quincy M.E.* He died in 1983.

ANTHONY PERKINS (actor, Norman Bates) appeared in such films as *Pretty Poison* (1968), *Catch-22*, and *WUSA* (1970), *Play It as It Lays* and *The Life and Times of Judge Roy Bean* (1972), *The Last of Sheila* (1973; which he co-wrote with composer Stephen Sondheim), *Mahogany* (1975), and *Remember My Name* (1978). In 1983 and 1986, he appeared again as Norman Bates in *Psycho II* and *Psycho III*, the latter of which he also directed, and *Psycho IV: The Beginning*. He directed *Lucky Stiffs* (1989), starred in *Edge of Sanity* (1989), *A Demon In My View* (1991). His last TV movie was *In a Deep Woods* (1992). He died in 1992.

RITA RIGGS (Wardrobe) assisted costume designer Edith Head on *The Birds* (1963) and *Marnie* (1964). She has collaborated with such directors as John Frankenheimer, Taylor Hackford, Arthur Penn, Richard Brooks, and John Huston, and dressed the stars of such films as *Seconds* (1965), *The Professionals* (1966), *Petulia* (1968), *Cinderella Liberty* (1973), *Night Moves* (1978), *Yes, Giorgio* (1981), *Deal of the Century* (1983), and *Mr. North* (1987). She was costume designer on *All in the Family*, *Good Times*, and *V.I.P.* Her most recent TV series was *10,000 Days* in 2010.

PEGGY ROBERTSON (assistant to Hitchcock) was an invaluable member of the Hitchcock "inner circle" on all the director's productions subsequent to *Psycho* right though much of the preparations for his last project, *The Short Night* (unfilmed). She died in 1998.

MARSHALL SCHLOM (script supervisor) worked on numerous post-Psycho films including *Beverly Hills Cop* (1984), *The Golden Child* (1986), *batteries not included* (1987), *Rain Man* (1988), *Postcards From the Edge* (1990), *Dead Again* (1991), *Malice*

(1993), *This Boy's Life* (1993) and *Dracula: Dead and Loving It* (1995). He has numerous credits on films directed by such greats as Billy Wilder, Stanley Kramer, and John Huston.

LEONARD SOUTH (camera operator, cinematographer) was Hitchcock's camera operator for fourteen films and was director of cinematography for the director's last, *Family Plot* (1976); he also worked on such other movies as *Thieves* (1977), *Herbie Goes to Monte Carlo* (1977), and *Amy* (1981). Less than a month before Hitchcock died in 1980, South was preparing to depart for Finland to shoot second-unit work for the director's final project, *The Short Night* (unrealized). South photographed the pilot film and two seasons of the television series *Designing Women*. He died in 2006.

JOSEPH STEFANO (screenwriter) produced television's best science fiction series of the sixties, *The Outer Limits*, and wrote the screenplays for such films as *The Naked Edge* (1961), *Eye of the Cat* (1969), and the television pilots for *Mr. Novak* and *Home for the Holidays*. In 1986, he wrote his first novel, *The Lycanthrope*. He wrote the screenplay for *Snowbeast* (1977) and *The Kindred* (1987). *Blackout,* from a Stefano screenplay, was released in 1989, and he developed for TV and wrote five episodes for *Swamp Thing* (1990). He wrote the screenplay and was a consultant for *Psycho IV: The Beginning* (1990). He died in 2006.

VAUGHN TAYLOR (actor, Mr. Lowery), the veteran character actor, appeared in *Diamond Head* (1962), *The Unsinkable Molly Brown* (1964), *The Russians Are Coming, The Russians Are Coming* (1966), *In Cold Blood* (1967), *The Ballad of Cable Hogue* (1970) and *The Gumball Rally* (1976). He died in 1983.

GEORGE TOMASINI (editor), the husband of the charming actress Mary Brian, star of such films as *The Virginian* (1929) and *The Royal Family of Broadway* (1930), cut such pictures as *The Misfits* (1961), *Cape Fear* (1962), and, for Alfred Hitchcock, *The Birds* (1963), and *Marnie* (1964). The brilliant and innovative editor died in 1964 at age fifty-five.

LURENE TUTTLE (actor, Mrs. Chambers) acted in such movies as *Ma Barker's Killer Brood* (1960), *Critic's Choice* (1963), *The Fortune Cookie* (1966), and *The Sentinel* (1977). She won an Emmy for her role in the TV series *Julia* and in the 1970s and 1980s was frequently a guest on *Dynasty, Trapper John M.D.*, and *Murder, She Wrote*. She died in 1987.

PSYCHO ON HOME VIDEO

Available on DVD and Blu-ray from Universal Studios Entertainment.

PSYCHO MUSICAL SCORE RECORDINGS

Psycho (Bernard Herrmann; National Philharmonic Orchestra, 1975; National Philharmonic Orchestra; Unicorn, out of print)

Alfred Hitchcock's Film Music (Bernard Herrmann; National Philharmonic Orchestra, 1985, Milan Records)

The Great Hitchcock Movie Thrillers (Bernard Herrmann; London Philharmonic Orchestra, 1996, London Compact Disc)

Psycho: The Complete Motion Picture Score (Joel McNeely; Royal Scottish National Orchestra, 1997, Varese Sarabande Compact Disc)

Psycho: Great Hitchcock Movie Thrillers (Various Artists and Orchestras: 1999, London Compact Disc)

THE FILMS OF ALFRED HITCHCOCK

Silent

The Pleasure Garden (1927)
The Mountain Eagle (1927)
The Lodger (1927)
Downhill (1927)
Easy Virtue (1927)
The Ring (1927)
The Farmer's Wife (1928)
Champagne (1928)
The Manxman (1929)

Sound

Blackmail (1929)
Juno and the Paycock (1930)
Murder! (1930)
The Skin Game (1931)
Number Seventeen (1932)
Rich and Strange (1932)
Waltzes From Vienna (1933)

The Man Who Knew Too Much (1934)

The 39 Steps (1935)

Secret Agent (1936)

Sabotage (1936)

Young and Innocent (1938)

The Lady Vanishes (1938)

Jamaica Inn (1939)

Rebecca (1940)

Foreign Correspondent (1940)

Mr. and Mrs. Smith (1941)

Suspicion (1941)

Saboteur (1942)

Shadow of a Doubt (1943)

Lifeboat (1944)

Spellbound (1945)

Notorious (1946)

The Paradine Case (1947)

Rope (1948)

Under Capricorn (1949)

Stage Fright (1950)

Strangers on a Train (1951)

I Confess (1953)

Dial "M" for Murder (1954)

Rear Window (1954)

To Catch a Thief (1955)

The Trouble with Harry (1955)

The Man Who Knew Too Much (1956)

The Wrong Man (1956)

Vertigo (1958)

North by Northwest (1959)

Psycho (1960)

The Birds (1963)

Marnie (1964)

Torn Curtain (1966)

Topaz (1969)

Frenzy (1972)

Family Plot (1976)

Television

For the series *Alfred Hitchcock Presents*:

"Breakdown" (1955)

"Revenge" (1955)

"The Case of Mr. Pelham" (1955)

"Back for Christmas" (1956)

"Wet Saturday" (1956)

"Mr. Blanchard's Secret" (1956)

"One More Mile to Go" (1957)

"The Perfect Crime" (1957)

"Lamb to the Slaughter" (1958)

"A Dip in the Pool" (1958)

"Poison" (1958)

"Banquo's Chair" (1959)

"Arthur" (1959)

"The Crystal Trench" (1959)

"Mrs. Bixby and the Colonel's Coat" (1960)

"The Horseplayer" (1961)

"Bang! You're Dead" (1961)

For *Suspicion*:

"Four O'Clock" (1957)

For *Ford Startime*:

"Incident at a Corner" (1960)

For *The Alfred Hitchcock Hour*:

"I Saw the Whole Thing" (1962)

A NOTE ON SOURCES

The cornerstone for my research was the invaluable Alfred Hitchcock Collection of the Margaret Herrick Library of the Academy of Motion Picture Arts and Sciences, donated by Patricia Hitchcock O'Connell. The papers attest to Mr. Hitchcock as the *complete filmmaker but a frustratingly incomplete record-keeper.* Nevertheless, the collection encompasses correspondence, production records, treatments, screenplays, and legal files for many post-1950s Hitchcock projects. I have also made use of The Billy Rose Theater Collection at the Library of Lincoln Center, New York, and of the American Film Institute Library, Los Angeles. The private collections of Frederick Clarke, Gary A. Smith, Paul Farrar, Sam Irvin, and Martin Kearns provided information and inspiration while supplementing material of my own.

For a general overview of a life in films, I found *Hitch* by John Russell Taylor and *The Art of Alfred Hitchcock* by Donald Spoto to be helpful. For analysis of the movie and others in the Hitchcock canon, one could hardly do better than *Hitchcock's Films* by Robin Wood and *Hitchcock—The Murderous Gaze* by William Rothman. The frame-by-frame breakdown book on *Psycho* by Richard J. Anobile was enormously useful for verifying visual memory.

Unless noted, most of my information on the making of the film stems from personal interviews with Mr. Hitchcock and his collaborators that I conducted from the winter of 1980 through the early spring of 1989. My first interview was with Hitchcock himself in January of 1980 at his offices at Universal. I was promised twenty minutes of a great man's valuable time. An hour later, he was still waving away his assistant, as if he were having a wonderful time being asked questions he must have heard a thousand times. Although battered in body and spirit, Hitchcock was, by turns, brilliant, acerbic, pedantic, lost in reverie, gossipy, and frustrated by the projects that he knew he would never make. I will never forget his grace, nor his rare good manners. Three months later, Hitchcock was dead.

I particularly want to salute the artists who were associated with Mr. Hitchcock and the making of the film *Psycho*. They shared happy and painful memories, gracefully endured my endless fussing and clarifying, and, in some cases, reviewed early drafts for accuracy: Harold Adler, Jack Barron, Saul Bass, Robert Bloch, Robert Clatworthy, Helen Colvig, Margo Epper, Hilton Green, Virginia Gregg, Mrs. Joseph Hurley, Paul Jasmin, Janet Leigh, Michael Ludmer, John McIntire, Jeanette Nolan, Tony Palladino, Anthony Perkins, Rita Riggs, Marshall Schlom, Leonard South, Joseph Stefano, H. N. Swanson, Lois Thurman, and Lurene Tuttle.

I hope this book will underscore the fact that, even for a Hitchcock, filmmaking, like living, is nothing if not a collaborative art.

SELECTED BIBLIOGRAPHY

Periodicals

Abramson, Martin. "What Hitchcock Does with His Blood Money." *Cosmopolitan*, January 1964.

———. "My Husband Hates Suspense." *Coronet*, August 1964.

Anonymous. "Pourquoi j'ai peur la nuit." *Arts*, no. 77, June 1, 1960.

Anonymous. "Hitchcock's Three Nightmares." *Newsweek*, January 24, 1966.

Anonymous. "Alfred Hitchcock Directs." *TV Guide* 4, 15 (1956):20-21.

Anonymous. "Horror, Humor and McGuffins." *TV Guide* 4, 43 (1956):17–19.

Anonymous. "Joan Harrison's Specialty: Murder." *TV Guide* 6, 10 (1958):17–19.

Anonymous. "An Old Master Opposes Sink-to-Sink TV." *TV Guide* 7, 7 (1959):17–19.

Anonymous. "Alfred the Great Shocker." *TV Guide* 9, 12 (1961):17-19.

Anonymous. "The Elderly Cherub That Is Hitchcock." *TV Guide* 13, 22 (1965): 14-18.

Brown, Royal D. "Herrmann, Hitchcock, and the Music of the Irrational." *Cinema Journal*, Spring 1982.

Clark, Paul Sargent. "Hitchcock's Finest Hour." *Today's Filmmaker*, November 1971.

Counts, Kyle. "The Making of Alfred Hitchcock's *The Birds*." *Cinefantastique* 10, 2 (Fall, 1980).

Crawley, Tony. "*Psycho!*" *Hammer's House of Horrors*, March 1978.

Foster, Frederick. "Hitch Didn't Want it Arty." *American Cinematographer*, February 1957.

Goodman, Ezra. "The World Is Now with Hitchcock." *New York Herald Tribune*, April 5, 1942.

Haber, Joyce. "Hitchcock Still Fighting Hard to Avoid the Conventional." *Los Angeles Times*, February 4, 1973.

Hitchcock, Alfred. "The Chase—Core of the Movie." *New York Times Magazine*, October 29, 1950.

———. "Murder—With English on It." *New York Times Magazine*, March 3, 1957.

———. "Why I Am Afraid of the Dark." *Arts: Lettres*, Spectacles, no. 7777 (June 1-7, 1960).

———. "The Woman Who Knows Too Much." *McCall's*, March 1956.

Knight, Arthur. "Conversations with Alfred Hitchcock." *Oui*, February 1973.

Martin, Pete. "I Call on Alfred Hitchcock." *Saturday Evening Post*, July 27, 1957.

Montagu, Ivor. "Working with Hitchcock." *Sight and Sound*, Summer 1980.

Natale, Richard. "There's Just One Hitch." *Women's Wear Daily*, June 16, 1972.

Rebello, Stephen. "Plotting With Alfred Hitchcock." *The Real Paper*, February 16, 1980.

———. "The Making of Alfred Hitchcock's *Psycho*." *Cinefantastique*, October 1986.

Roche, Catherine dela. "Conversation with Hitchcock." *Sight and Sound*, Winter 1955–1956.

Whitcomb, Jon. "Master of Mayhem." *Cosmopolitan*, October 1959.

Books

Anobile, Richard J., ed. *Psycho: The Film Classics Library*. New York: Avon Books, 1974.

Armes, Roy. *A Critical History of the British Cinema*. London: Oxford University Press, 1978.

Bloch, Robert. *Psycho*. New York: Simon & Schuster, 1959.

Bogdanovich, Peter. *The Cinema of Alfred Hitchcock*. New York: Museum of Modern Art Film Library/Doubleday, 1963.

Boucher, Anthony, ed. *The Quality of Murder*. New York: E.P. Dutton, 1962.

Bouzereau, Laurent. *The DePalma Cut*. New York: Dembner, 1988.

Brill, Lesley. *The Hitchcock Romance*. Princeton, N.J.: Princeton University Press, 1988.

Brosnan, John. *The Horror People*. New York: St. Martin's, 1976.

Cameron, Ian, ed. *Movie Reader* ("Suspense and Meaning" and "The Mechanics of Suspense"). New York: Praeger, 1972.

Carringer, Robert L. *The Making of Citizen Kane*, Berkeley: University of California Press, 1985.

Chase, Donald. *Filmmaking: The Collaborative Art*. Boston: Little, Brown, 1975.

Corliss, Richard. *Talking Pictures*. New York: Overlook Press, 1974.

Deny, Charles. *Dark Dreams*. New York: A. S. Barnes, 1977.

Deutelbaum, Marshall, and Leland Poague, eds. *A Hitchcock Reader*. Ames: Iowa State University, 1986.

Durgnat, Raymond. *The Strange Case of Alfred Hitchcock*. Boston: The MIT Press, 1974.

Eames, John Douglas. *The Paramount Story*. New York: Crown, 1985.

Everson, William K. *Classics of the Horror Film*. Secaucus: Citadel, 1974.

Eyles, Allen, Robert Adkinson, and Nicholas Fry, eds. *The House of Horror*. London: Lorrimer, 1973.

Freeman, David. *The Last Days of Alfred Hitchcock*. New York: Overlook Press, 1984.

Green, Jonathan. *The Greatest Criminals of All Time*. New York: Stein & Day, 1980.

Greenberg, Harvey R., M.D. *The Movies on Your Mind*. New York: Saturday Review Press/E.P. Dutton, 1975.

Grierson, John. "Directors of the Thirties," in *Film: An Anthology*, edited by Daniel Talbot. Berkeley: University of California Press, 1966.

Haley, Michael. *The Alfred Hitchcock Album*. Englewood Cliffs, N.J.: Prentice-Hall, 1981.

Hammond, Lawrence. *Thriller Movies*. Secaucus: Derbibooks, 1975.

Hardy, Phil, ed. *The Encyclopedia of Horror*. New York: Harper & Row, 1986.

Harmetz, Aljean. *The Making of The Wizard of Oz*. New York: Limelight Editions, 1977.

Harris, Robert A., and Michael S. Lasky. *The Films of Alfred Hitchcock*. Secaucus: Citadel, 1976.

Head, Edith, and Jane Kesner Ardmore. *The Dress Doctor*. Boston: Little, Brown, 1959.

Higham, Charles, and Joel Greenberg. *The Celluloid Muse*. New York: Signet, 1972.

Hirschorn, Clive. *The Universal Story*. New York: Crown, 1985.

Jara, Rene et al., eds. *The Paradigm Exchange*. Minneapolis: University of Minnesota, 1981.

King, Stephen. *Danse Macabre*. New York: Berkley Books, 1982.

La Valley, Albert, ed. *Focus on Hitchcock*. Englewood Cliffs, N.J.: Prentice-Hall, 1972.

Leff, Leonard. *Hitchcock & Selznick*. New York: Weidenfeld & Nicolson, 1987.

Low, Rachel, and Roger Mahvell. *The History of the British Film, 1896-1950*. London: George Allen & Unwin, 1948.

MacDonald, John M. *The Murderer and His Victim*. Chicago: Charles C. Thomas, 1961.

McCarty, John, and Brian Kelleher. *Alfred Hitchcock Presents*. New York: St. Martin's Press, 1985.

McGilligan, Pat. *Backstory*. Los Angeles: University of California Press, 1986.

Modleski, Tania. *The Women Who Knew Too Much*. New York: Methuen, 1988.

Moldea, Dan E. *Dark Victory: Ronald Reagan, MCA, and the Mob*. New York: Viking, 1986.

Naremore, Michael. *Filmguide to Psycho*. Bloomington/London: Indiana University Press, 1973.

Pechter, William S. *Twenty-four Times a Second*. New York: Harper & Row, 1971.

Perkins, V. F. *Film as Film*. New York: Viking, 1972.

Perry, George. *The Films of Alfred Hitchcock*. New York: E.P. Dutton, 1965.

————.*Hitchcock*. New York: Doubleday, 1975.

Phillips, Gene D. *Alfred Hitchcock*. Boston: Twayne Publishers, 1984.

Powell, Michael. *A Life in Movies*. New York: Knopf, 1986.

Rohmer, Eric, and Claude Chabrol. *Hitchcock*. New York: Frederick Ungar, 1979.

Rothman, William. *Hitchcock—the Murderous Gaze*. Boston: Harvard College, 1982.

Ryall, Tom. *Alfred Hitchcock & the British Cinema*. Urbana and Chicago: University of Illinois Press, 1986.

Sarris, Andrew. *Interviews with Film Directors*. New York: Avon, 1967.

Schecter, Harold, *Deviant*, New York: Pocket Books, 1989.

Schickel, Richard. *The Men Who Made the Movies*. New York: Atheneum, 1975.

Shipman, David. *The Great Movie Stars, the International Years*. New York: St. Martin's, 1973.

Sinyard, Neil. *The Films of Alfred Hitchcock*. New York: Gallery Books, 1986.

Spoto, Donald. *The Art of Alfred Hitchcock*. New York: Hopkinson and Blake, 1976.

————. *The Dark Side of Genius: The Life of Alfred Hitchcock*. Boston: Little, Brown, 1983.

Taylor, John Russell. *Hitch: The Life and Times of Alfred Hitchcock*. New York: Pantheon, 1978.

Thomson, David. *America in the Dark*. New York: William Morrow, 1977.

————. *A Biographical Dictionary of Film*. New York: William Morrow, 1981.

————. *Overexposures: The Crisis in American Filmmaking*. New York: William Morrow, 1981.

Truffaut, François. *Hitchcock*. New York: Simon & Schuster, 1967.

Weldon, Michael. *The Psychotronic Dictionary of Film*. New York: Ballantine, 1983.

Wollen, Peter. *Readings and Writings: Semiotic Counter Strategies*. *London*: Verso, 1982.

Wood, Robin. *Hitchcock's Films*. New York: A.S. Barnes, 1965.

Yacowar, Maurice. *Hitchcock's British Films*. Hamden, Connecticut: Archon, 1977.

ACKNOWLEDGMENTS

Thanks, first to Julian Bach and Ann Rittenberg for their passion for the original book manuscript way back when, let alone for their suggestions, decency and old-world agentry. Deep and lasting gratitude, especially, to Mary Evans, Rachel Vogel and everyone at Mary Evans Inc for their years of unflagging advocacy, brilliance and integrity. Appreciation to David Colden whose impeccable good sense and know-how I wish I'd had from dayone. My thanks go out to publisher Catheryn Kilgarriff of Marion Boyars Publishers for keeping the flame alive in the U.K. and to Jack Shoemaker of Counterpoint Press and Soft Skull Press for this film tie-in edition. My special salute, also, to Soft Skull's wonderful, patient production manager Emma Cofod for her professionalism and ability to turn around on a dime. To producers Alan Barnette and Tom Thayer, great appreciation for their stick-to-itveness and endless capacity for reinvention; to Tom Pollock, specifically, and to Ivan Reitman and all the executives at The Montecito Picture Company, big thanks as well. A grateful bow to the decision makers at 20th Century Fox and Fox Searchlight, let alone to the incredible Team *Hitchcock* studio publicity and promotions team including Melissa Holloway, Lauren Hochberg, James Lewis, Angela Johnson, Sonia Freeman, Barry Johnson, Jen Crocker,

Ruth Busenkell and Isabelle Sugimoto. For support, kindnesses, encouragement, laughter, and for so many other reasons, I am forever grateful to Lou D'Elia. Mrs. Joseph Hurley, Frederick S. Clarke, Paul Farrar, Marshall Schlom, Gary A. Smith, and Ron Harvey were so selflessly helpful in tracking down reference material. Without the unconditional love and companionship of my beloved Miou-Miou, Minerva, Jasmine, Barnaby, Nicky, Gus, and Benjamin this journey would never have been anywhere near as much fun. And without Gary Rubenstein, the whole thing would be unthinkable.

INDEX